IMAGES
of America

MARTINSVILLE AND THE WASHINGTON VALLEY

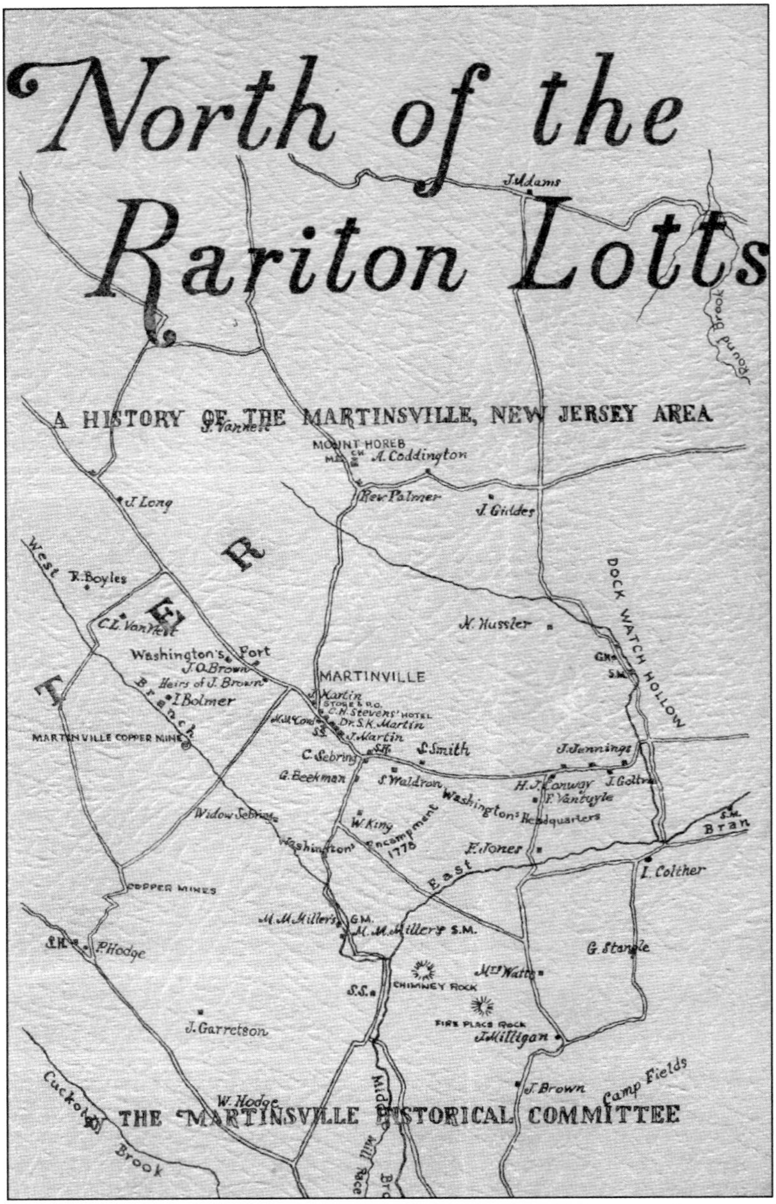

The cover of *North of the Rariton Lotts*, a 1975 history of the Martinsville area, features this map depicting Mount Horeb to the north, Dock Watch Hollow to the east, Chimney Rock to the south, and the valley road heading northwest toward Pluckemin. Martinville (the original spelling) is in the center; a store, post office, and the locations of Washington's encampments are noted. (Author's collection.)

On the Cover: "The ice is safe!" As word spread up and down the valley that the reservoir was safe for skating, all ages grabbed their skates and headed down to join the fun. In 1940, from left to right, are (first row) Beverly Brown, Phyllis "Fluff" Bartle, and Jeanette Van Nest; (second row) Clara Hulse and Freda Yehle. (Courtesy Freda Yehle.)

IMAGES
of America

Martinsville and the Washington Valley

Patricia Valentine Whitacre
and the Martinsville Community Center

ARCADIA
PUBLISHING

ISBN 978-0-7385-7571-1

Published by Arcadia Publishing
Charleston, South Carolina

Printed in the United States of America

Library of Congress Control Number: 2011920701

For all general information, please contact Arcadia Publishing:
Telephone 843-853-2070
Fax 843-853-0044
E-mail sales@arcadiapublishing.com
For customer service and orders:
Toll-Free 1-888-313-2665

Visit us on the Internet at www.arcadiapublishing.com

To our children, with the hope that they will pass this glimpse into a period of American history on to future generations

Contents

Acknowledgments 6

Introduction 7

1. A Melting Pot of Neighbors 9
2. Farm Life in the Valley 29
3. Businesses in the Community 49
4. A Village Up in Flames 59
5. Wartimes Over the Years 69
6. Leisure Activities for All Ages 83
7. Survivors in the Path of Progress 119

ACKNOWLEDGMENTS

We must first express our gratitude to our forebears who chose Martinsville and the Washington Valley in which to live and raise their families. The core of our research team included Coddington cousins Judy Hecker, Barbara Marton, and Karen Swart; Jane Waldron Gandolfe, whose mother, Ruth, helped to compile *North of the Rariton Lotts*; and Joan M. Newman, who also coauthored that book. Without the extensive research that preceded the 1975 work, including interviews with elderly residents and details of the surviving evidence of Washington's encampments, much valuable historical information would have been lost.

Thanks to the Internet, we have been able to brainstorm with people from Maine to Florida and from Long Island to the Hawaiian Islands to assemble a collection of memories and mementos. While we appreciate the input of numerous others, limited space restricts our acknowledgments to those whose photographs appear within.

The following list includes the three-letter code that identifies the source of each photograph, and we have included family names of those who no longer bear them: John Alker (ALK), Edward Anderson (AND), Ina Mae Bartle (IMB), Isaac Bartle (IKE), Paul Bartle (DOC), Alfred Beronio (BER), Joanne Bixler (BIX), Walter Hubacek Blejwas (HUB), Nancy Hulse Brett (HLS), Jean Valentine Cahill (JVC), Vicki Charles (VCH), Edwin Coddington (ECD), Lois Poffley DeGhetto (POF), Shirley Bartle Dennis (SBD), Brent Duxbury (DUX), Nora Waldron Fetzer (NWF), Jane Waldron Gandolfe (JWG), Louis Geschwindner (GSH), Raymond Haines (HNS), Irene Van Nest Hall (IVN), Judy Coddington Hecker (JCD), James Housten (HST), Eleanor Pepper Kells (PEP), Nancy Gilbride Killeen (GBD), Ann Kurtz (KTZ), David London (LND), Frances Cramer Longo (SIS), Sal Longo (SAL), Martinsville Volunteer Fire Department (MFD), Barbara Coddington Marton (BCD), Marian Vactor Meyer (VAC), Dorothy Mason Moore (MSN), Paul Morin (MRN), Joan Newman (JMN), Karen Byrne Norris (BRN), Ellen Geschwindner Opdyke (EGS), John D. Roberts (RBT), Johanna Rooda (RDA), Vera Musialowski Slowey (MUS), Joseph Smerdon (SMR), Karen Coddington Swart (KCD), Richard Thum (THM), Frances Brarens Toleno (FBR), Robert Tunison (TUN), Patricia Valentine Whitacre (PVW), Irwin Wishnow (WSH), and Freda Yehle (YLE).

INTRODUCTION

A hamlet in the valley between two ridges of the Watchung Mountains in New Jersey and only 40 miles west of Manhattan, Martinsville retained its rural atmosphere long after the flatlands to the south had lost their original identity. The objective of this book is to portray the life and times of the residents of this area during the first half of the 20th century.

Chimney Rock is perched atop a cliff at the entrance to the cleft in the First Watchung Mountain through which traffic enters the valley from the south. It stands like a surveyor's monument to define the boundary between the hills and farm fields to the north and to the south, the densely populated, brightly lit corridor spreading eastward towards New York.

Native Americans had lived here for at least a thousand years. People with a sharp eye might still find arrowheads in a freshly plowed field. Some have found buttons, musket balls, and other objects left behind by George Washington's troops. The geology of the area attracted the first white men as copper was found in the basaltic ridges of ancient lava flows. The glaciers that stopped north of the mountain ridges in several periods created huge lakes as they melted. As these waters drained into the valley, depositing sand that would compress into sandstone as well as clay for later brick-making, they created habitats for the dinosaurs whose footprints have been found here and for the fish whose fossils have also been discovered. Seams of coal were deposited as the swamplands dried, and finally, rich farm soil covered the valley floor.

Families were large in the early days, often with a dozen or more children. It was a close-knit community in which much of the social life revolved around activities at the Martinsville and Mount Horeb churches. The church was the place where new life was welcomed and where families bade farewell to loved ones. People met and sometimes married, while others became lifelong friends. Sunday afternoons were a time when neighbors, still dressed in their Sunday best, might gather on each other's porches for tea or lemonade and cookies or a fancy layer cake.

After 1920, the Martinsville Community Club, which later was renamed the Martinsville Community Center (MCC), was another hub of social activity and joint community projects. As Doc Bartle, son of the village blacksmith, observed in 1971, "In those days, it took a newcomer 25 years to be considered a native. Now you can make it in about six months."

As people of different nationalities got to know their neighbors, there were amusing incidents. When Sis Longo brought a lasagna casserole to a Cub Scout covered-dish supper, one young Cub, with spaghetti sauce and mozzarella cheese on his chin, declared, "I never knew that cooked bubble gum tasted so good!"

Emily Baist, the local midwife, was horrified when the Byrnes named their new daughter Hazel: "Ach, who would name a baby Esel?" The word *esel* meant "jackass" in her native German. In many families, when the parents did not want their children to know what they were saying, they spoke to each other in the native tongue. It was common when someone sneezed to hear a response of, "Gesundheit!" Another anecdote tells of the Byrnes, who had placed in their dooryard garden a small sign reading, "Gemütlichkeit," which means the feeling of a cozy, relaxed atmosphere. One day they called for Dr. Allegrante. Upon following the Byrnes' directions, the doctor thought he had mistakenly found the home of a Mr. and Mrs. Gemütlichkeit and knocked on the door to ask where the Byrnes lived.

Tales of early adventures as people transitioned from horse and buggy to automobiles have been handed down. It was not uncommon to see a Model T owner with his arm in a sling from being kicked as he turned the crank to start the car. During a bitter cold winter, a broken windshield was temporarily replaced by a section of tar paper with a small hole through which the driver could peer at the road while chatting nonchalantly with his passenger. An occasional passenger invariably opened the conversation with, "You are covered by accident insurance, aren't you?"

People here grew up imbued with a familiarity with the natural world around them. They knew where to look near springs for watercress, which was rumored to have been brought by Joshua Martin from his native England. A stand of honeysuckle invited one to stop to suck drops of nectar from the base of each blossom. Schoolchildren might detour through a field on the way home to find a four-leaf clover. If the path was through woods, they might startle a grouse or discover the first bloodroots to open in spring. As goldenrod began to bloom in summer fields, they knew the carefree days of summer were about to end, and school began again. They learned to whistle on acorn caps, and one family called to each other outdoors by whistling the *cheer-cheer-cheer* call of the cardinal instead of disturbing the peace by shouting, "Where are you?"

Families who were blessed with abundant water shared with others. Dairy farmers kept their products in the springhouse on the Cramer farm, and when neighboring wells went dry, they filled large milk cans with water from the Cramer well. Schoolchildren stopped there to fill water jars to go with their lunches. The Goltra brothers had a well in their front yard where neighboring children were welcome to quench their thirsts. After drawing a bucket of water, the procedure was to swish the water three times in the dipper, dumping it back into the well each time. The dipper was then considered clean enough for drinking.

The people of Martinsville have realized their good fortune in living here, and through the Fresh Air Fund they have opened their homes to children from the inner city for two summer weeks at a time, introducing them to rural living. One young boy refused to join his young hosts who had pitched a tent and planned to spend the night there. He could not understand why anyone would choose to sleep on the ground when there was a perfectly good bed in the house. Another visitor reported many years later to his hosts that his three visits with them had changed his life. He had returned home to Spanish Harlem, told all his friends that there was a whole different world out there, and had succeeded in making his way into that better world.

Jessie Smalley witnessed the entire 20th century in her 106 years here. She had visited other parts of America and kept abreast of current events. In a 1990 interview she declared, "We have a wonderful country. We need to take care of it." Her favorite saying was, "Life is a difficult riddle."

Many who had the good fortune to grow up in the special environment of the Martinsville area have followed careers or families to other parts of the world. However, they might challenge any notion that presumes they have moved to a world that is better than that of their rural childhood in Martinsville and the Washington Valley.

One

A Melting Pot of Neighbors

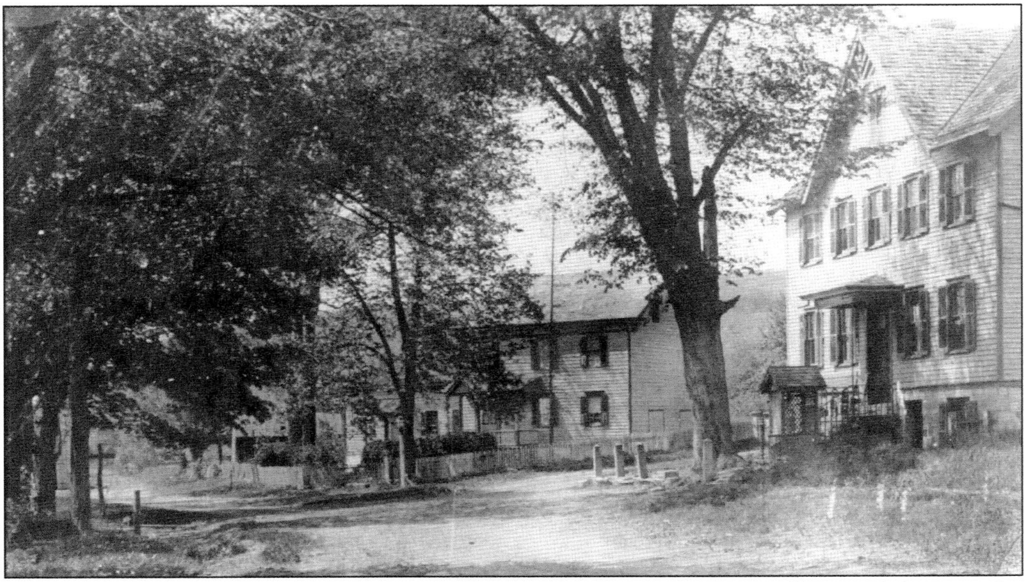

A stagecoach stop at the intersection of Mount Horeb and Washington Valley Roads became the nucleus of the hamlet of Martinsville, named after the first postmaster, Absalom Martin, in 1828. By 1873, W. Richardson owned the farmhouse later owned by Joseph Van Nest. A blacksmith and a wheelwright shop were opposite the hotel. Hitching posts are in front of the hotel in this photograph from about 1911. An Exxon station and a bank now occupy this corner. (IKE.)

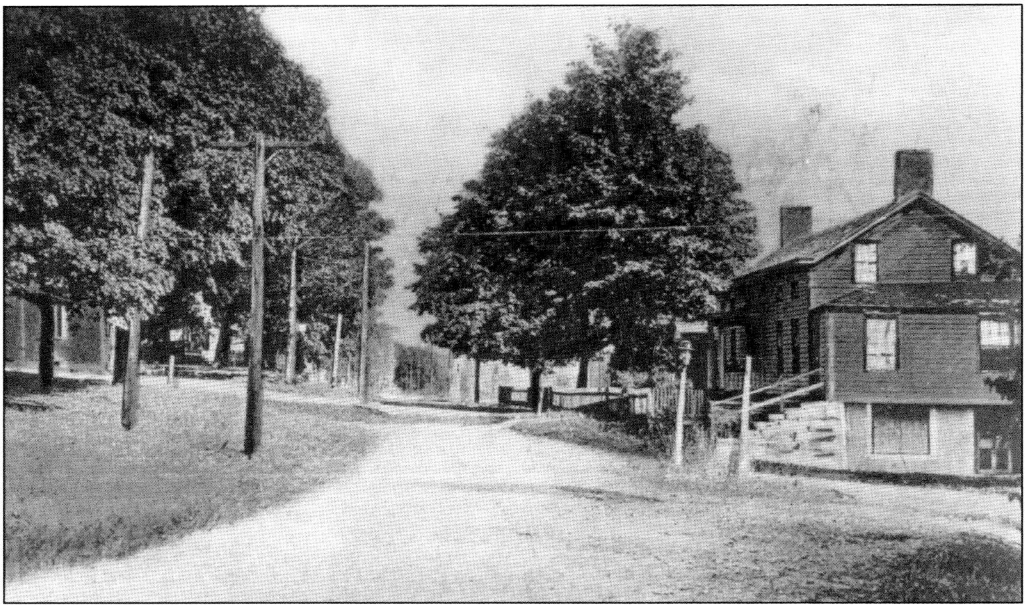

East of the Mount Horeb Road intersection, the C.L. Waldron store occupied the southwest corner of Washington Valley and Chimney Rock Roads, and by 1873, a schoolhouse was located on the north side. In this 1911 view, a kerosene streetlamp is atop a post at the base of the Waldron stone steps, and the brick base of the general store appears beneath the trees on the left. (IKE.)

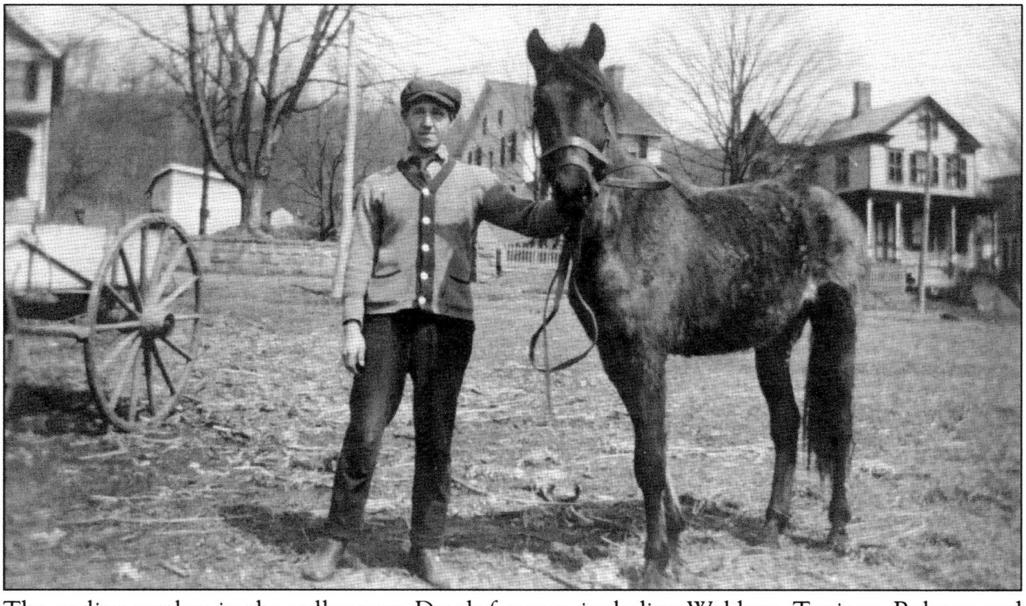

The earliest settlers in the valley were Dutch farmers, including Waldron, Tunison, Bolmer, and Goltra. In 1920, Arthur Waldron and his horse named Sunday stand before two houses, which survive to the present. Arthur was the fifth generation since Daniel Waldron settled in Dock Watch Hollow in the early 1700s and the ninth generation from Joseph Waldron, who first settled in New Amsterdam. Arthur married Valentina Coombs, who later became postmistress. (JWG.)

Johannes Van Nest's 1752 marriage to Aeltje Tunison, whose family had owned land here since the early 1700s, added another Dutch settler to the valley. In the early 20th century, Johannes's cousin Joseph Van Nest married Bessie Bolmer, descended from yet another early settler. Pictured on their wedding day in 1920 are William Van Nest, another of Johannes's cousins, and Violette Tunison of Bound Brook. William's sister Sarah married Reuben Coddington. All six were lifelong residents. (IVN.)

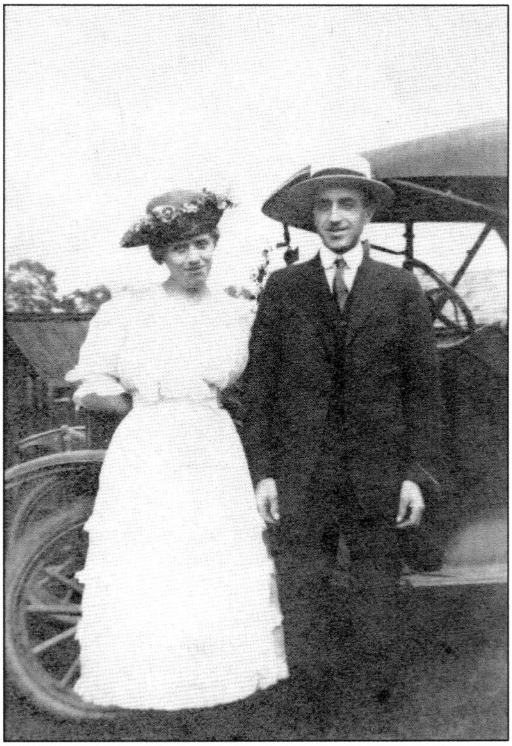

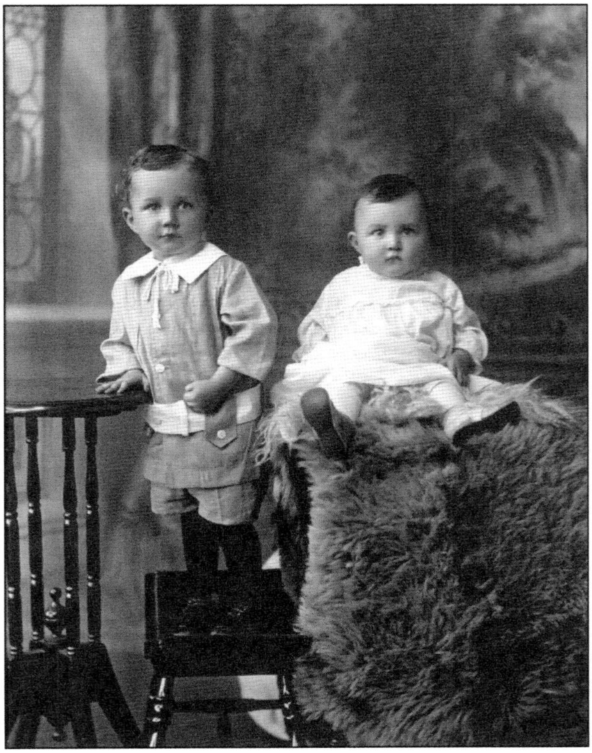

Adding English roots to the melting pot of neighbors were Isaac Coddington and his wife, Sarah, who settled in Warren Township in the mid-1700s. Pictured in 1918, William (left) and Harold Coddington were the sons of Sarah Van Nest and Reuben Coddington, whose livestock and extensive apple and peach orchards supplied markets in Bound Brook, North Plainfield, and New Brunswick. Reuben also served as a Somerset County freeholder. (KCD.)

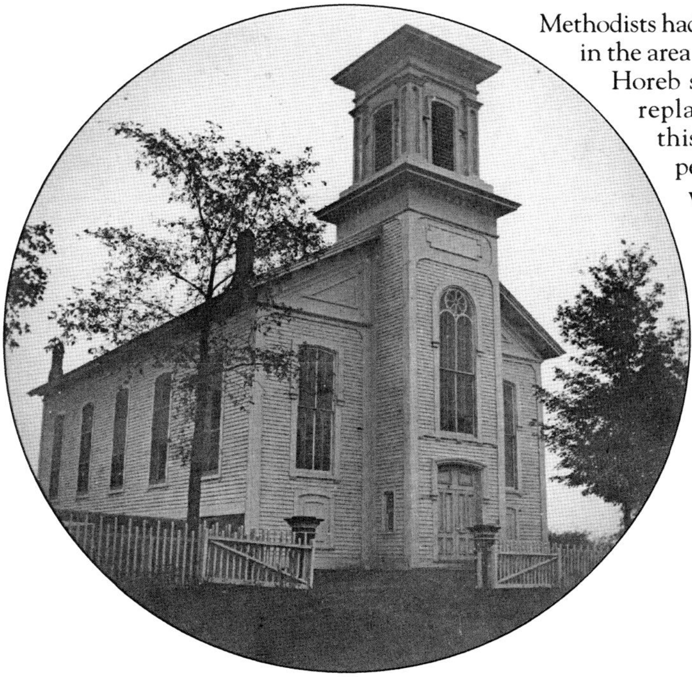

Methodists had been meeting in private homes in the area named after the biblical Mount Horeb since the 1770s. In 1867, they replaced their first church with this classic, white frame building perched atop a hill. The parish, with a mailing address of Martinsville, covered an area from Warrenville and Mount Bethel in the east, north to Liberty Corner, west to the upper Washington Valley, and south to Chimney Rock. (TUN.)

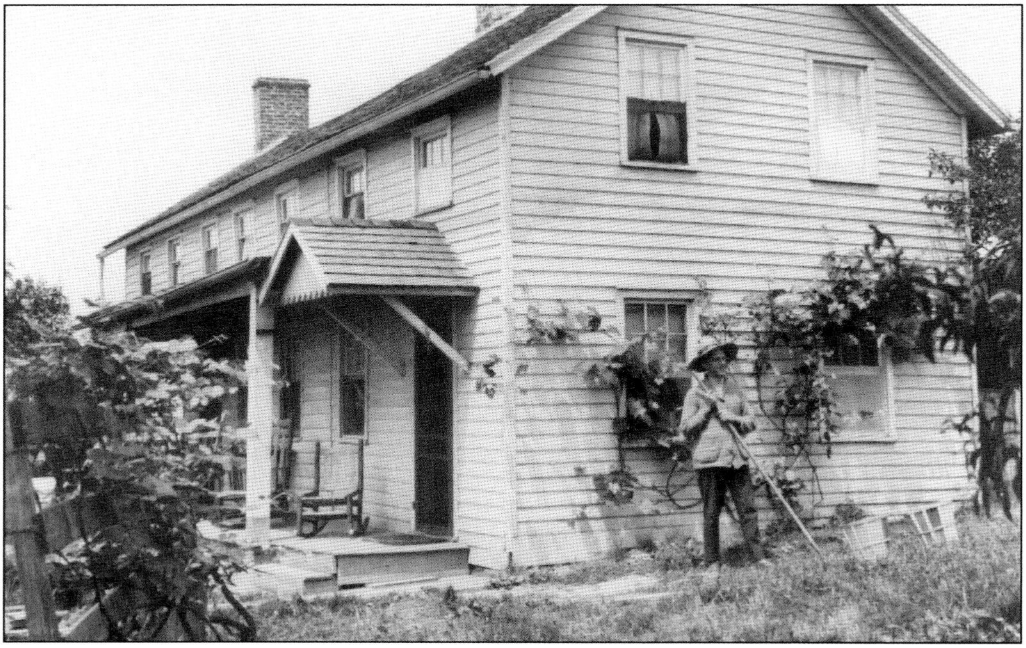

A new pastor in 1892 scolded the congregation for building such a handsome church while providing this primitive parsonage for its pastor. He added that he could not afford a horse and carriage on his modest salary, and the territory was too large to serve on foot. Early church members' names included Badgley, Bartle, Bolmer, Codington, Coddington, Coon, Coriell, Davis, Doty, Giddes, Goltra, King, Linbarger, Mundy, Martin, Nuse, Perrine, Roberts, Thum, Totten, Tunison, Vactor, Van Nest, Voorhees, Waldron, and Zimmerman. (TUN.)

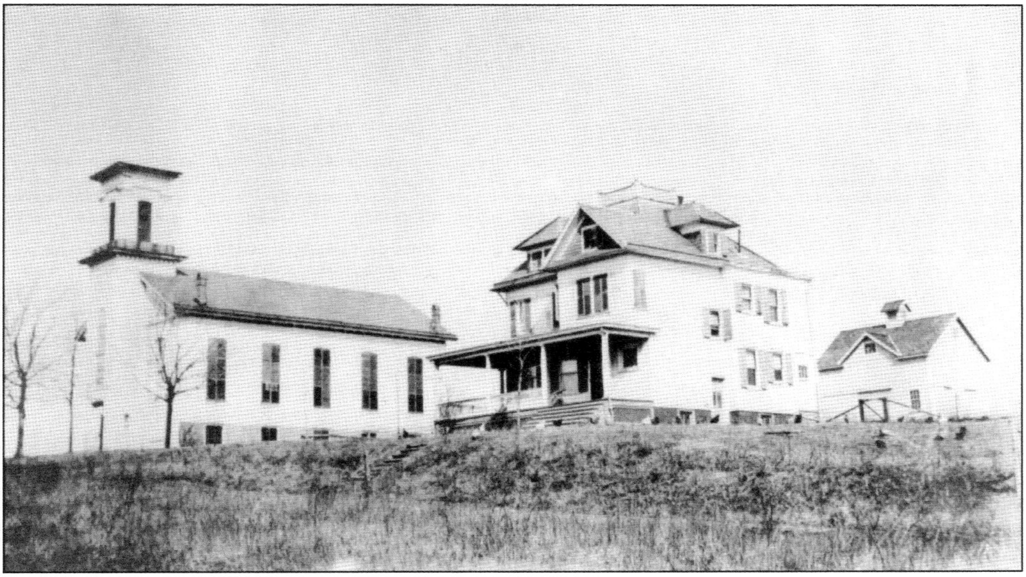

A new parsonage was built in 1904, by which time the pastor also served the Springdale and Martinsville churches with morning, afternoon, and evening services. One spring day in 1889, however, it was decided that the pastor should not continue on to Springdale because of the "wretched condition of the road." In 1979, this picturesque setting was chosen for the filming of the movie *Simon*, starring Alan Arkin. (TUN.)

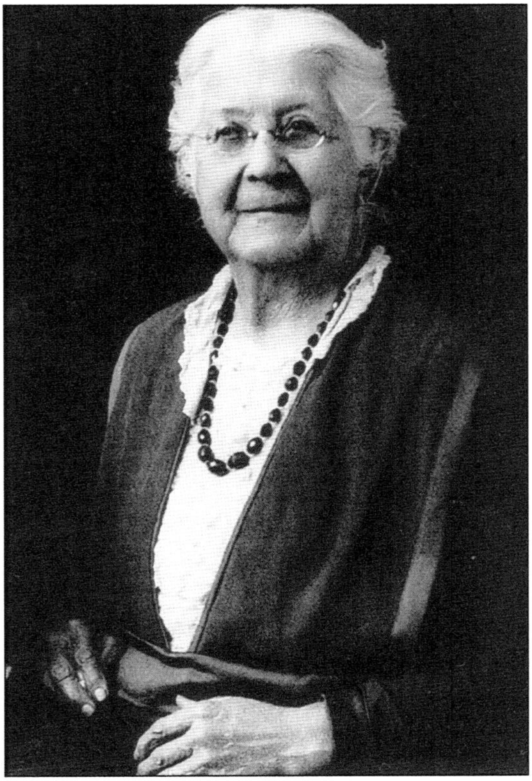

Originally Veghte, Vactor is another early Dutch name. Blacksmith Bartley Vactor's family was in Martinsville by 1850. Son William, also a blacksmith, married Harriet Davis, sister of wheelwright George Davis. William served in the Civil War and was active in the temperance movement. Harriet, seen in this 1929 photograph, lived the last of her 96 years with son Raymond, his wife, Jennie, and granddaughter Ethel, who later married Arnold Napoleon. (VAC.)

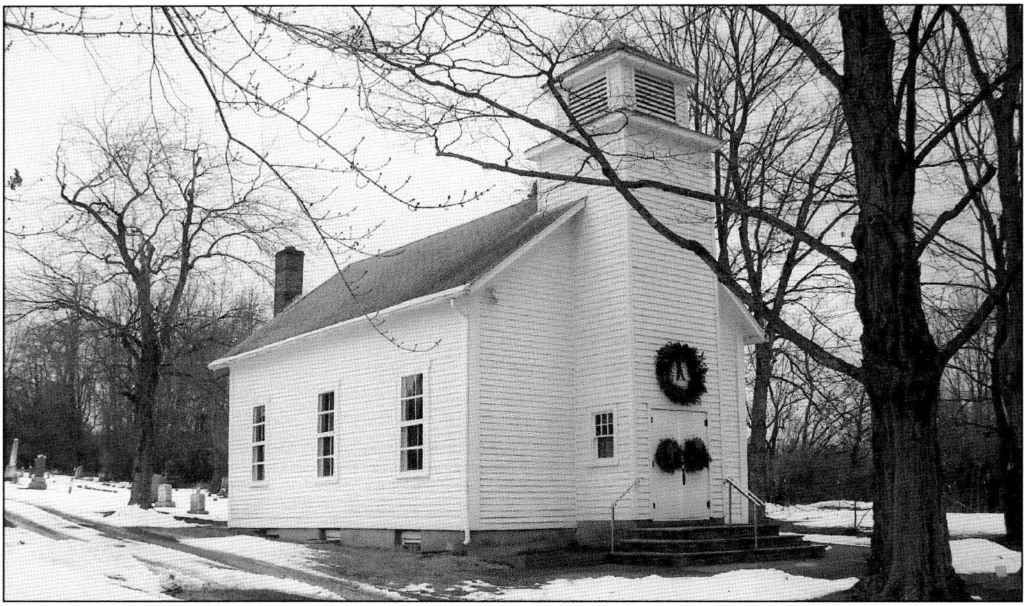

The Springdale Methodist Church in Warren Township, dating to at least 1839, was served by the Martinsville post office. Burials in the cemetery include the names Mundy, Waldron, Smalley, Thum (Toms), and the Goltra family. Bachelor brothers Floyd, George, John, and Newton Goltra lived together near the center of Martinsville. In 1964, the last surviving brother, Floyd, passed away at age 89. (PVW.)

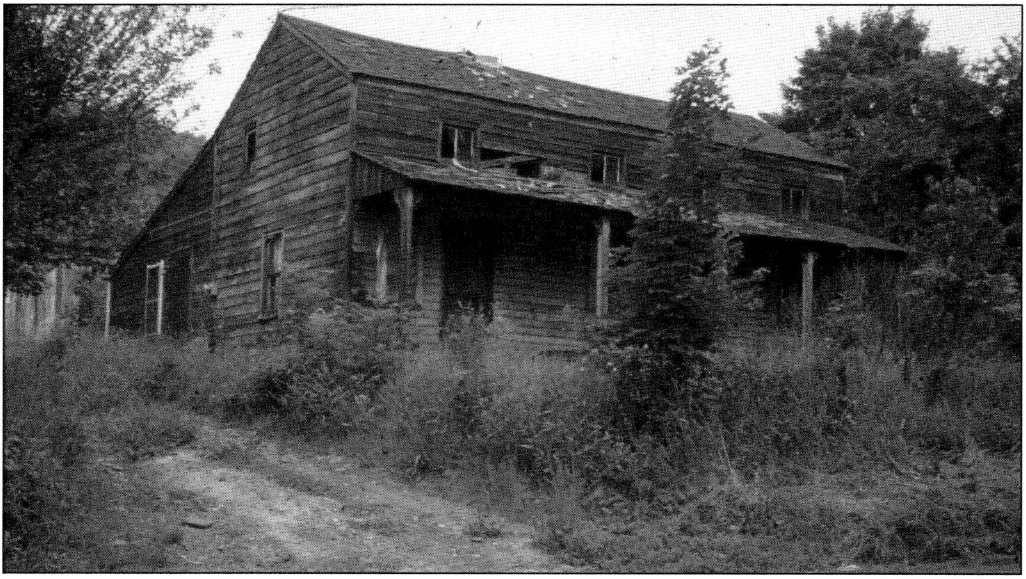

The Goltra brothers lived in this house, where they raised most of their own food and resisted such 20th-century improvements as indoor plumbing or central heat. They only installed electricity in their final years. By the light of kerosene lamps, they studied their stacks of *National Geographic* magazines. They had framed collections of butterflies, and while on rambles in area woodlands with neighbor children, Newton pointed out wildflowers, warning the children never to pick the rare bottle gentians. (ECD.)

Jacob and John Thum were the sons of wheelwright Frederick Toms, a German immigrant. Jacob, pictured around 1900, and his wife, Elizabeth, did not have children. Brother John was widowed by 1900, with son John F., who married Jennie Giddes in 1905, and daughters Anna, who married Bernard Gilbride, and Mamie. Gilbride's parents were from Ireland. Middle Brook near Gilbride Road is also known as Toms Brook. (GBD.)

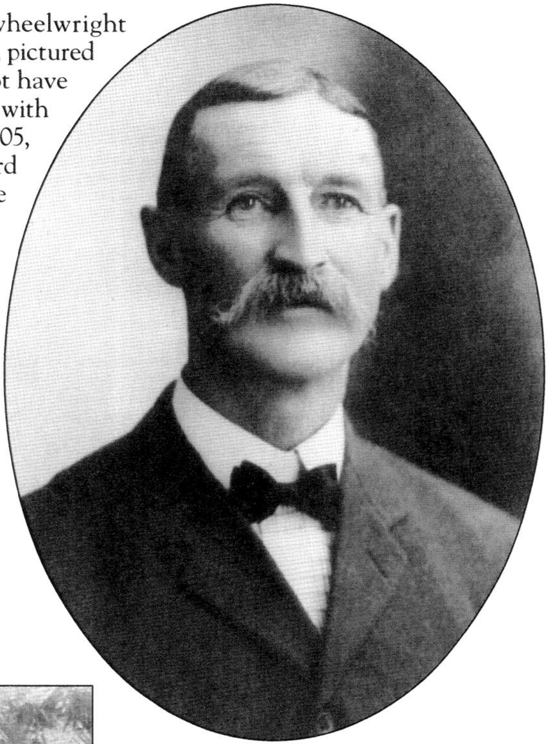

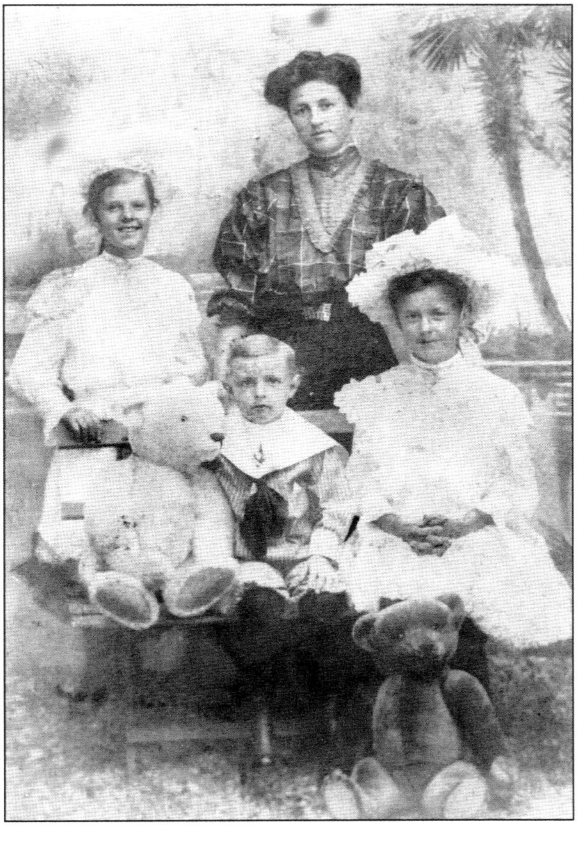

When Anna Thum Gilbride posed in 1920 with her three children, from left to right, Anna Loretta (eldest), Bernard, and Mary Lou, they included the children's teddy bears. Inspired by the story of Pres. Theodore Roosevelt's good sportsmanship in sparing the life of a bear while on a hunting expedition in 1902, toy makers in Germany and America began producing the cuddly stuffed toys. With Roosevelt's permission, they were called teddy bears. (GBD.)

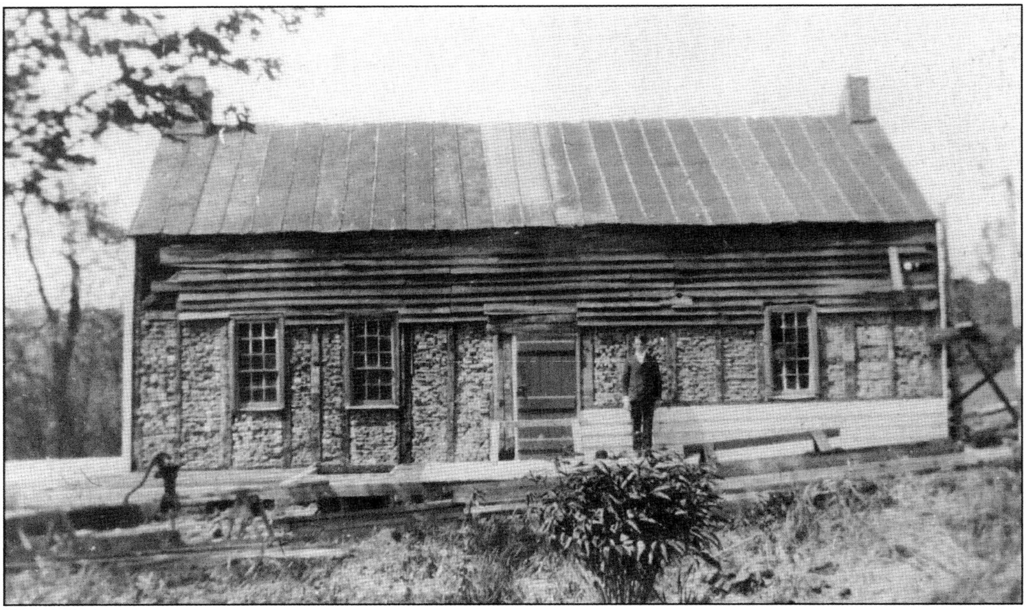

Joshua and Maria Doty Martin built this house before 1766 on a bluff above the present bridge over Toms Brook on Gilbride Road. Martin operated both a gristmill and a sawmill here. In this 1907 photograph, the clapboards have been removed to reveal stone-filled frame construction, an early method of insulation. The house survives. Joshua's son, Absalom, was the first postmaster. (IKE.)

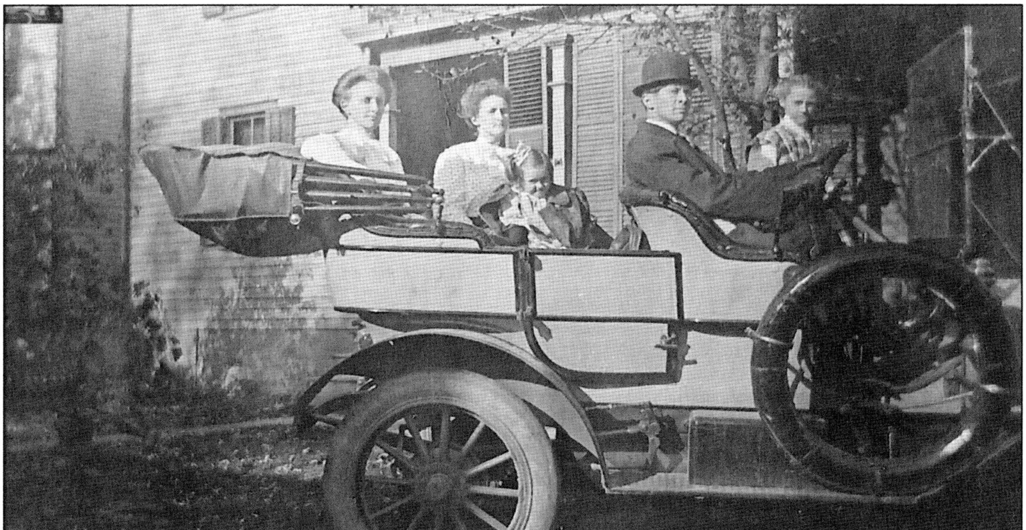

Thomas Roberts emigrated from Wales and married Lettie Van Nest in 1840. Their son John Peter Roberts was the father of John David (J.D.) Roberts, pictured in the family automobile in 1908. From left to right are Louisa Colthar and J.D.'s wife, Hattie Van Nest Roberts, with Louisa's daughters, Ruth and Gladys. Hattie and her sister-in-law Bessie Bolmer Van Nest kept extensive diaries detailing life in the Martinsville area. (RBT.)

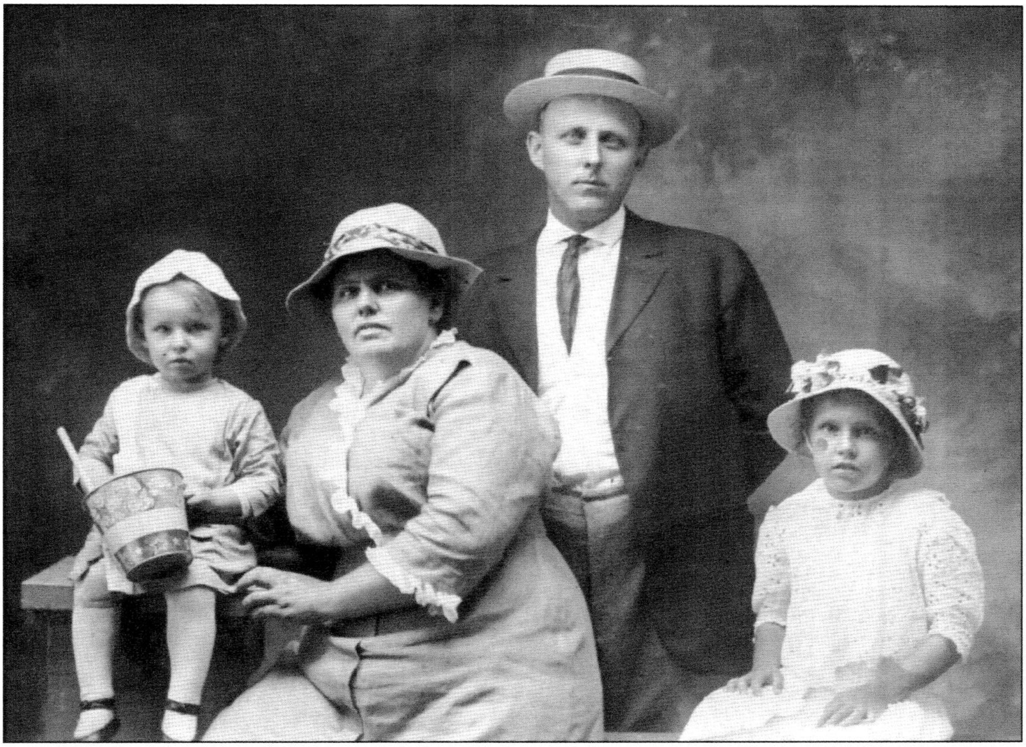

John and Sarah Bartle came from Yorkshire, England, in 1843 with their children William, Isaac, Ellis, John, and Hannah. Ellis then married another Sarah, who bore 14 children. Seven of their sons—William Ellis, Isaac, John, Edward, James, Albert, and Fred—and several daughters lived in Martinsville by 1900. Albert and his wife, Lillian Giddes, are pictured in 1915, with son Arthur and daughter Dorothy. Albert was foreman of his brother's stone quarry. (IKE.)

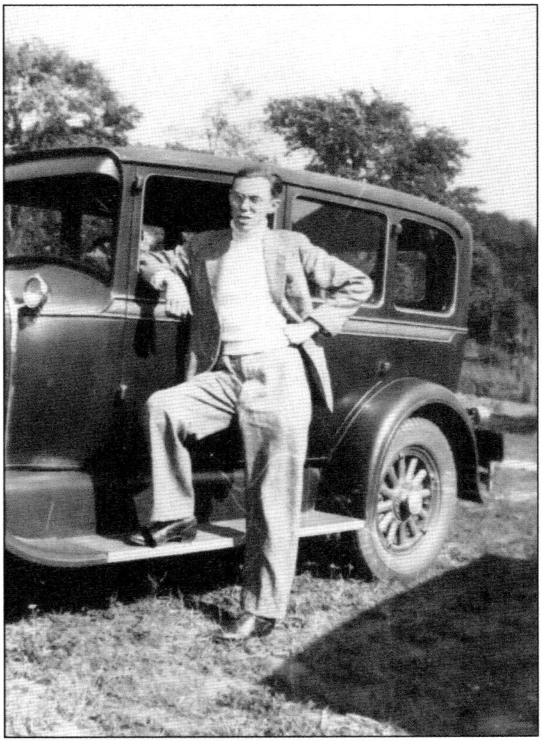

Fred Bartle, whose wife was Doris Van Winkle, became the village blacksmith. Their son Franklin Way Bartle was an avid photographer whose many photographs helped document village life. Known affectionately by all as "Doc," for his scholarly personality, he appears in 1932 beside the family automobile. He was active in community affairs, appearing in dramatic productions and serving as president of the Martinsville Community Club, later renamed Martinsville Community Center. (DOC.)

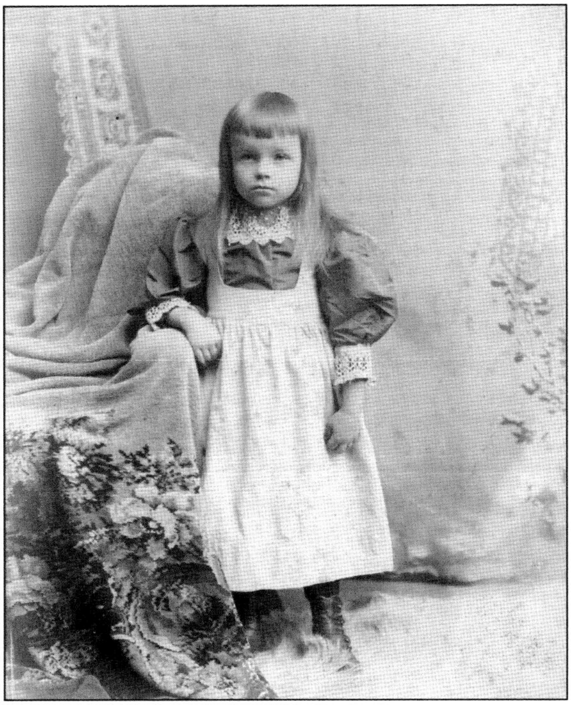

William Ellis Bartle, who married Elizabeth Zimmerman, was an astute businessman who employed his brothers John, Isaac, and Albert in the stone quarry begun by his father about 1875. At one time, he owned all the land between the ridges of the two mountains from Chimney Rock Road to Newmans Lane. He was also a philanthropist whose generosity benefited his community. His daughter Jessie appears in this 1896 photograph. (JCD.)

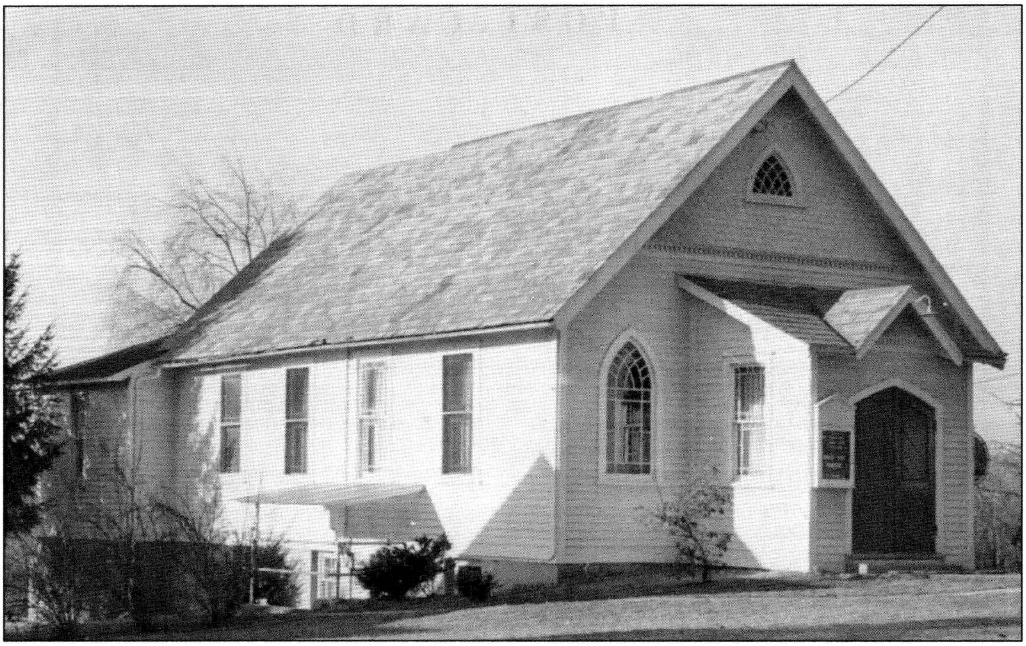

Martinsville Methodists met in private homes until 1894, when the Mount Horeb and Springdale churches sponsored the building of the Martinsville Methodist Church, and the three churches shared a pastor. Neighbors lent chairs, and Lyng's store provided kerosene lamps for the opening service in the new church. Edwin Smalley, whose father had been pastor of all three churches, was lay preacher and Sunday school superintendent for 25 years. (KCD.)

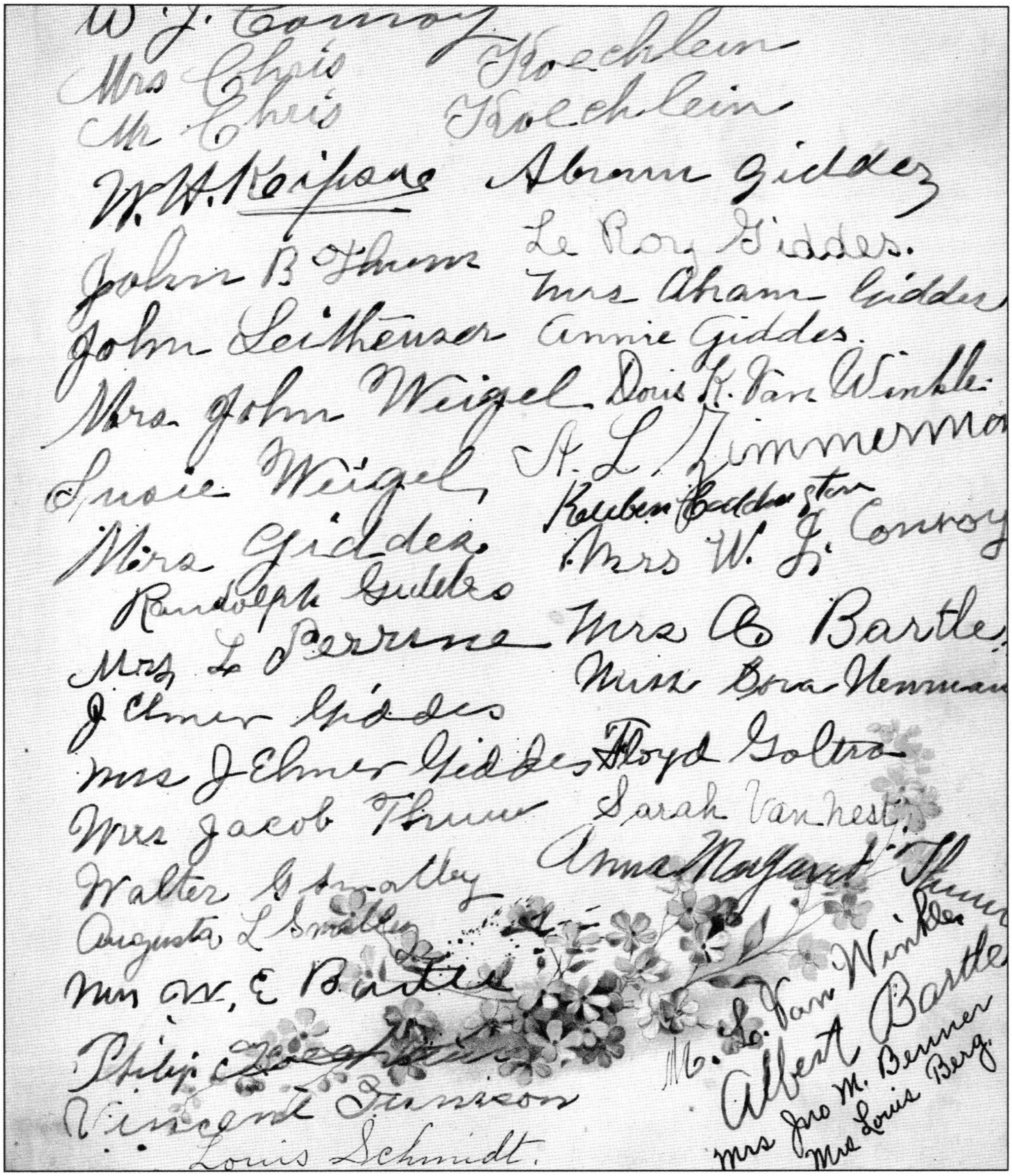

Signatures in the guest book at the 1905 wedding of John F. Thum and Jennie M. Giddes fill four pages and record more than 100 neighbors. Over 40 old-family names include Abbott, Bartle, Benner, Berg, Conroy, Coddington, DeMott, Durling, Goltra, Haines, Jetter, Kipsey, Koechlein, Mallett, Martin, McGowan, Newman, Nuse, Opdyke, Perrine, Smalley, Schmidt, Skillman, Smith, Spencer, Totten, Tunison, Van Nest, Van Winkle, Voorhees, Walton, Way, Weigel, and Zimmerman. Several of the single young people in attendance later married fellow guests. On this page decorated with forget-me-nots, Reuben Coddington's autograph appears several spaces above Sarah Van Nest's, whom he later married. M.L. Van Winkle was the mother of Doris Van Winkle, who would marry Fred Bartle. A.L. Zimmerman was a relative of Elizabeth Zimmerman, who signed with her married name of Mrs. W.E. Bartle. Floyd Goltra attended, but he would remain a bachelor all his life. (THM.)

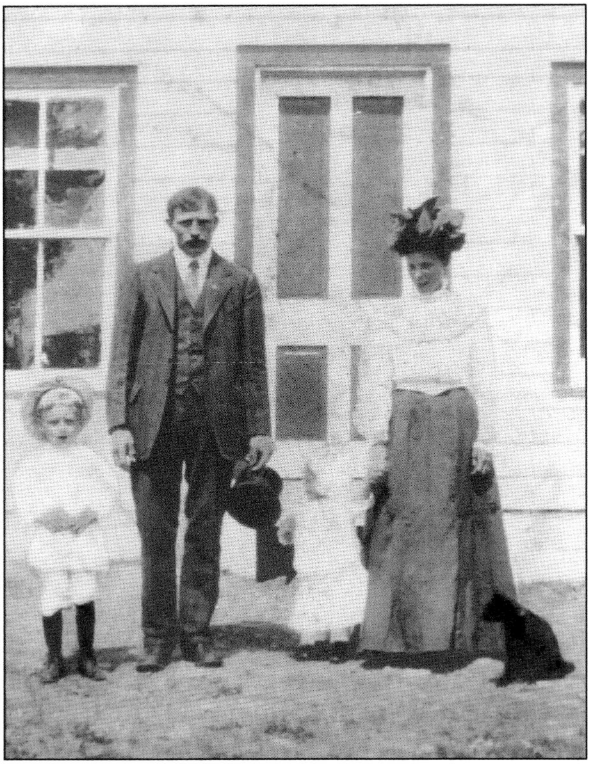

The William and Mabel Mason family dressed in their finest for this 1910 family portrait with son Albert, daughter Florence, and the family cat. William's brother Dennis lived next door on Mount Horeb Road. Both worked in the stone quarry and were sons of German immigrant Henry Mason. William's home is now gone, but family members continue to live in Dennis and Amelia's house across from the Reuben Coddington farm. (MSN.)

In 1918, the Bartle and Smalley families gathered at the Bartle homestead on Chimney Rock Road for the wedding of Jessie Bartle and Edwin Smalley. Several guests were in uniform, but the groom, standing tall beside his bride with her bouquet, had not yet left for World War I. The farm fields later grew Lofts Grass Seed and are now the site of Loft Farm townhouses and Chimney Rock County Park. (IKE.)

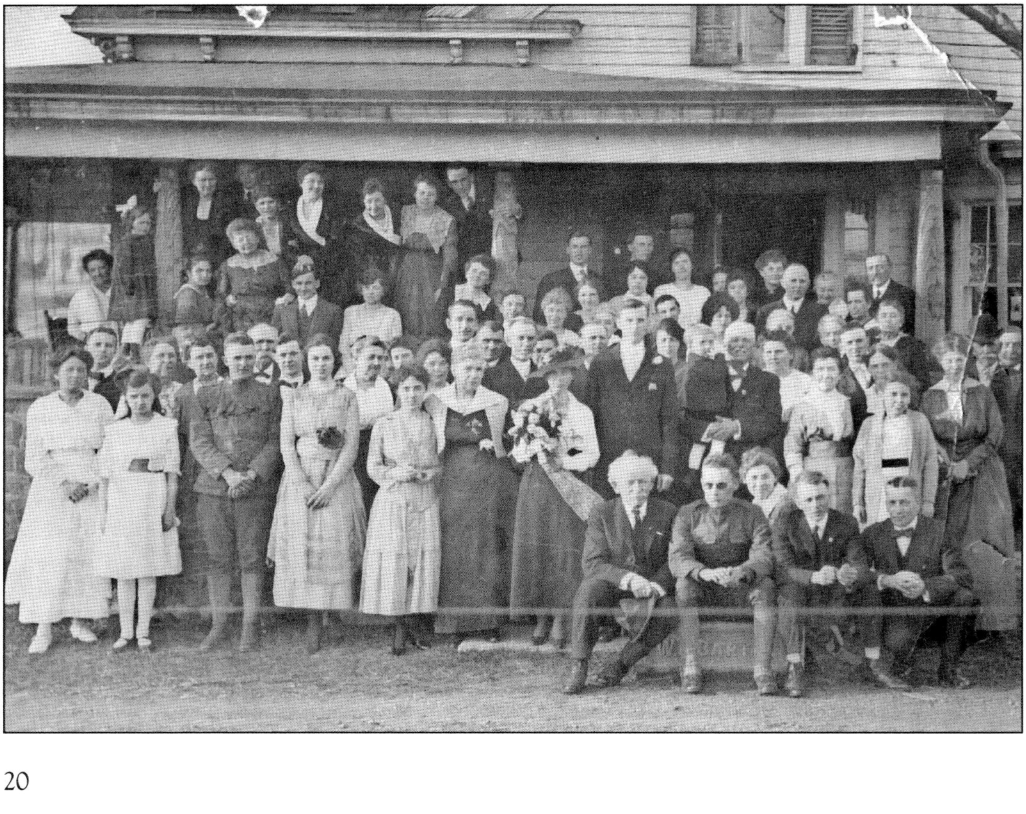

In the early 20th century, immigrants from other parts of Europe joined the melting pot of neighbors. Esther Petho came from Hungary and married German immigrant Charles Yehle. They settled on Chimney Rock Road in Martinsville in 1921. Esther embroidered the skirt panel for the outfit she wears here, and a dressmaker then created the ensemble. The embroidered panel is the prized possession of her daughter Freda. (YLE.)

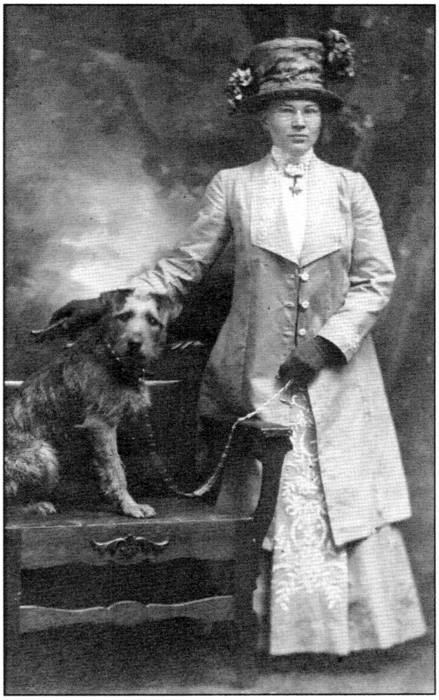

Machinist Rudolph Hubacek came to America from Slovakia in 1914, followed by Marie Nemec in 1917, the year they married and posed for this photograph. They moved to Gilbride Road in 1932 with their children Bertha, Marie, and Rudolph. Daughter Marie married Walter Blejwas, and they and their three children, Walter Jr., Thomas, and Virginia, lived with Marie's parents for many years. Their neighbors were the Gilbrides, Kubisches, and Peppers. (HUB.)

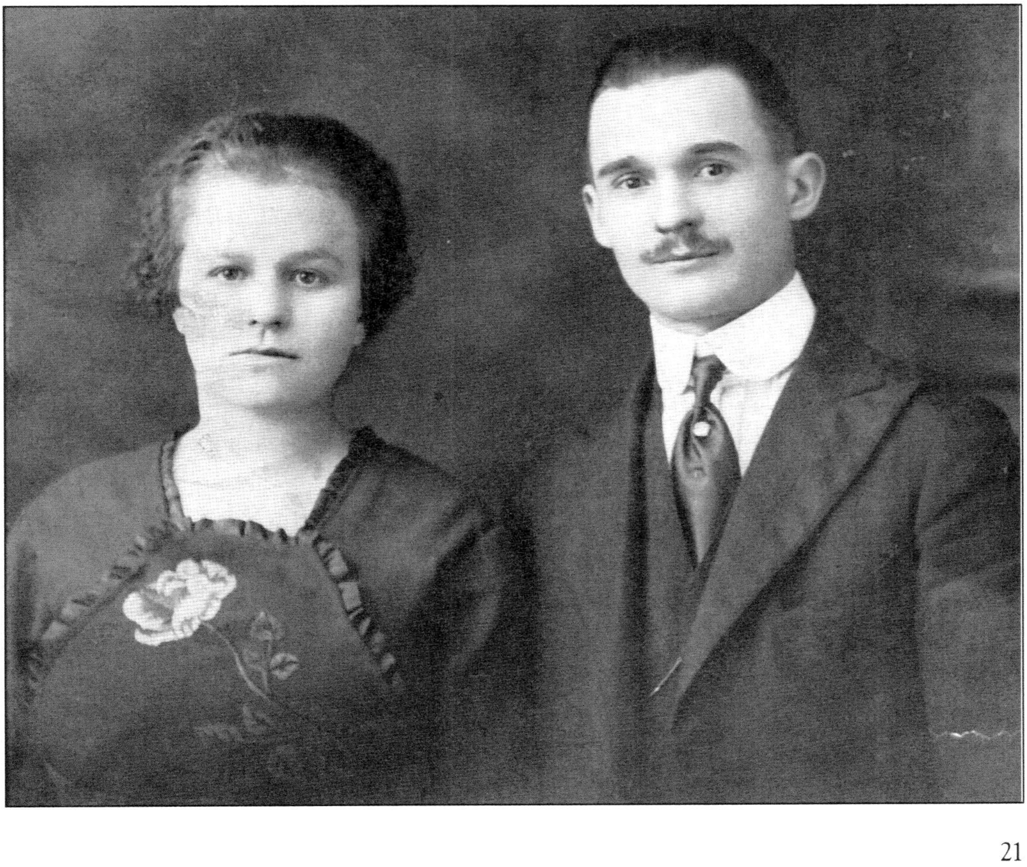

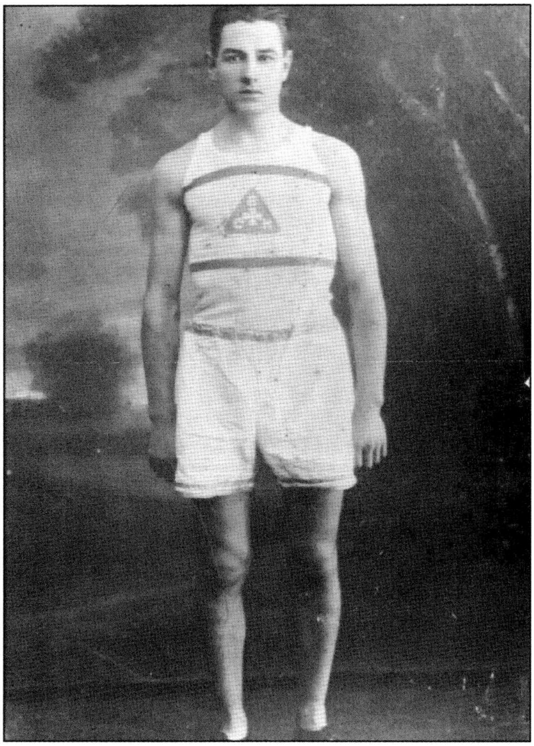

When the 1919 National Prohibition Act ended Edward Byrne's career in New York as an imitator of fine French liqueurs, he brought his family to Mount Horeb. Having placed fifth in the 1915 Boston Marathon with a time of two hours and 37 minutes, Byrne's running a few miles to his new employment as a chemist in Bound Brook was an easy jog. Of Irish and German parentage, he refused an invitation to lend his talents to the local underground bootlegging operation. (PVW.)

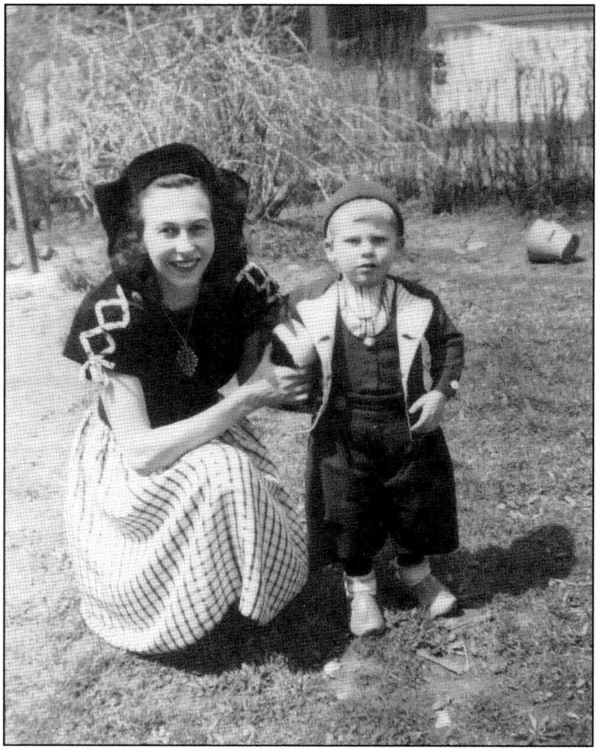

Faced with difficult living conditions in postwar Holland in 1946, Antoinette Rooda poses with her three-year-old son Gonthar in his traditional Dutch outfit with balloon pants and wooden shoes before they fled to America. She brought $5 and a trunkful of antiques to sell. Her husband, John, and daughter, Johanna, followed later. The family located in the Mount Horeb area, 250 years after the first Hollanders had settled here. (ROD.)

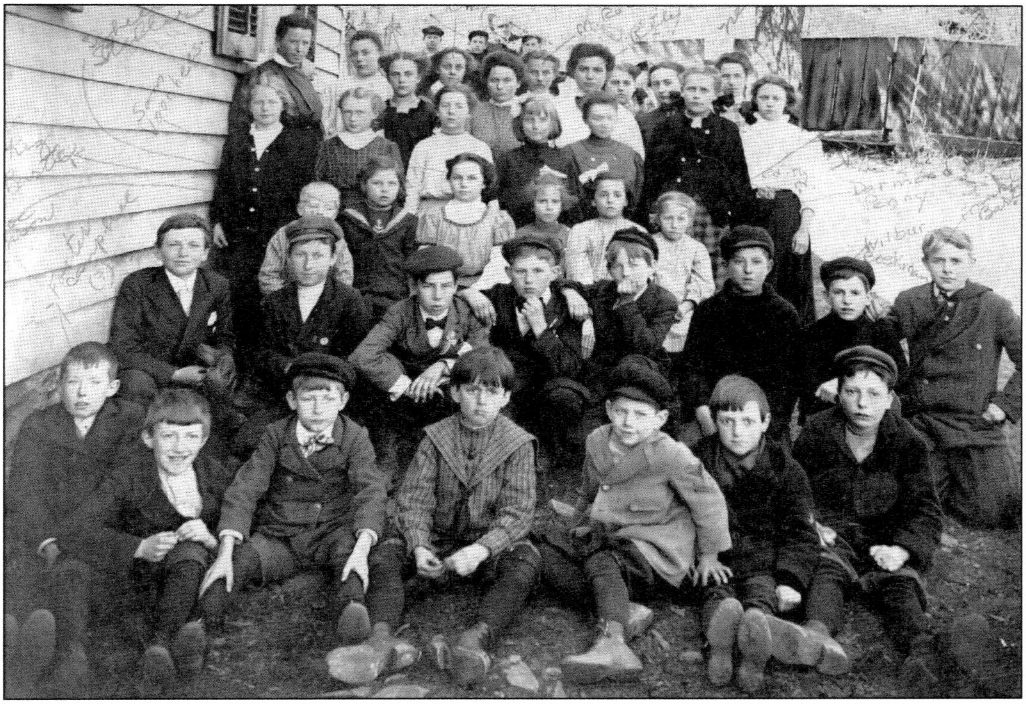

All eight grades of Martinsville School are assembled with their teacher, Addie Opdyke, in 1909. Names written on the side of the photograph, from top to bottom, are (left row) Miss Opdyke, Sybella Stieler, Sam Voorhees, Kiz Bartle, Joe Mason, and Foster Campbell; (right row) Minnie Ackerback, Darmond Penny, Wilbur Beekman, and Franklin Bartle with hand in pocket. Note the caps, black stockings, high shoes, and the cobbled soles on the shoes in the first row. (IKE.)

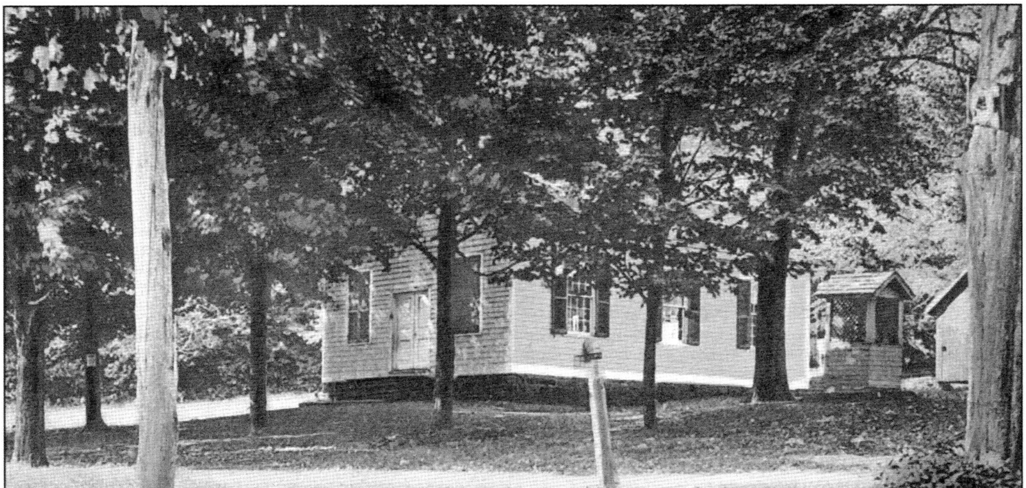

The Dutch settlers believed in education for their children. The first school was built in 1734 in the Vosseller Avenue and Gilbride Road area east of the village. A second school was constructed in 1751 several miles west of the village at Mount Vernon Road. The third school, located at the head of Chimney Rock Road, was built in 1820 and replaced in 1861 by the building pictured. (VCH.)

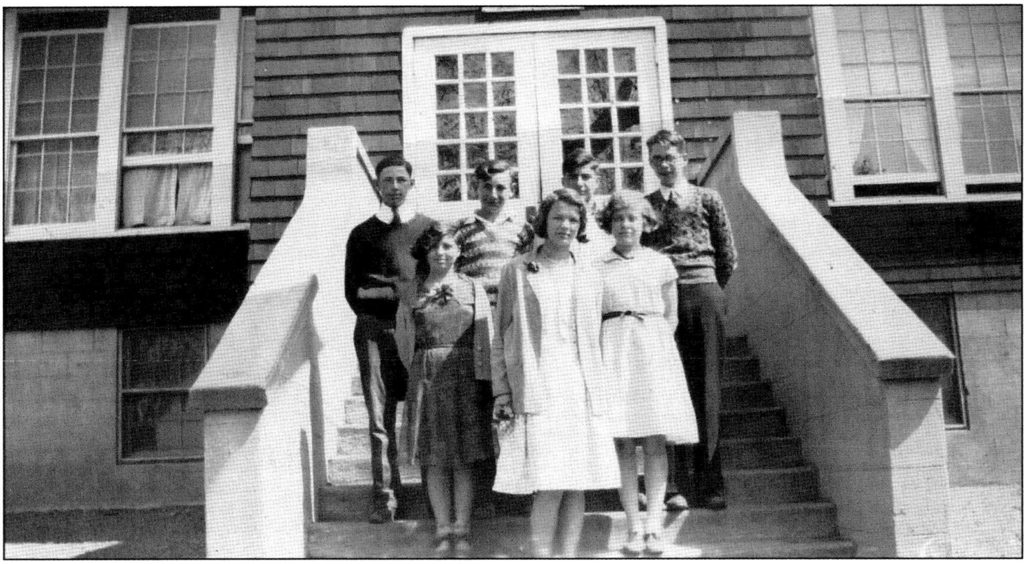

Florence Wilde's eighth-grade class in 1931 consisted of seven students. They are, from left to right, (first row) Frances "Sis" Cramer, Eleanor Byrne, and Ethel Vactor; (second row) Paul Moody, Richard Feudtner, Ted Mastapeter, and John Perrine. The Perrines were longtime residents who had a large poultry farm on Vosseller Avenue for many years. The Cramer and Mastapeter families added Italian roots to the melting pot. (PVW.)

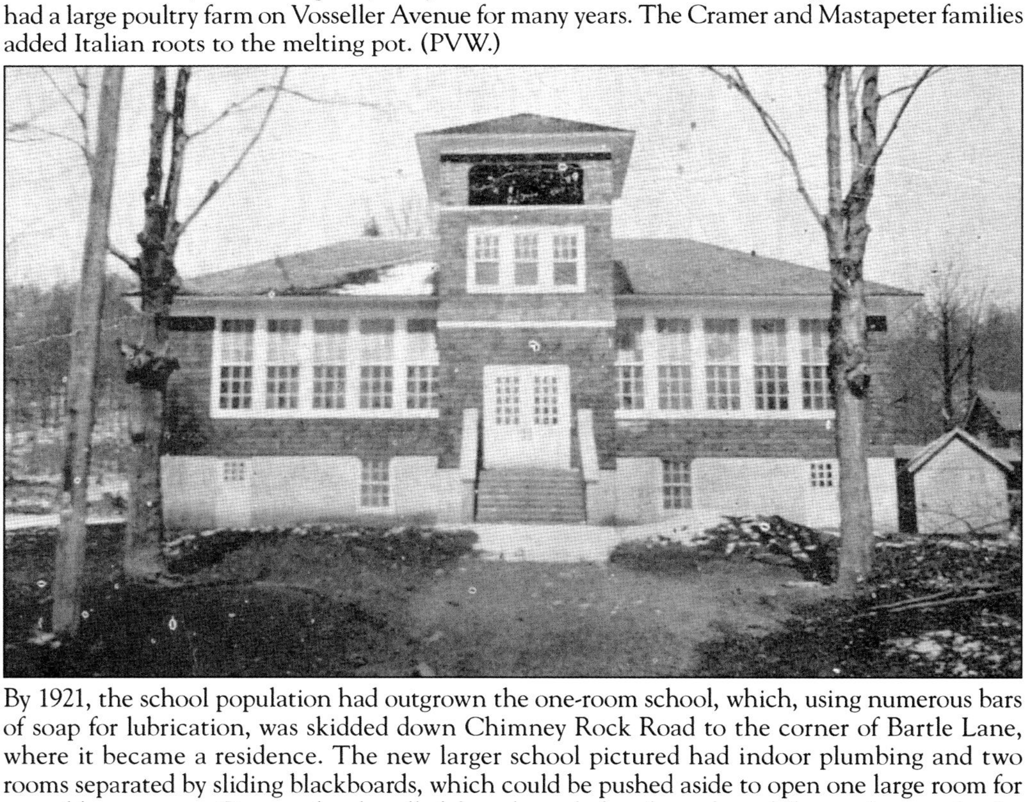

By 1921, the school population had outgrown the one-room school, which, using numerous bars of soap for lubrication, was skidded down Chimney Rock Road to the corner of Bartle Lane, where it became a residence. The new larger school pictured had indoor plumbing and two rooms separated by sliding blackboards, which could be pushed aside to open one large room for assembly programs. One teacher handled first through fourth grades, while another taught the upper four grades. (FBR.)

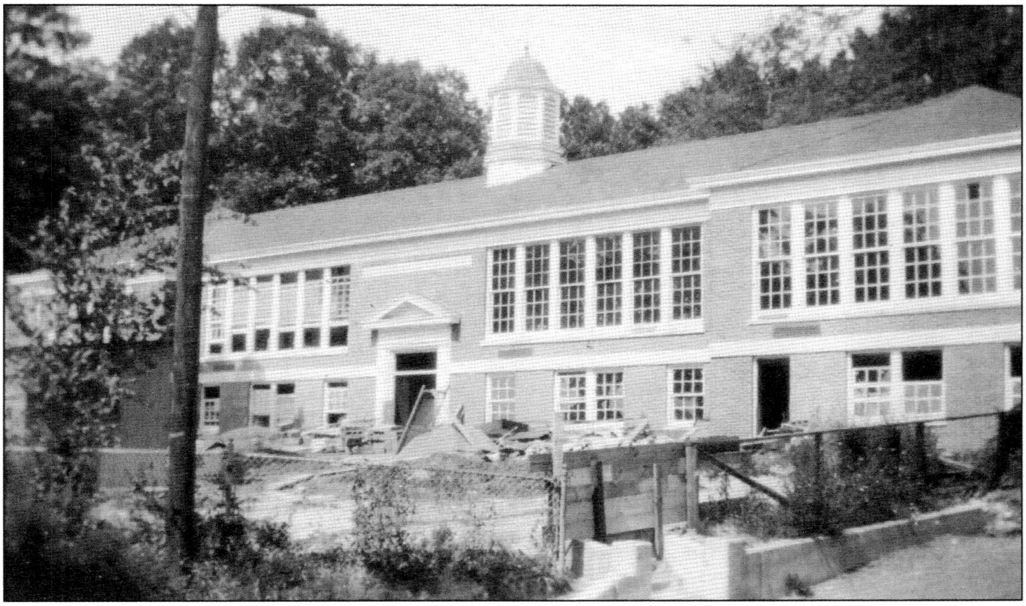

As the school population continued to expand, a four-room addition was necessary by 1934. A classroom was added at each end, with a kindergarten room beneath the western room, on left in this photograph, and an all-purpose room beneath the new classroom on the eastern end. A library, with a piano for glee club rehearsals, and a storage room occupied the original two ground-floor spaces. The school closed in 1978 and is now a professional building, which continues to be a focal point at the head of Chimney Rock Road. (HNS.)

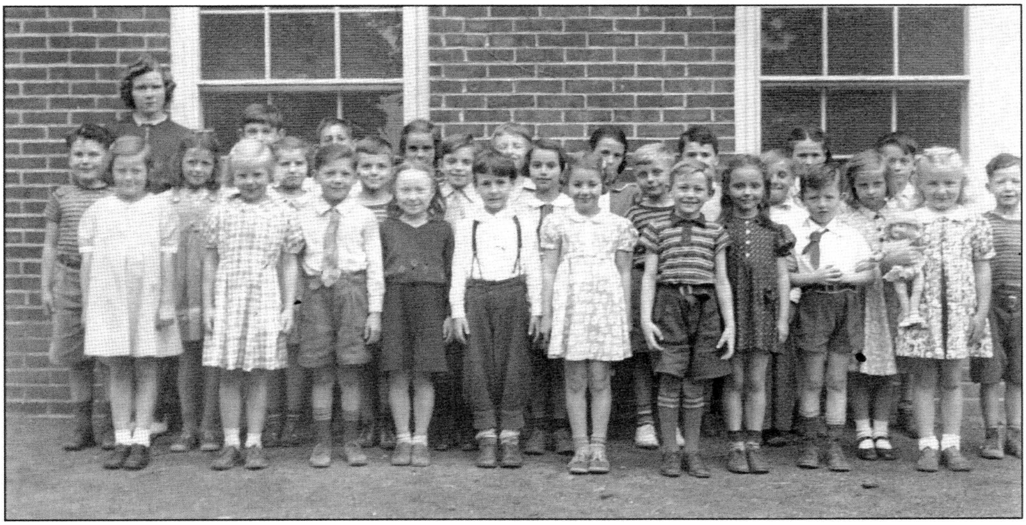

Clothing in Miss Lytel's 1938 first and second grades differed from that in 1909. From left to right are (first row) Shirley Anderson, Esther Sauer, Pat Boglioli, Betty Stumpp, John Long, Beverly Miller, James Hicklin, Nancy Mitchell, unidentified, and Arlene Olson; (second row) ? Sullivan, Betty Parry, Shirley Cunningham, Herb Totten, John Frankhauser, Meryl Brown, Richard Davis, Andrew Myer, Catherine Van Heusen, and Bill Mingle; (third row) Miss Lytel, unidentified, Bob Grab, Lorraine Totten, Kenny Wilson, Sally Richards, Jack Papen, Elaine Papen, and David London. (LND.)

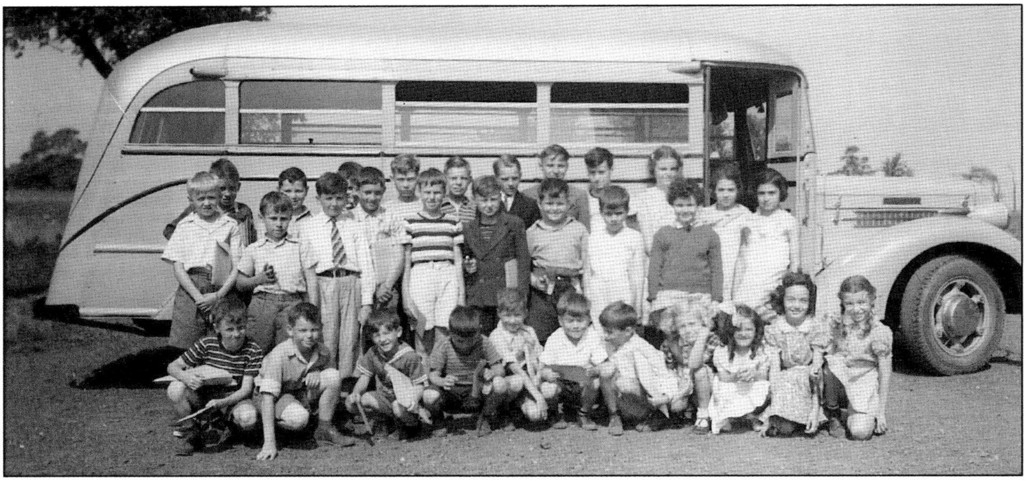

In the 1930s, high school students rode to Bound Brook with Franklin "Chick" Bartle on his mail run. Chick, who had lost an arm in World War I, had to take his hand off the steering wheel to shift gears, while his passengers held their breaths. Raymond Haines then began transporting younger students (pictured) to the Martinsville School and older students to Bound Brook High School in a single yellow bus, which expanded to an extensive fleet over the years. Pictured is one of his 1940s vehicles. (HNS.)

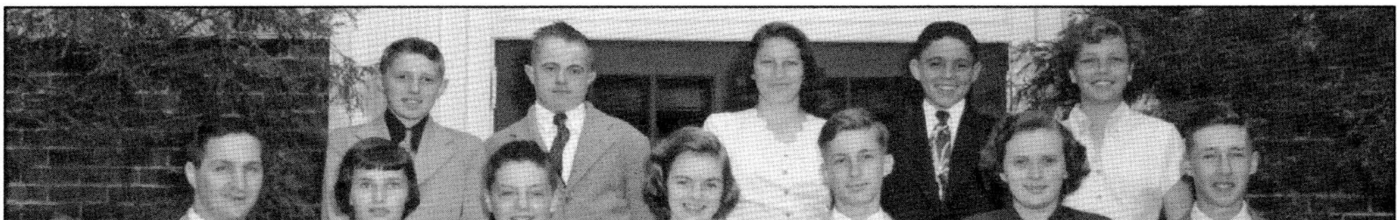

By 1950, the eighth grade had doubled in size from the 1931 enrollment. The class included, from left to right, (first row) Bob Rodgers, Margaret Tullo, Tom Biddle, and Roberta Wait; (second row) Margaret Tingley, Ed Hoyt, Pat Valentine, Bill Kozic, Edna Conyk, and Warren Stein; (third row) George Matalenas, Edward Mayer, Rose Tullo, Patsy Martino, and Beverly Davis. Walter Kritzberger was the teacher, and Adelaide Kenny was principal. (PVW.)

Commencement daisy chains have long been a tradition, as evidenced by this photograph from the early 1900s. Martinsville continued the tradition for many years, as children brought bunches of daisies to school and scoured the surrounding fields for additional blossoms the day before graduation. Long ropes of loosely braided strips of cotton sheets, stored year after year, were soaked in water so that the flowers would stay fresh as their stems were woven into the braids. (PVW.)

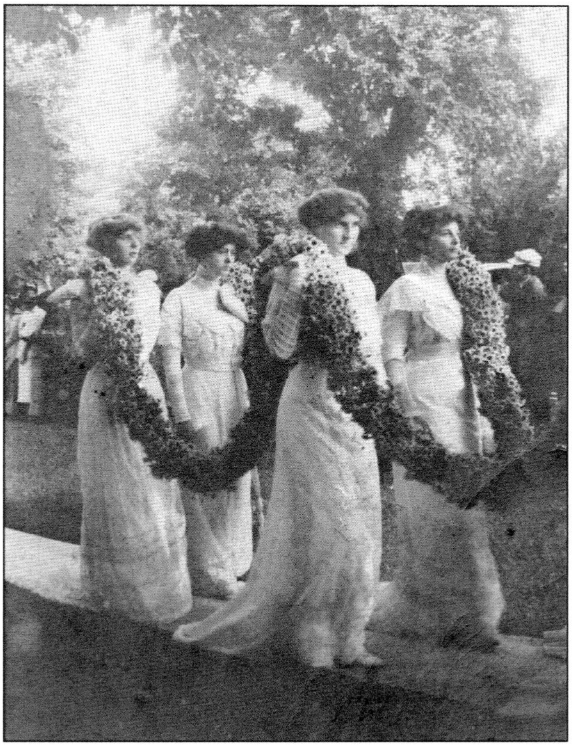

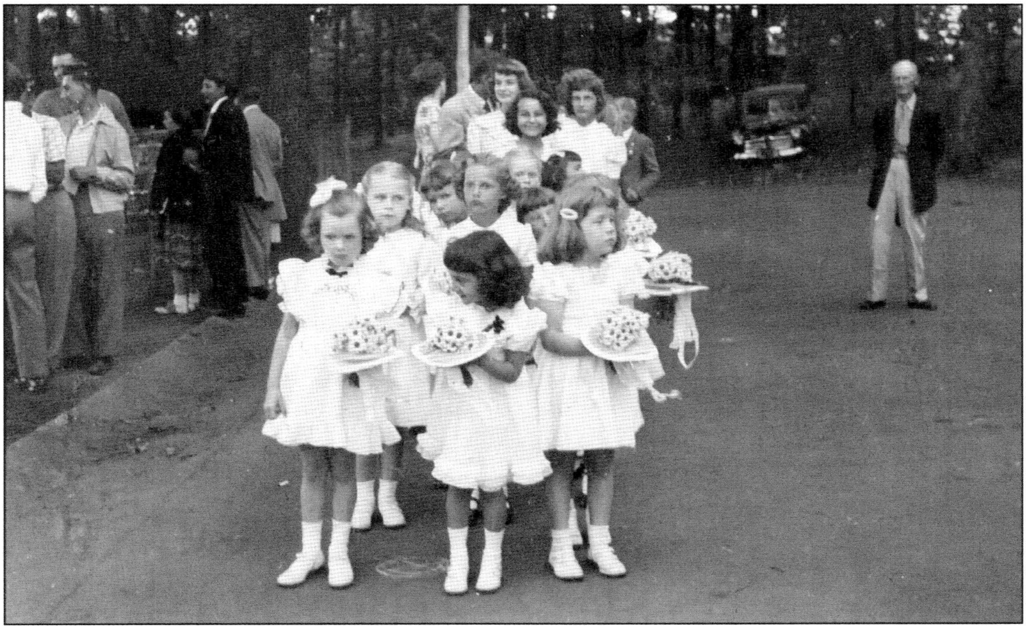

Younger girls dressed in pastels held the daisy chain to line the processional route. In this 1949 photograph, the daisy chain had been replaced by nosegays of daisies held by the unidentified younger girls, while members of the glee club wait behind them. From left, beside teacher Walter Kritzberger, are Pat Valentine, Margaret Tullo, and Margaret Tingley. (EGS.)

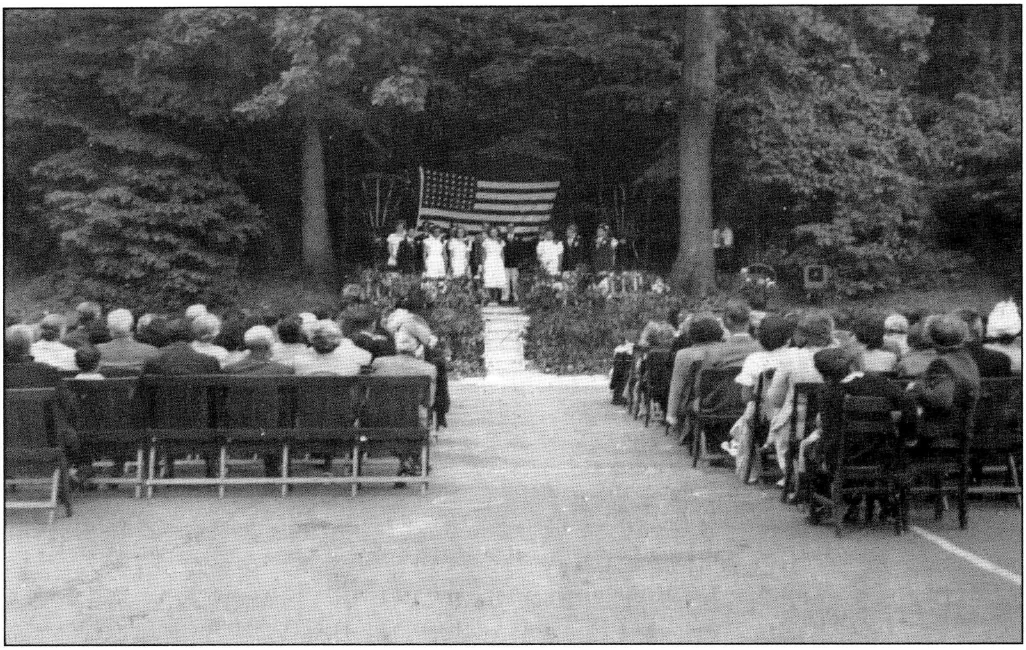

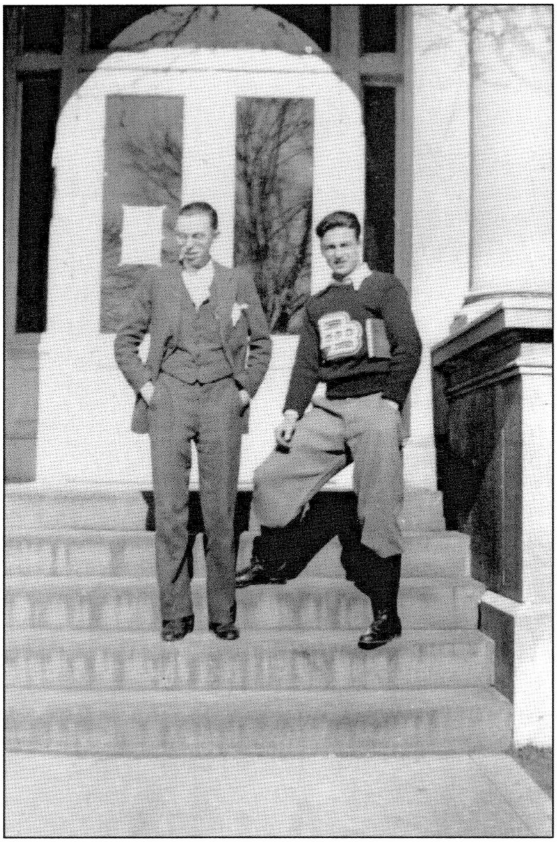

Until 1939, commencement ceremonies had been held in the adjacent Martinsville Community Club. Thereafter, the ceremony was held on the playground behind the school where a stage had been dug out of the edge of the woodland to form a raised platform. Here, rambler roses are wound into trellises beside the flag, and the stage is decked with flowers from residents' gardens. (EGS.)

High school was the next step for graduates. Most attended Bound Brook High School, while others went to Somerville High School. In 1933, on the steps of Bound Brook High School, Doc Bartle (left) and Bernard Gilbride demonstrate the varied fashions for the scholar, with Doc's three-piece suit, and for the athlete, with Bernie's varsity athletic letter proudly displayed on his sweater. Knickers continued to be fashionable. (DOC.)

Two

Farm Life in the Valley

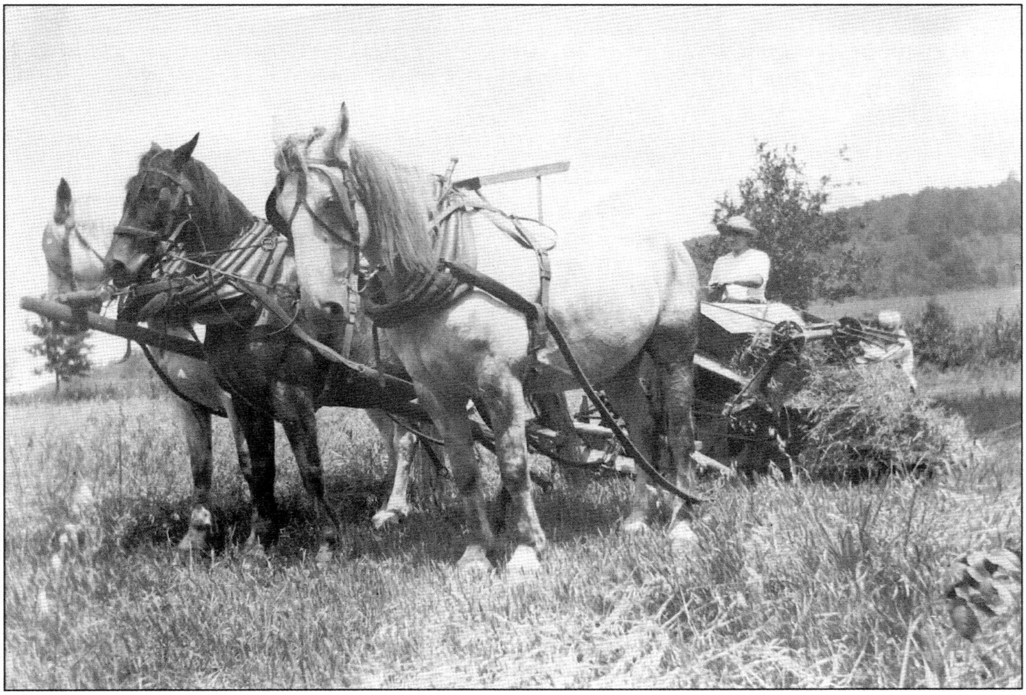

Farming in the rich soil of the Washington Valley was a way of life here long after other areas to the south had become urbanized. Horses not only hauled wagons and other farm equipment but also walked on treadmills to power large threshing machines. The three sturdy horses on the Musialowski farm in this 1920s photograph are pulling a binder, which is forming sheaves of grain to be loaded onto a wagon. (MUS.)

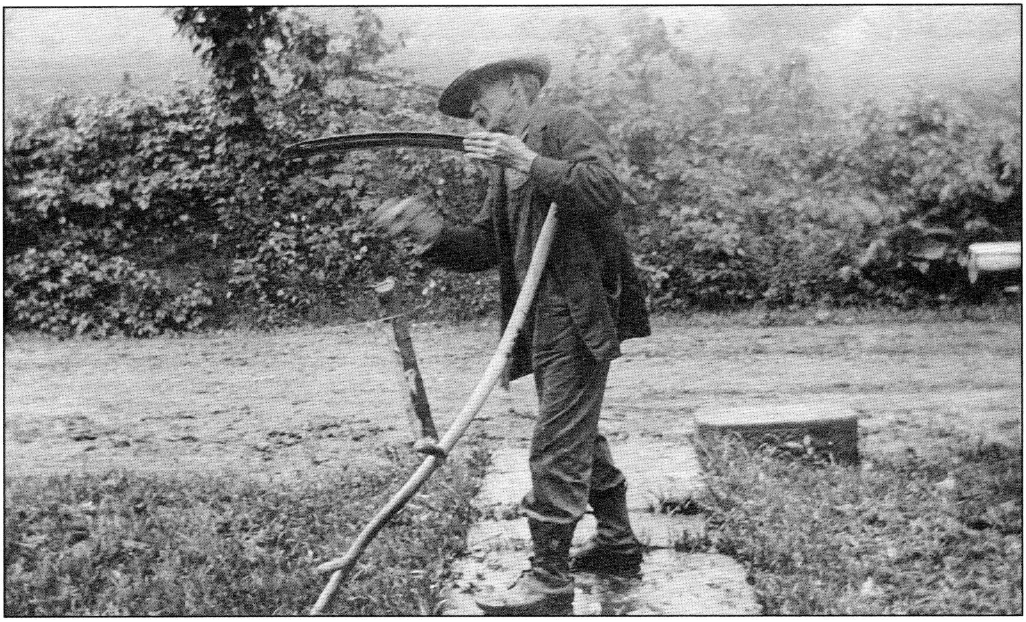

The scythe had been in use since Roman times, its design hardly changing over the centuries. After the invention of mowing machinery, it continued to be a necessary tool for uneven ground, hard-to-reach places, and for edging a field. In this 1903 photograph, John Peter Roberts sharpens his scythe on the Roberts family farm in the Spring Run area. (RBT.)

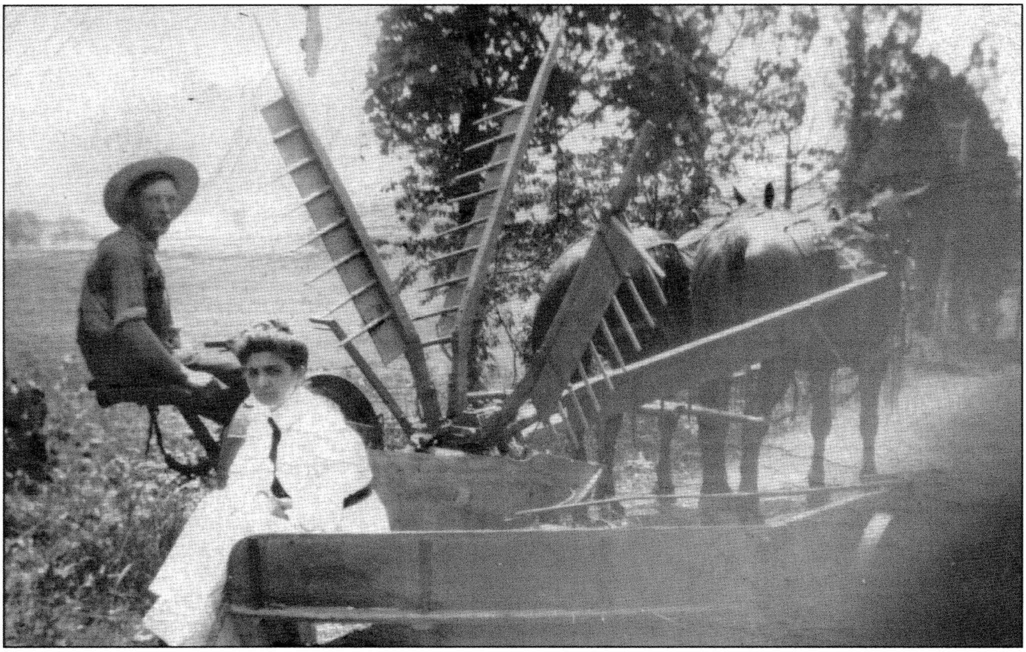

The reaper, invented by Cyrus McCormick, made it possible to harvest ten acres a day, compared to two or three acres by manual labor. The revolving rakes on this model swept the cut grain off the table to distribute it for drying in the sun before gathering it into sheaves. The workers in this 1910 photograph on the Bartle farm are unidentified. (JCD.)

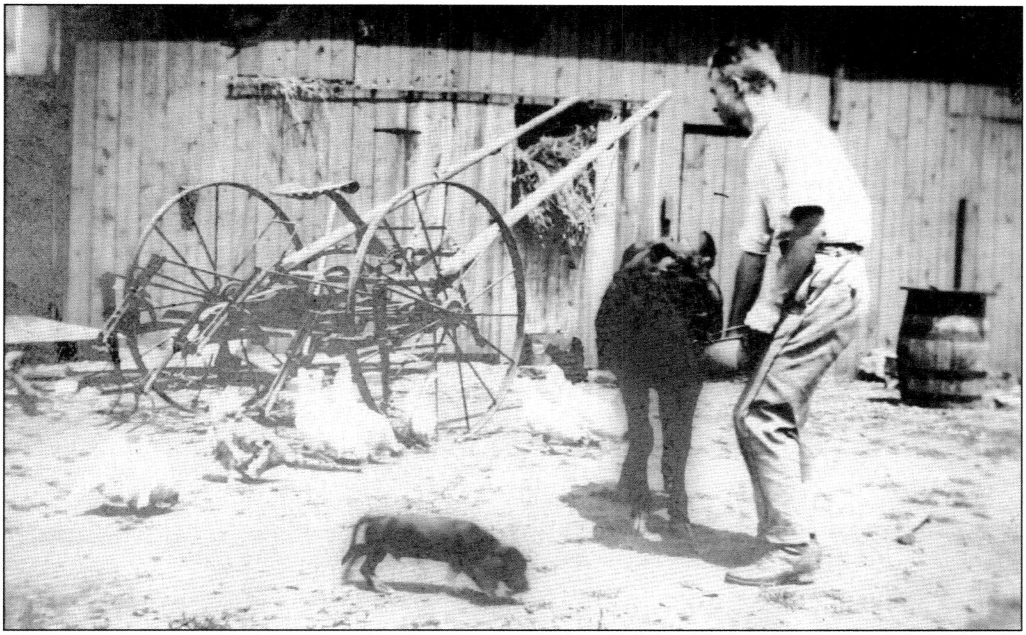

A dachshund—reputed to be more efficient at mouse control than the traditional cat—patrols the barnyard beside Stanley Bartle in 1910. The hay tedder model parked here employs a single three-pronged fork to lift and turn the hay in the field as it dries. Wider, more elaborate tedders had multiple sets of forks or an entire row of teeth to turn a wider swath across the field. (JCD.)

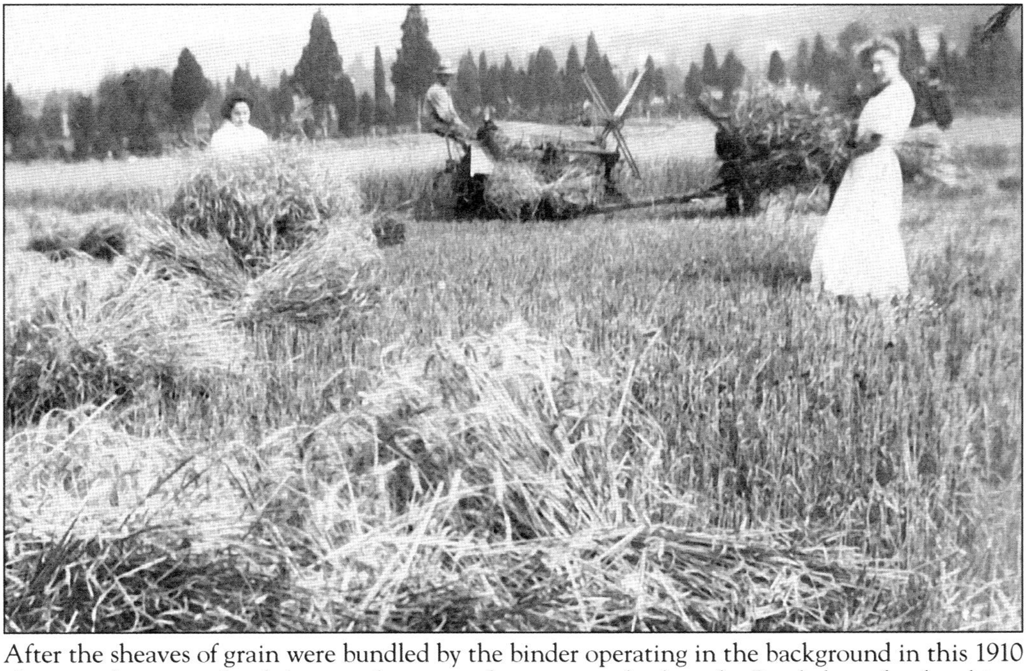

After the sheaves of grain were bundled by the binder operating in the background in this 1910 photograph, women haul them to the wagon for transport back to the Bartle barn for threshing. The rows of cedar trees edging the field were the pioneer plants that would quickly invade any field left fallow for a few years. They made fragrant Christmas trees. (JCD.)

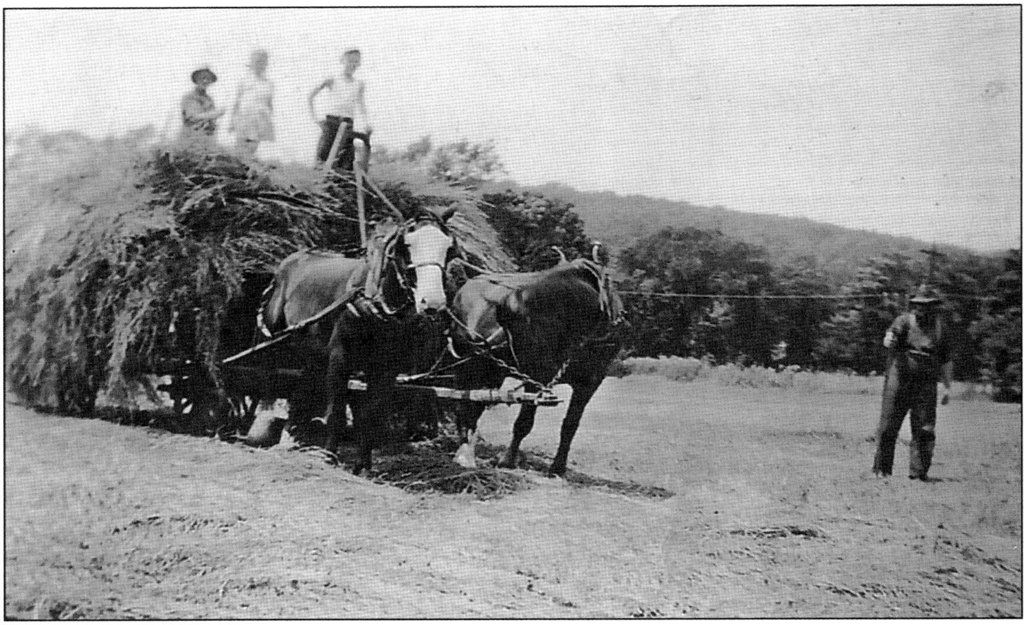

Harvesting was a hot, dusty summer job. A favorite thirst-quencher was switchel, or haymakers' punch, which might be described as farmers' Gatorade. The mixture of cider vinegar, water, and honey or molasses, sometimes with a dash of ginger, was more refreshing than plain cold water. In Joe Van Nest's field atop the load, from left to right, are unidentified, Shirley Anderson, and her brother Ed; Van Nest supervises from the ground. (AND.)

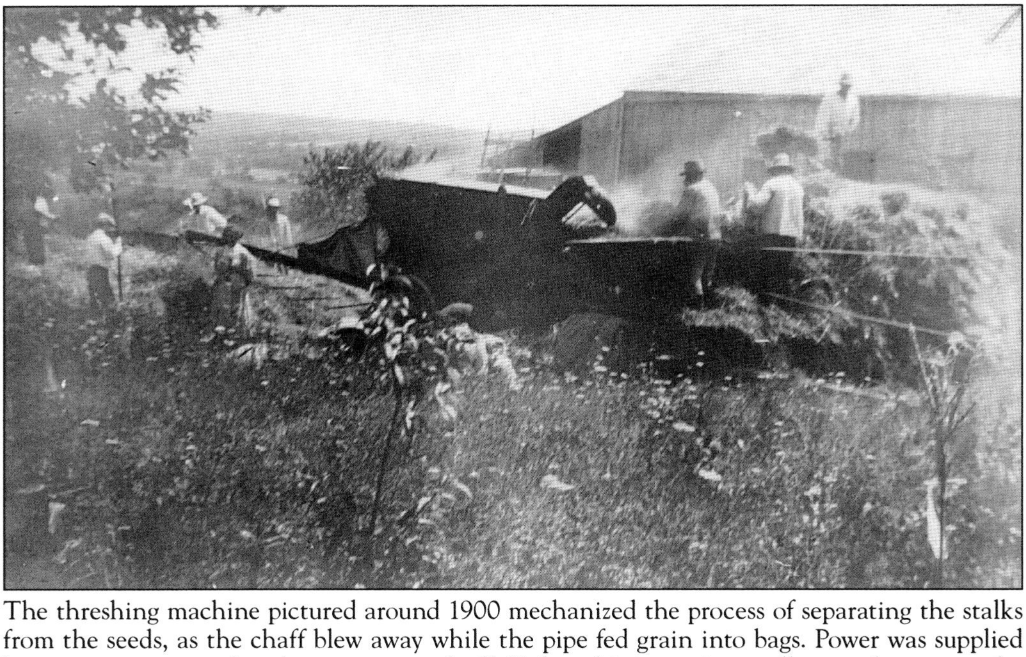

The threshing machine pictured around 1900 mechanized the process of separating the stalks from the seeds, as the chaff blew away while the pipe fed grain into bags. Power was supplied by a steam engine or by a horse on a treadmill. Before this invention, stalks were beaten on the threshing floor of the barn using a flail, which is a long-handled object with a two-foot-long beater attached by a leather thong. (JCD.)

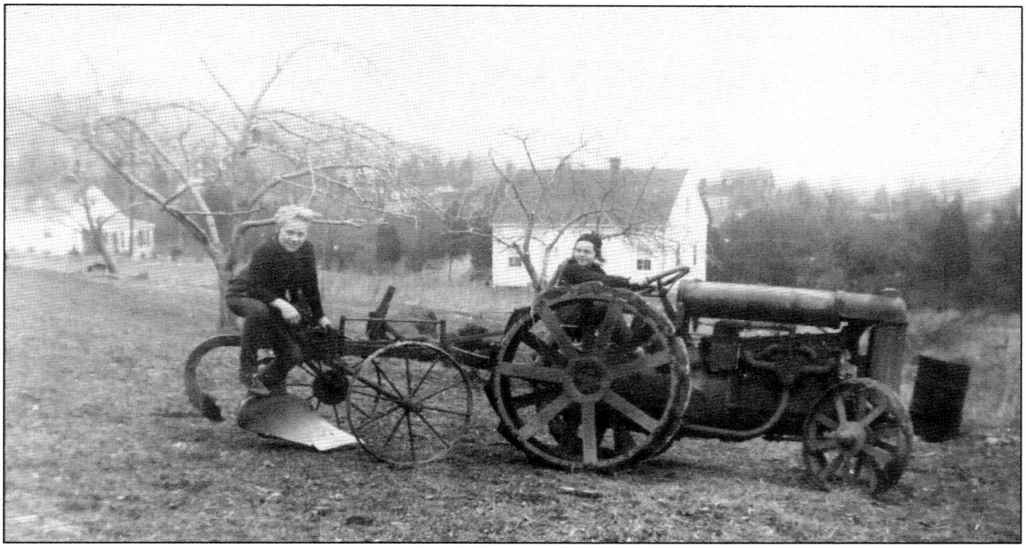

Henry Ford held a lifelong dream of making farming easier. His first small, lightweight Fordson tractor, introduced in 1916, made it possible for small farmers to own one of the vehicles. It was cheaper to maintain than horses. Owned by Edwin Smalley, Harold Coddington, and Chick Bartle, the tractor driven here in 1945 by Brent Duxbury, with Fluff Bartle on the plow, appears to be identical to a 1917 Fordson. (DUX.)

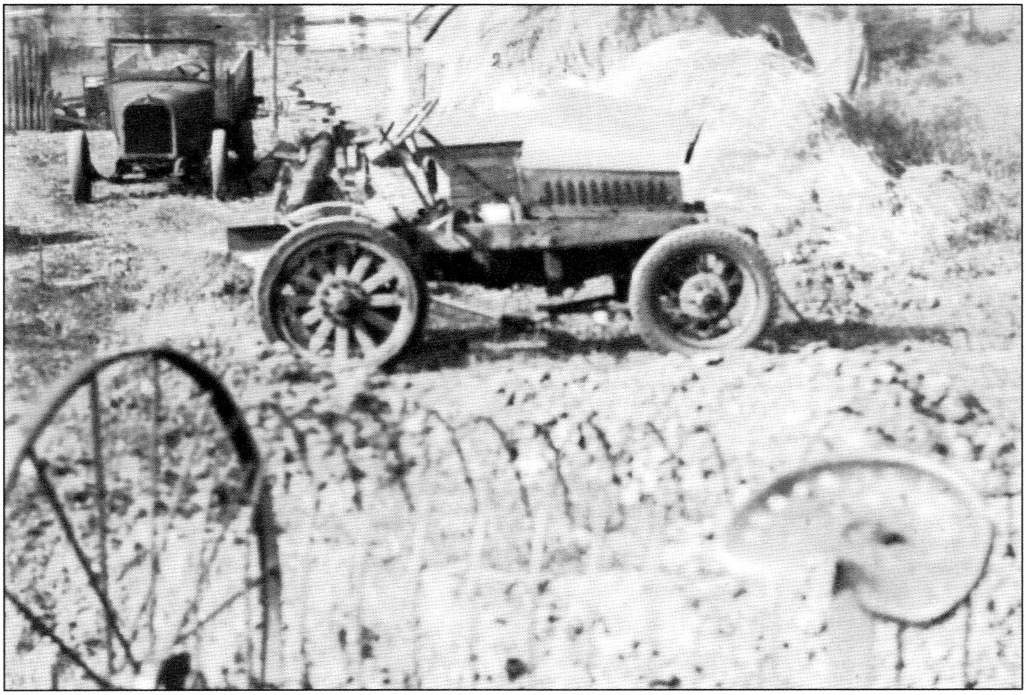

Even more popular than its Fordson tractors were conversion kits sold by Ford with which old Model A or Model T trucks could be converted into functional tractors. In Martinsville, Mort Clark, Bill Laire, and Ken Tingley built several of these units in Laire's garage and dubbed them C-L-T tractors. Pictured is one example, which was used on the Musialowski farm. (MUS.)

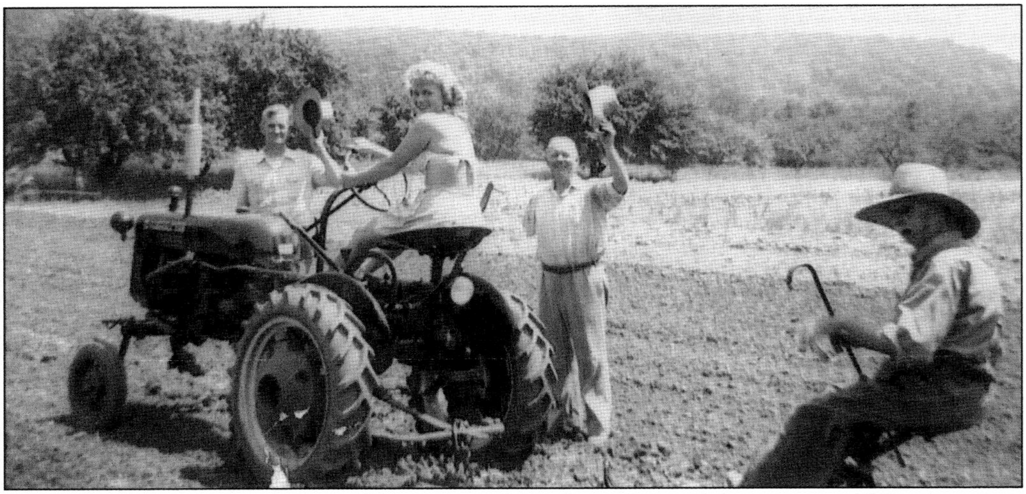

After World War II, Smalley, Coddington, and Bartle exchanged their trusty old Fordson for a new Farmall Cub. Written on the back of this 1948 photograph are the words: "Thrill of the new tractor!" Celebrating its arrival are, from left to right, Edwin Smalley, Fluff Bartle, Chick Bartle (who lost an arm in World War I), and Frank Wahl. (SBD.)

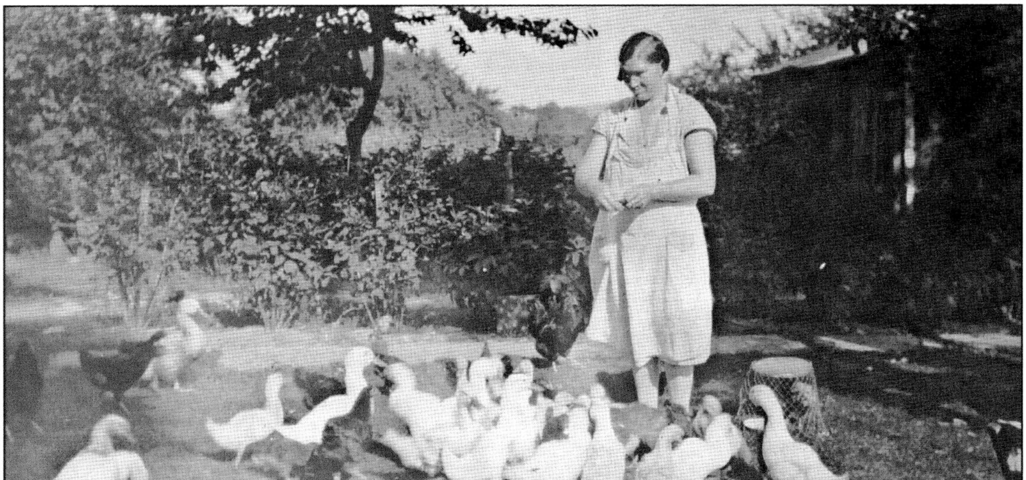

Country families kept at least a few chickens for family consumption, but Esther Yehle also kept ducks. Her ample apron was standard apparel for housewives. It might carry eggs or vegetables or kindling for the woodstove. It was also handy for carrying a hot pan or drying one's hands. She always kept a few nickels in her apron pocket to treat neighboring children who came to visit. (YLE.)

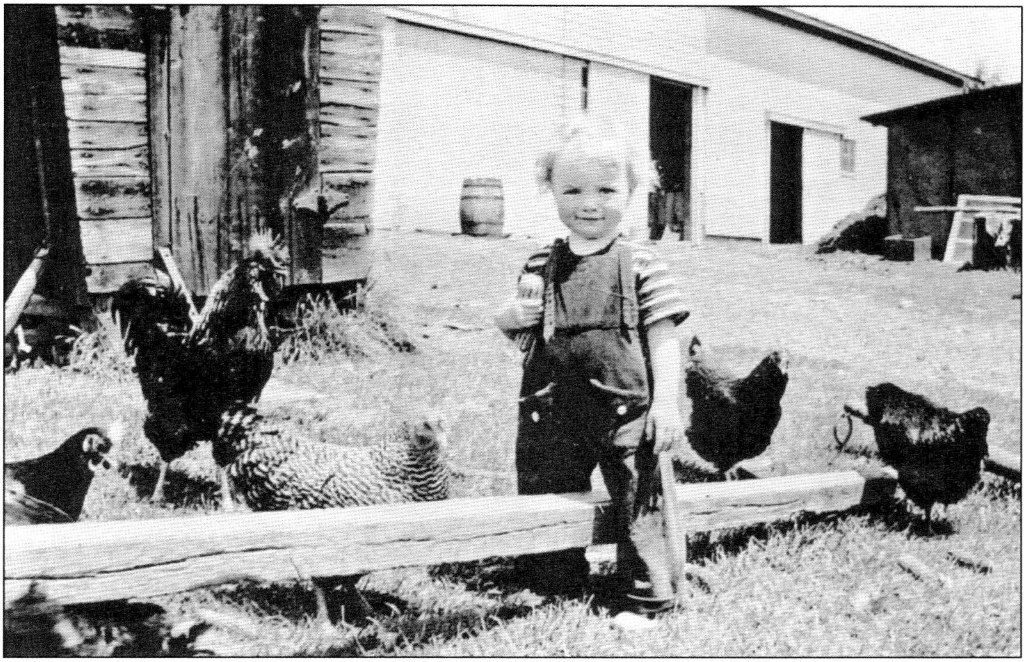

Hoping for a few kernels of corn, chickens on the William Van Nest farm gather around Pat Valentine in 1938. Farmers had a variety of devices for shelling corn, from hand-operated, one-cob-at-a-time shellers invented in 1850 to large-scale, machine-driven implements. Until the development of husking machinery, husking the corn was also a tedious hand operation, made lighter by inviting friends for a husking bee. (PVW.)

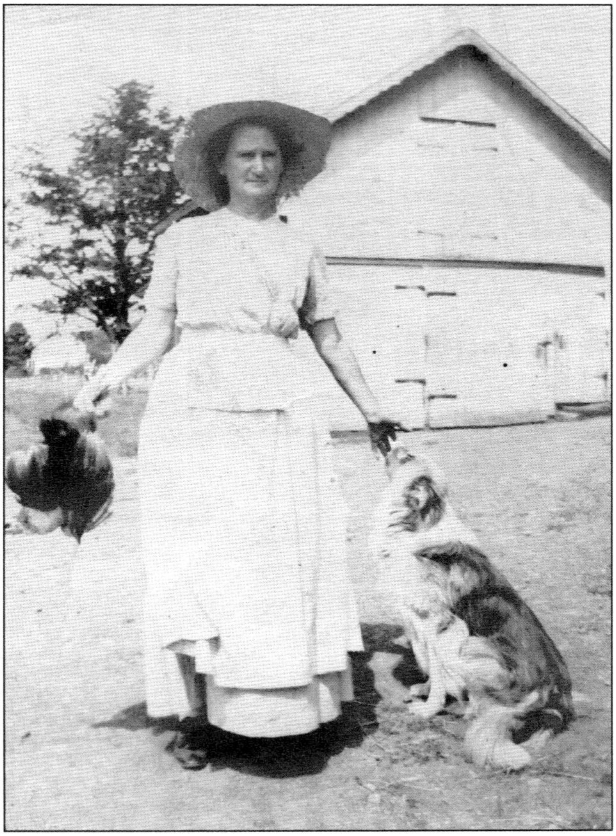

Preparing chicken for Sunday dinner began with decapitating the fowl—perhaps an ornery rooster or an old hen from the flock. This step accomplished, the family dog in this photograph gives new meaning to the phrase "finger lickin' good" before the chicken is dunked in boiling water to facilitate plucking the feathers—all unfamiliar tasks to most modern cooks. Tougher birds became stew, while younger ones were delicious roasted or fried. (JCD.)

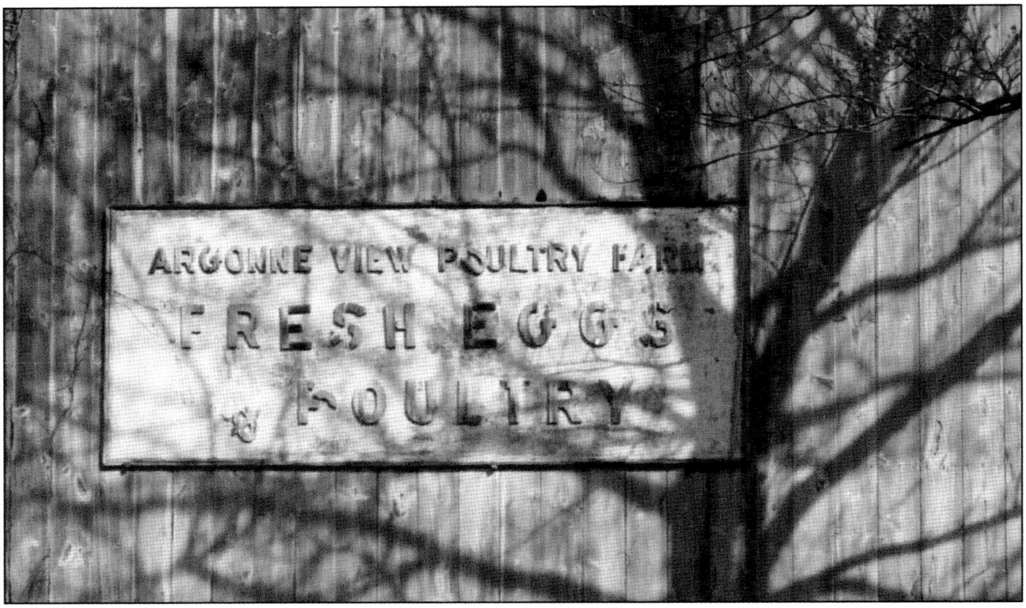

A few families in the valley had large-scale poultry farms. The Perrines on Vosseller Avenue supplied the eastern area of the valley, while the Wishnow family owned the Argonne View Poultry Farm in the western part of the valley. Neighbors recall stopping at the farm on the way home from church on Sunday mornings to buy several dozen eggs for a large family breakfast. Wishnowitz was the original family name, which added Russian roots to Martinsville's melting pot of neighbors. (WSH.)

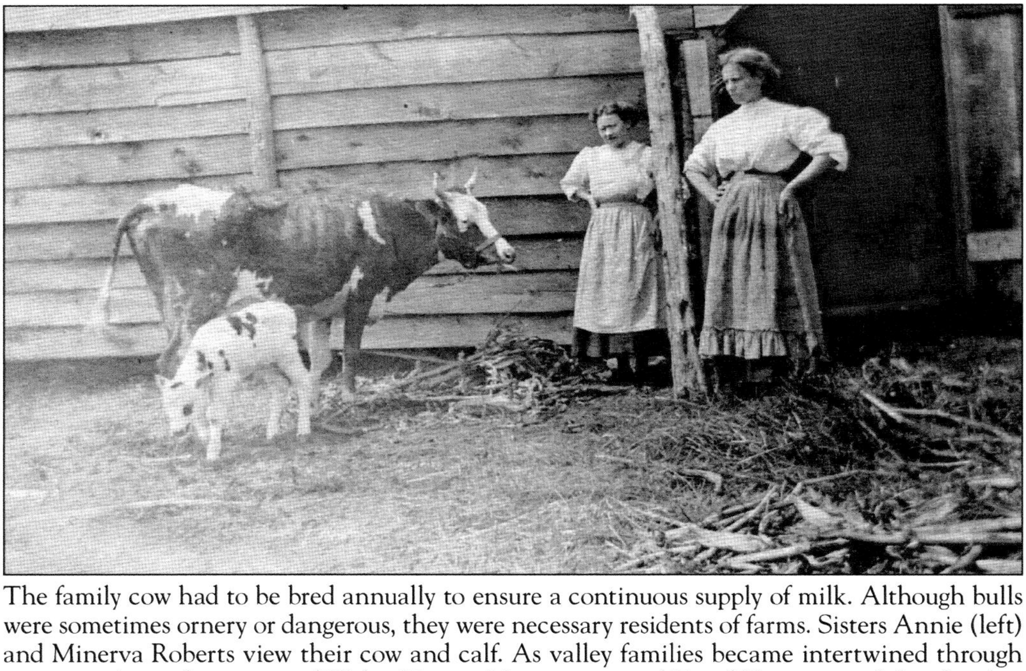

The family cow had to be bred annually to ensure a continuous supply of milk. Although bulls were sometimes ornery or dangerous, they were necessary residents of farms. Sisters Annie (left) and Minerva Roberts view their cow and calf. As valley families became intertwined through marriage, Annie later married Walter Totten, Minerva married David Housten, and their brother George Roberts married Sarah Bartle. (RBT.)

David London (pictured) and his father, Abraham, alternated the chore of milking the family cow early each morning. On school days, this meant that David had to complete the milking before cleaning up to go to school. David later studied agriculture at Rutgers University and employed innovations to improve production on the family farm at the eastern end of Washington Valley Road just before the road drops down to Dock Watch Hollow. (LND.)

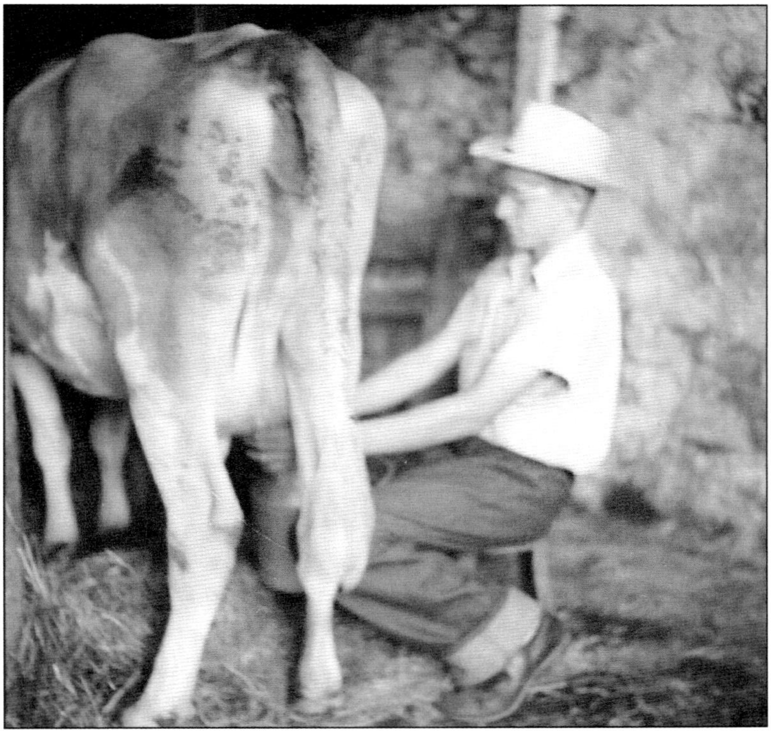

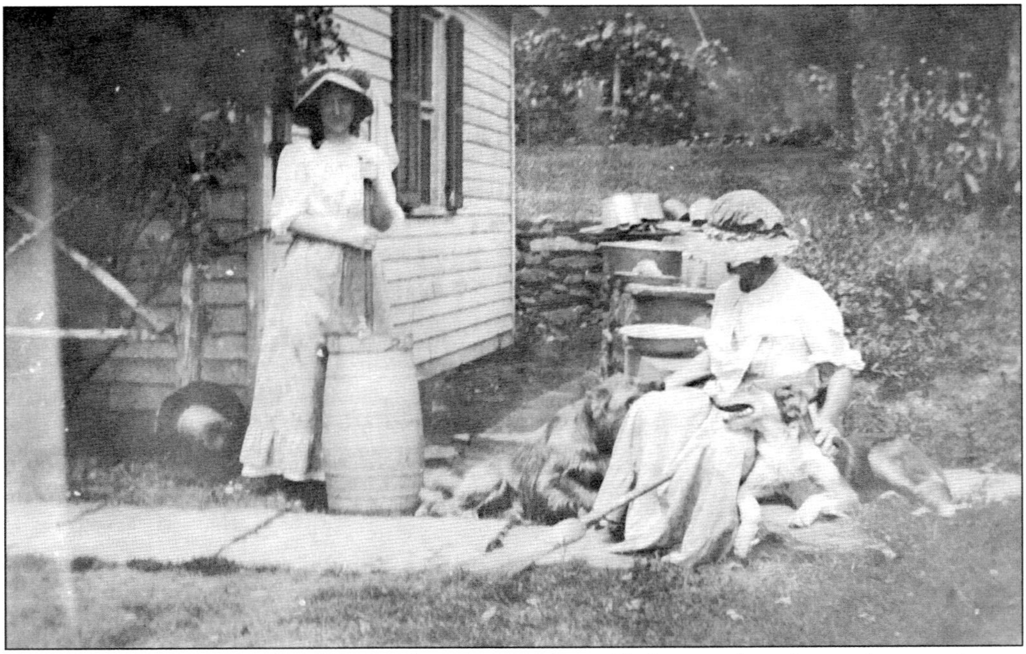

One of the many chores that fell into the category of so-called women's work was churning butter from the cream that rose to the top of milk before the days of homogenized milk. After the lumps of butter were extracted from the churn, the remainder was buttermilk, a delicious, refreshing drink. Two Smalley women take turns at the churn in this 1929 photograph. (JCD.)

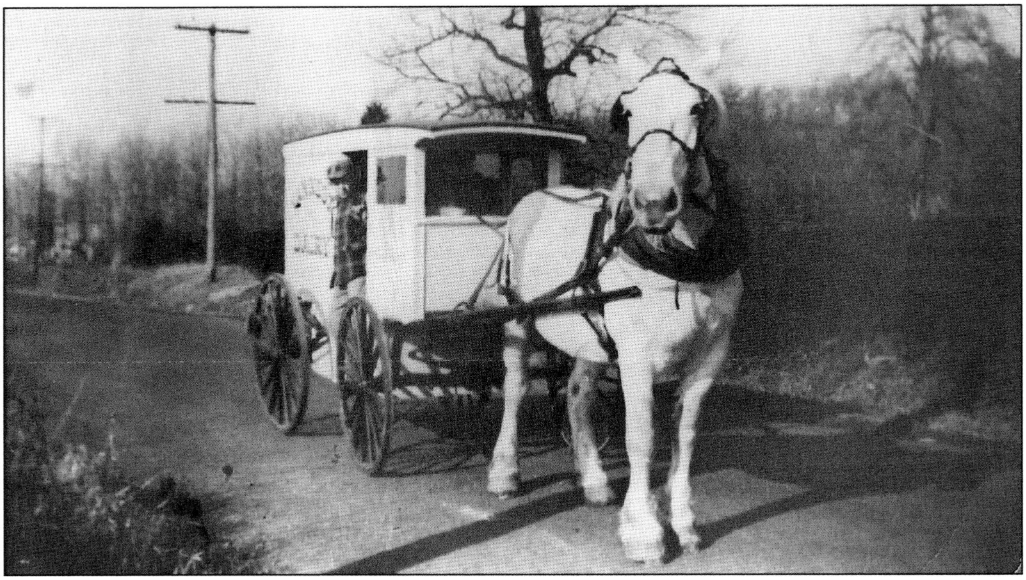

Joseph T. Van Nest's dairy was a major supplier of milk to residences and to schoolchildren. Ed Anderson delivered milk with the Van Nest horse and wagon. Jack Bartle, who had a smaller dairy farm on Bartle Lane, sold only raw milk, claiming that it was unnecessary to pasteurize his milk because he strained out the germs. Here, Ed Anderson prepares to deliver milk to another customer. (AND.)

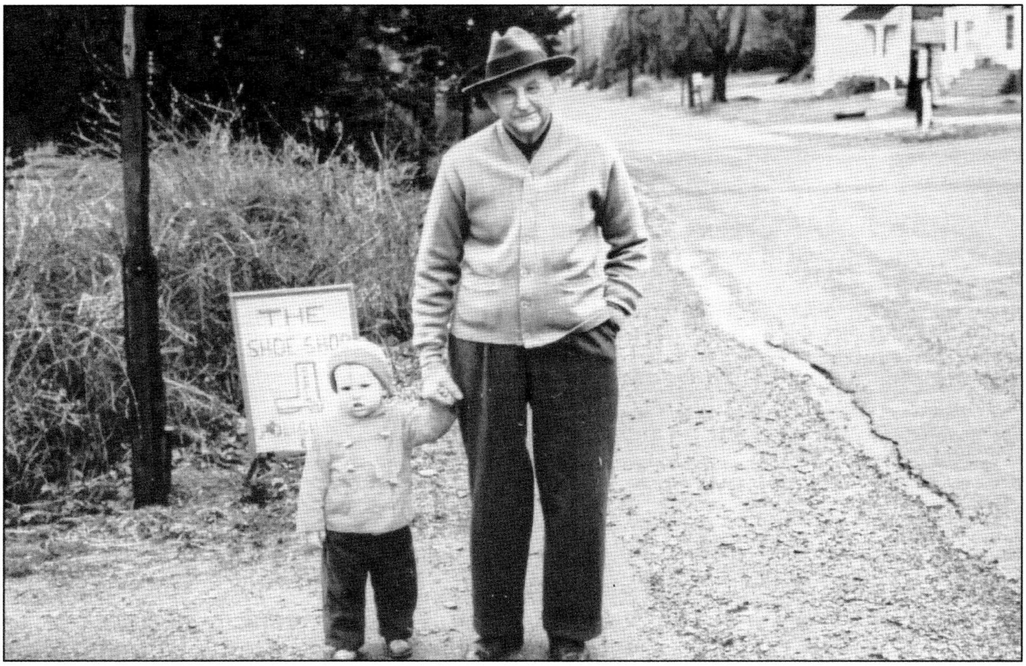

Joe Van Nest pauses with an unidentified child in front of Fred Bartle's blacksmith shop, where a sign also points to a shoe repair shop. The Van Nest farmhouse is in the background at the corner of Mount Horeb Road where an Exxon station now stands. His barns were across the road. (IKE.)

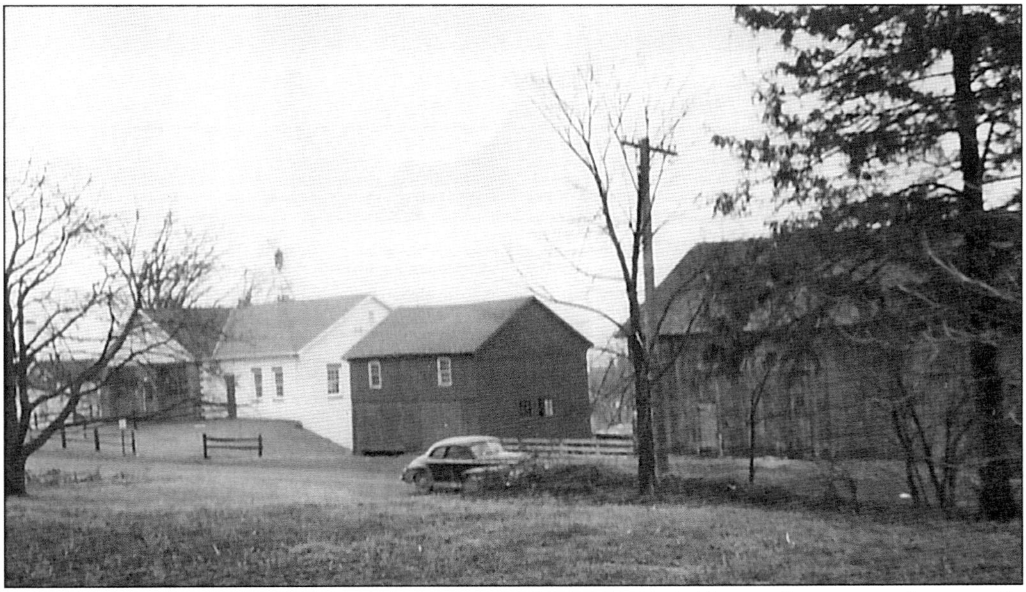

The two Van Nest barns sheltered dairy cows and stored hay. Additionally, one resident recalls how children amused themselves: "We might stop to watch the barber or the blacksmith, or better yet, jump out of the loft in the Van Nest barn and land on bales of hay." When the siren went off at the adjacent white firehouse, visible in this photograph, children checked the station blackboard for the location and raced off on their bikes to witness the action. (AND.)

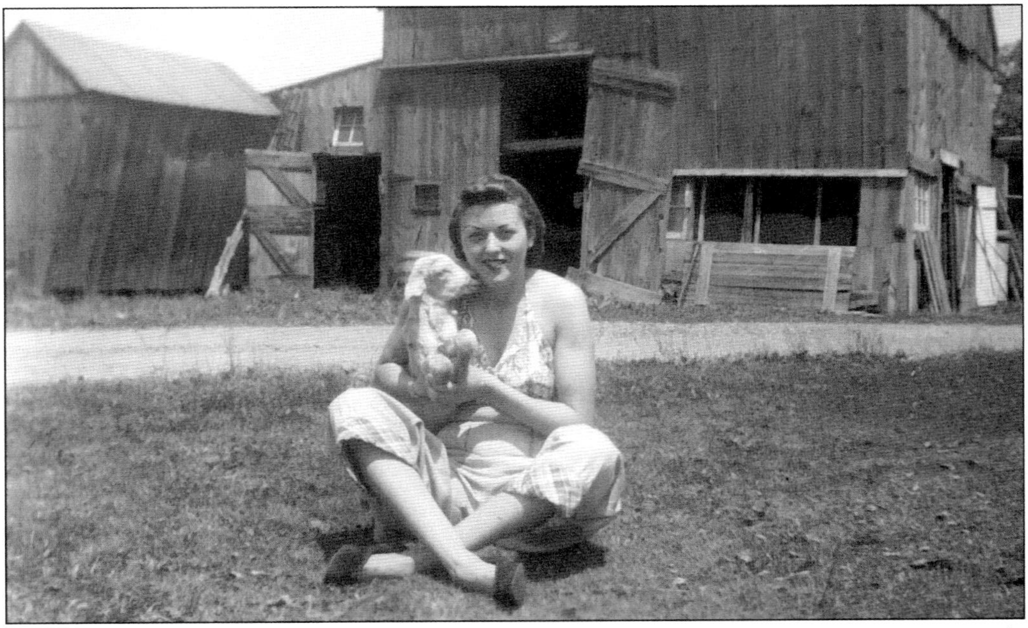

In 1911, John and Laura Brarens moved to the former Horace Coddington farm in Mount Horeb, where they raised their eight children and Toggenburg goats. The breed is known for high milk production, and the Toggenburgs' gentle nature makes them ideal pets. The Brarens' daughter Frances, who holds one of the kids in this 1939 photograph, remembers bringing newborn kids into the kitchen on very cold nights and bottle-feeding them. (FBR.)

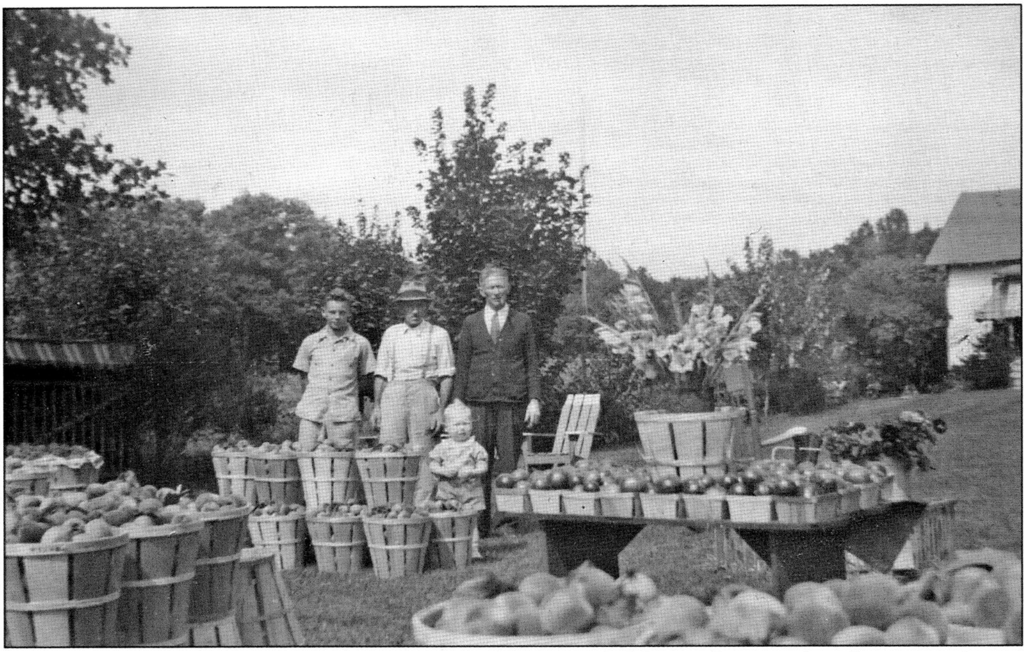

The apple orchards that wound through the valley provided fruit, of course, but they were also an ideal place for children to build forts, as were the woods covering the mountainsides. Raymond Haines's farm stand was one of several in the valley marketing produce over the years. In 1941, from left to right, are Ken Peterson, Raymond Haines, and brother-in-law John D. Roberts with young Ray Haines in front. (RBT.)

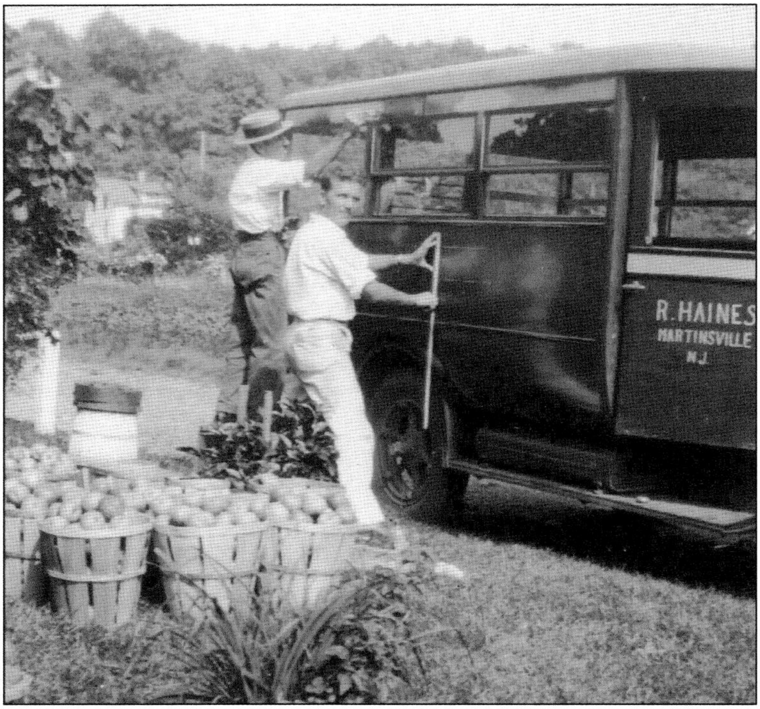

Raymond Haines (left) used his school bus to deliver farm produce to markets in surrounding towns during the summer. His assistant is unidentified. Teenagers earned 10¢ a basket to pick produce at the local farms. They recalled that it took a long time to fill a basket with beans or peas, while a basket of cucumbers filled faster but was much heavier to carry. (HNS.)

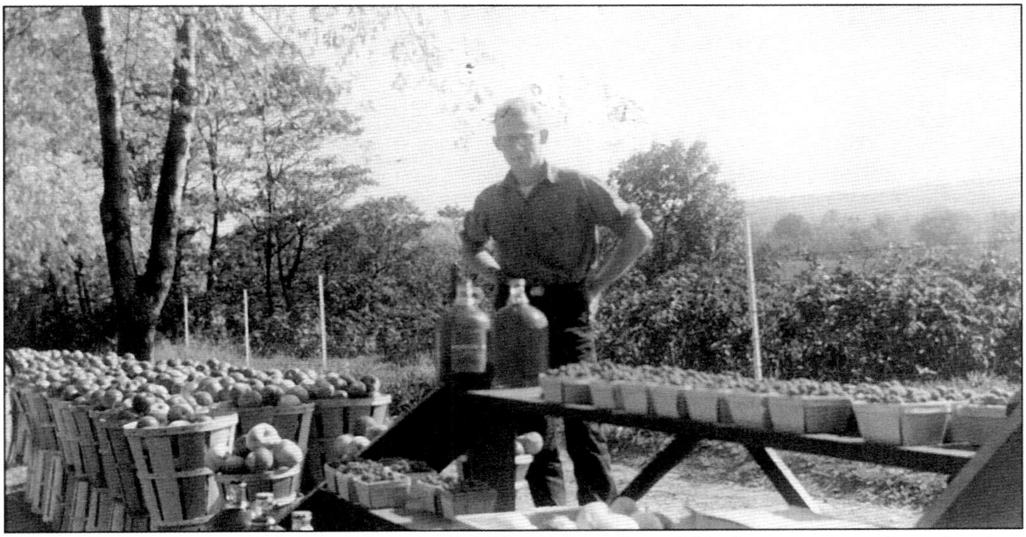

David London tends the family farm stand in this September 1954 photograph with apples that are fresh and crisp and cider known as a local delicacy. The strawberry baskets contained late-summer, everbearing strawberries, and gourds were displayed on the lower shelf. The Londons installed irrigation lines, which increased production above that of neighboring farms. David's grandparents were born in Russia. (LND.)

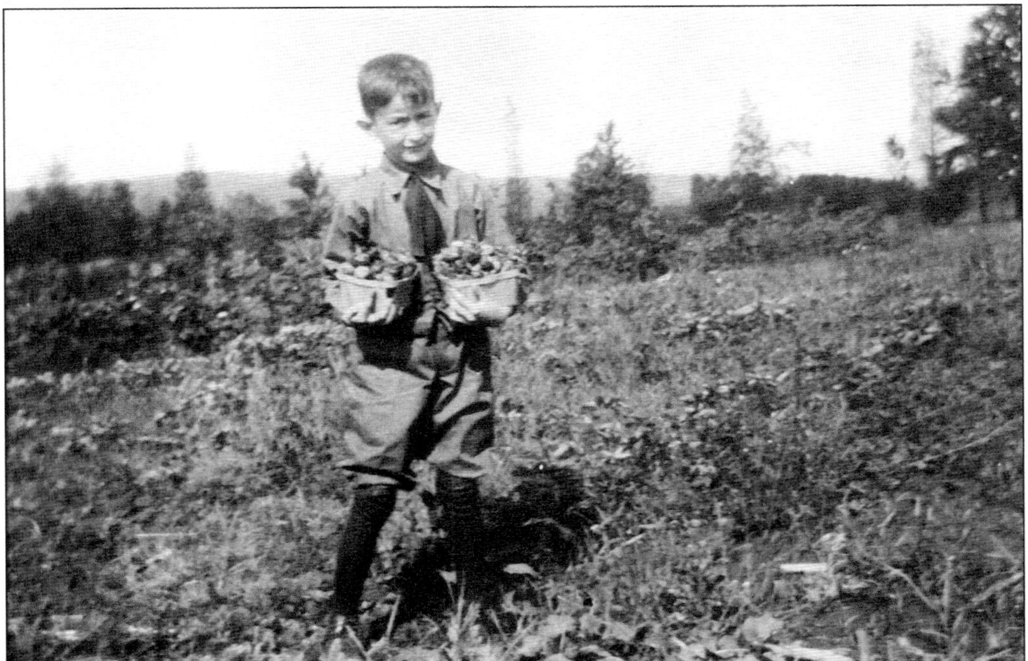

In this 1919 image, John Lester Roberts has gathered strawberries in June, the month of church strawberry festivals and when children took turns turning the crank on the ice cream maker to create strawberry ice cream. Mothers made jam to spread on freshly baked bread in colder months. Wild strawberries are smaller than cultivated berries, but they have a more concentrated flavor. Later, there would be wild blackberries, black raspberries, and red wineberries to pick. (RBT.)

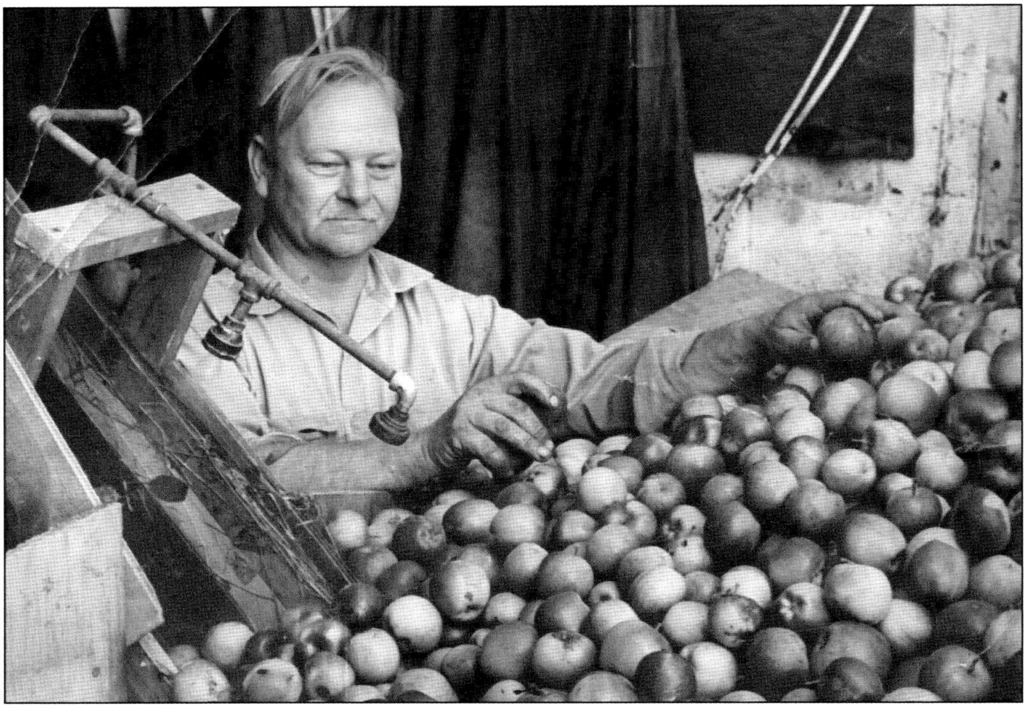

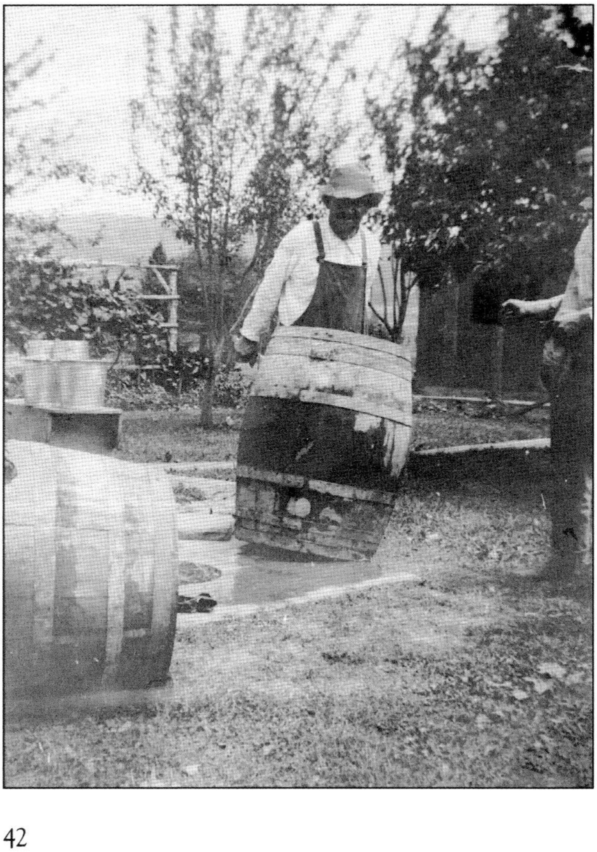

Cider from the Musialowski apples was famous up and down the valley. In this 1960 photograph, Joseph Musialowski is sorting and washing the apples before pressing them for cider. Hanging behind him are the cloths used in the pressing process. Schoolchildren visited the farm to learn how cider was made and to enjoy samples of fresh cider and apples. (MUS.)

Several 30-gallon barrels of cider were fermented for a year's supply on a small farm. All ages, including babies at bedtime, drank hard cider. Europeans brought the practice of home brewing beer and wines, a necessary skill in their homelands where water was often too polluted for safe drinking. They later distilled brandy known as applejack. Cider was also made into vinegar, important in pickling and food preservation, and elderberry wine was another homemade delicacy. (JCD.)

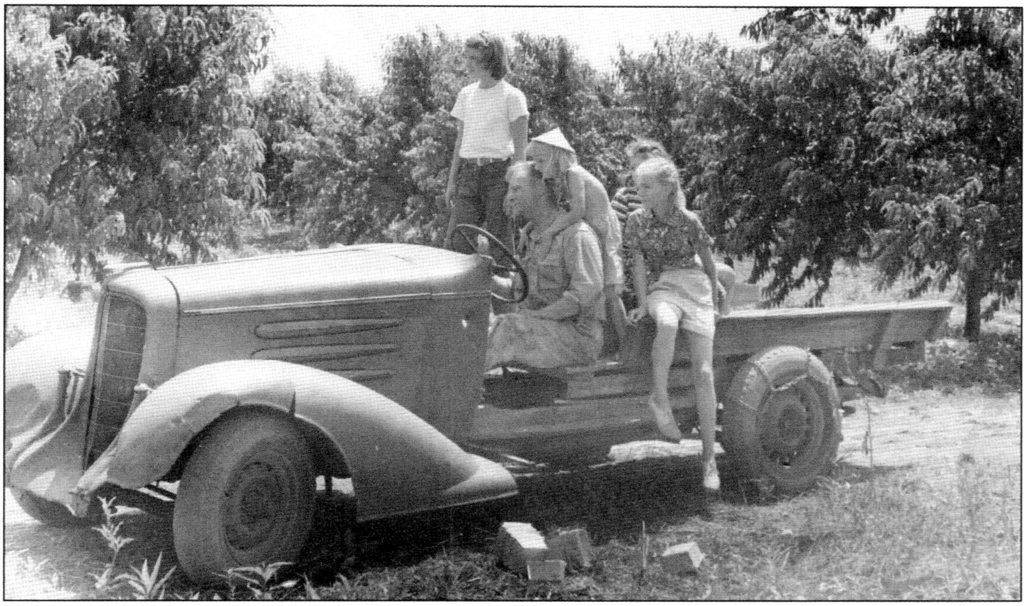

Joe Musialowski chauffeurs, from left to right, Susan Steinback, Joan Musialowski (hugging her father), unidentified, and Patti Musialowski. Strawberry baskets dropped beside the truck indicate that the girls had been picking berries from the field adjacent to the peach orchard in this 1951 photograph. The Musialowski peaches were the basis of many a delicious dessert in August and easily rivaled June's strawberries as favorites. (MUS.)

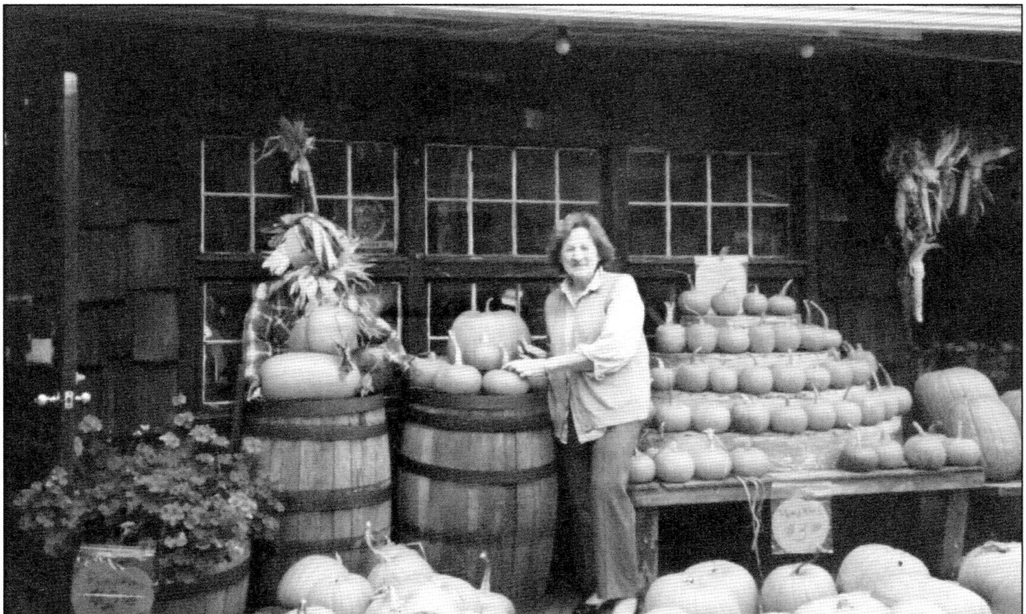

Mildred Musialowski created attractive displays of her husband's produce as the season progressed. The family farm stand was a favorite stop for weekend drivers through the picturesque Washington Valley. Called "Cricket" by the children and adult art students of her Cricket Corner Studio, Mildred also led a Girl Scout troop and contributed her artistic talents to community projects. (MUS.)

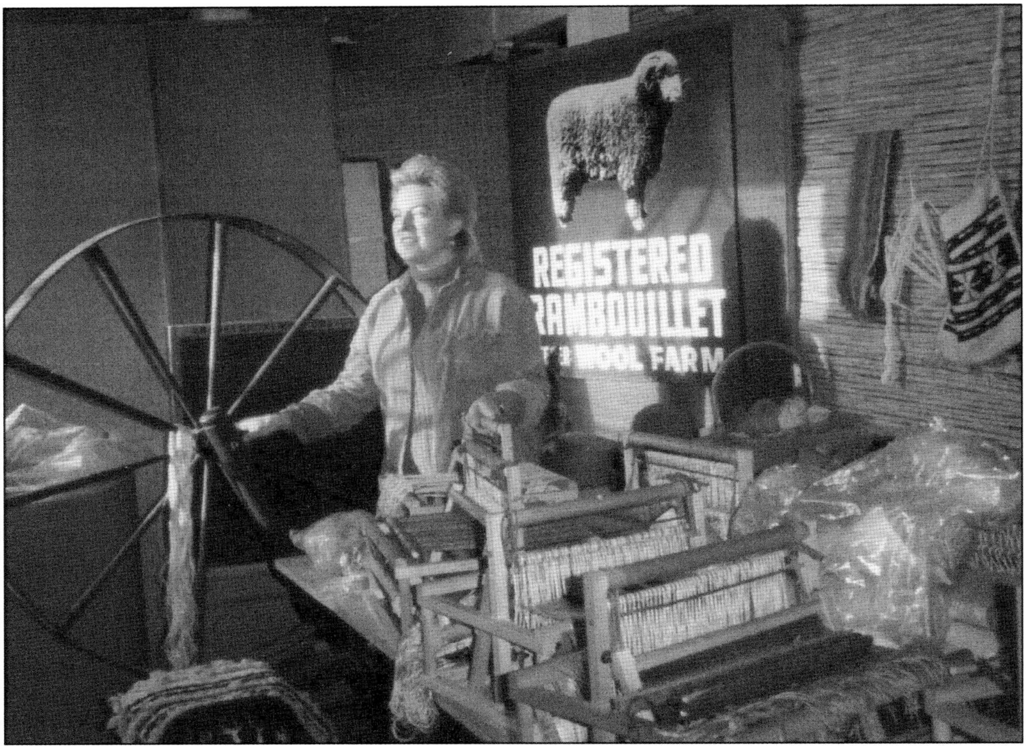

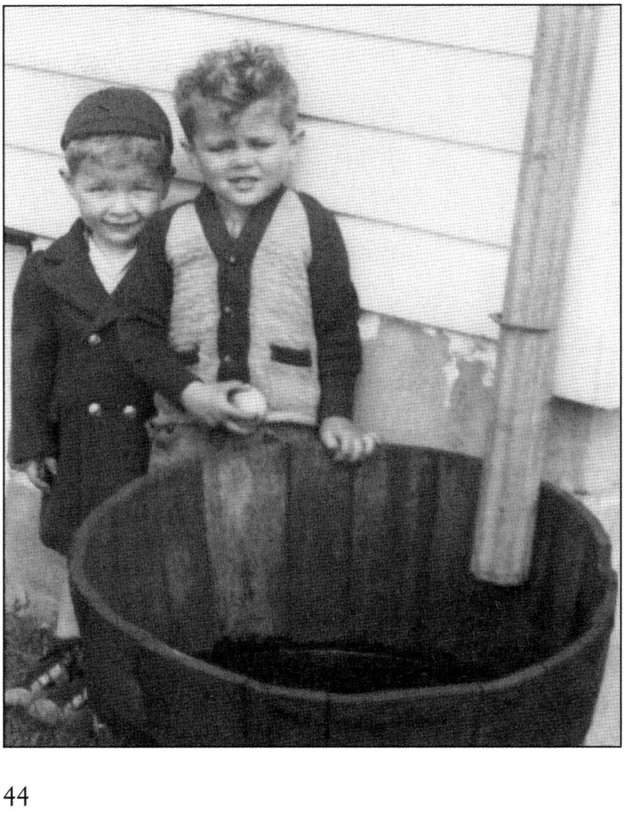

Daughter Patti Musialowski studied Fiber Arts at McGill University and started her own wool farm on the family property. She raised Rambouillet sheep, dyed the wool with natural plants, and spun it into yarn on her grandmother's spinning wheel. Pictured in 1968, she created many decorative and wearable items. She also taught college-level spinning and weaving classes and demonstrated the from-sheep-to-shawl process to visiting elementary schoolchildren. (MUS.)

Two Brarens grandchildren stand beside the family rain barrel. The barrel collected water from gutters on the roof to provide housewives with soft water for laundry. To avoid having mosquitoes breed in the water, some families kept a fish or two in the barrel to dine on the wriggling mosquito larvae. (FBR.)

Rainwater was also captured by roof gutters and stored in large underground cisterns with pumps. Here, Lester Roberts assists his mother, the former Hattie Van Nest, with the family laundry. Children also enjoyed splashing in the washtub in hot weather. (RBT.)

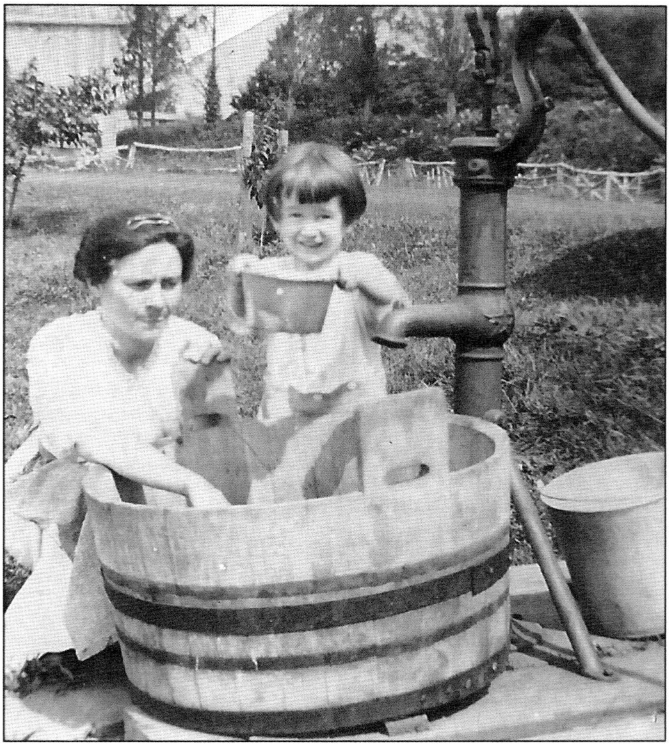

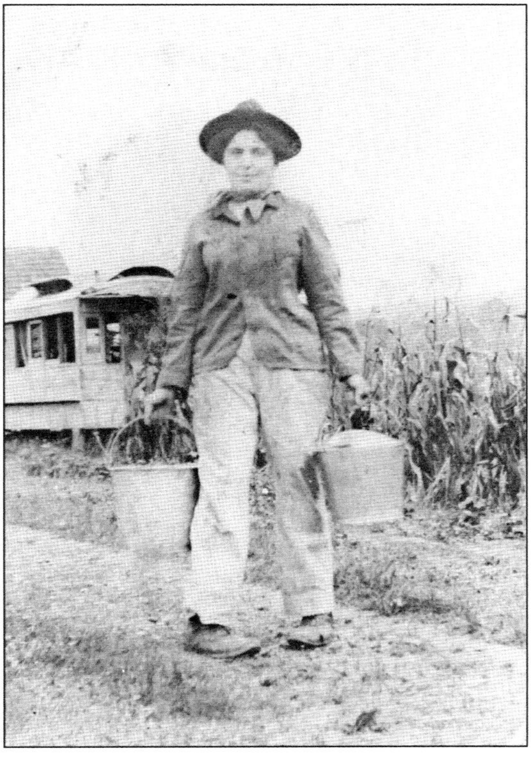

Safe drinking water had to come from a well, which, for convenience in watering the animals, was frequently located nearer to the barn than to the house. In this photograph, Agnes Thum Roberts carries water and feed buckets on the Perrine farm in 1912. She is wearing masculine clothing at a time when most women, including her sisters-in-law Annie and Minerva Roberts (see page 36) wore dresses while doing farm chores. (IKE.)

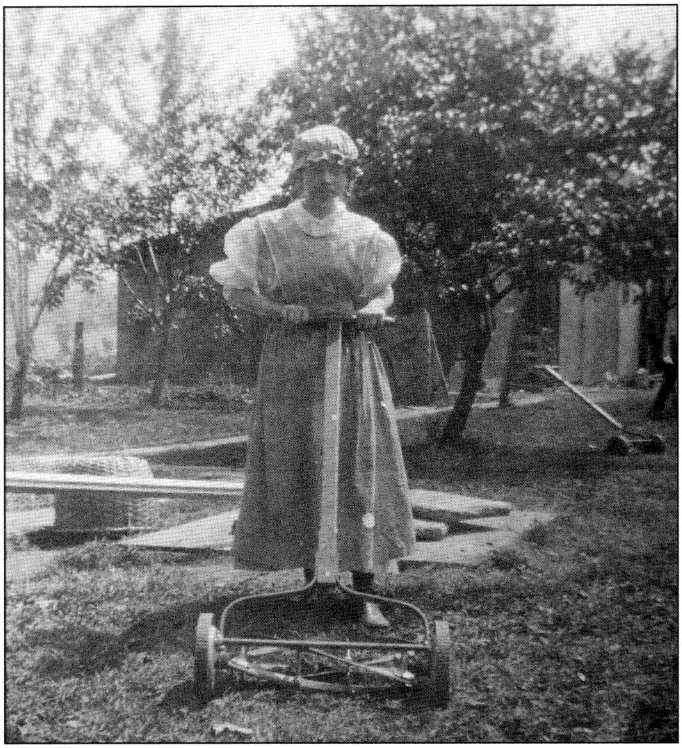

Lawn mowing was another chore that might fall to the women, unless children were available for the task. Here, Jessie Bartle Smalley tackles the job, while a second mower stands idle in the background in case help might arrive. One father recalled waiting until a suitor of his daughter arrived; he would then begin to mow the lawn, whereupon the visitor would quickly offer to help. (JCD.)

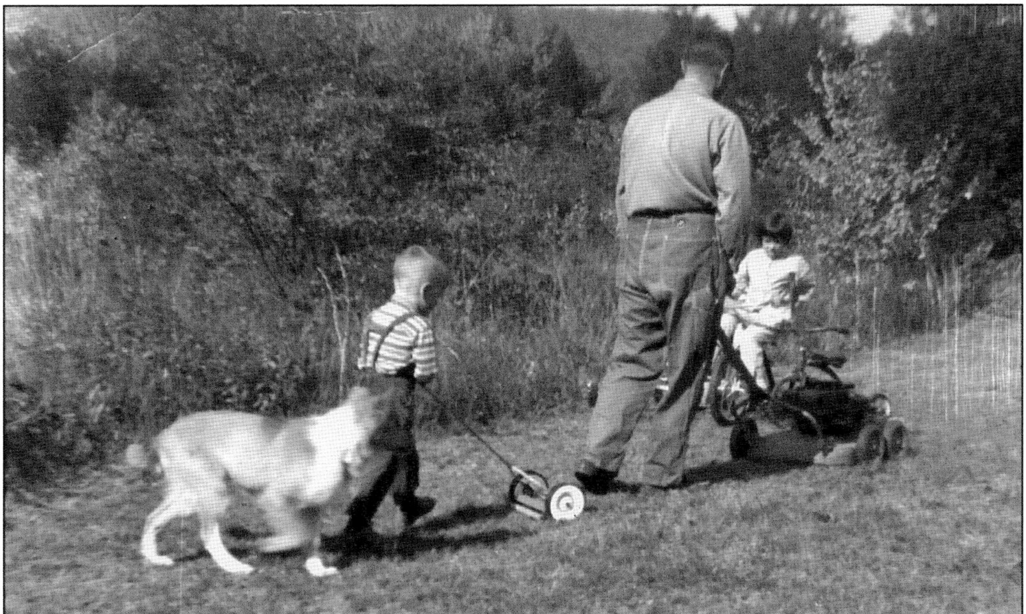

Once power mowers arrived, men could gallantly relieve "the little lady" of this chore. In 1957, young Paul Bartle follows his father, Doc Bartle, while neighbor Kathy Russell steers clear of the flying grass from the mower. The Russells' collie Bonnie joined the action, roaming freely as most dogs did in those times. (DOC.)

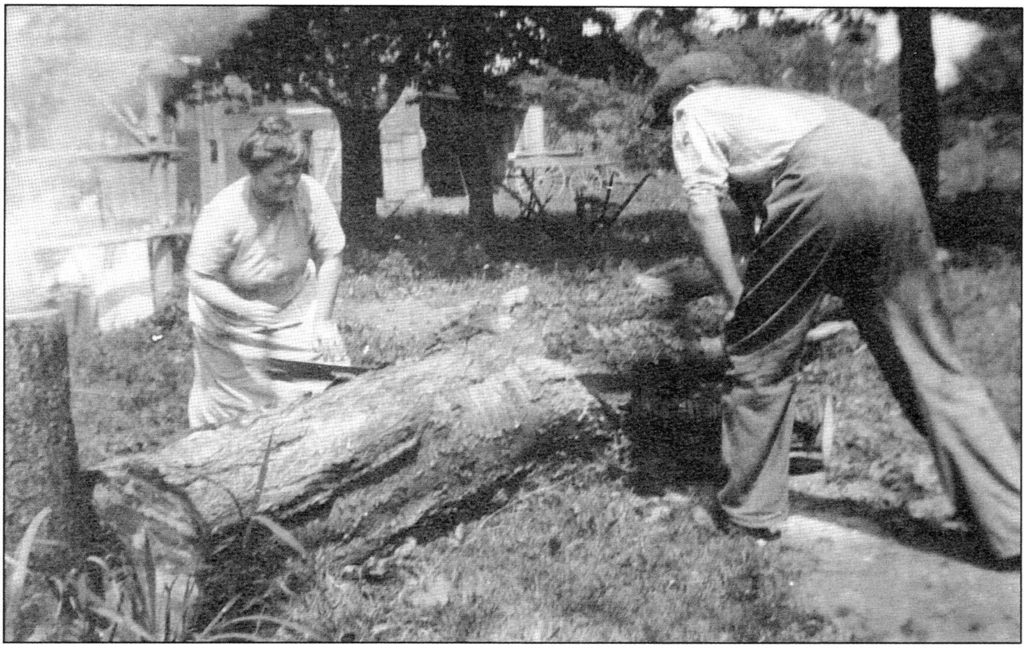

Before chainsaws were available, cutting large logs required a two-man saw. It became a two-person saw when Laura Brarens helped husband John in 1915. John could then split the logs into firewood using an axe or splitting wedges and a sledgehammer. (FBR.)

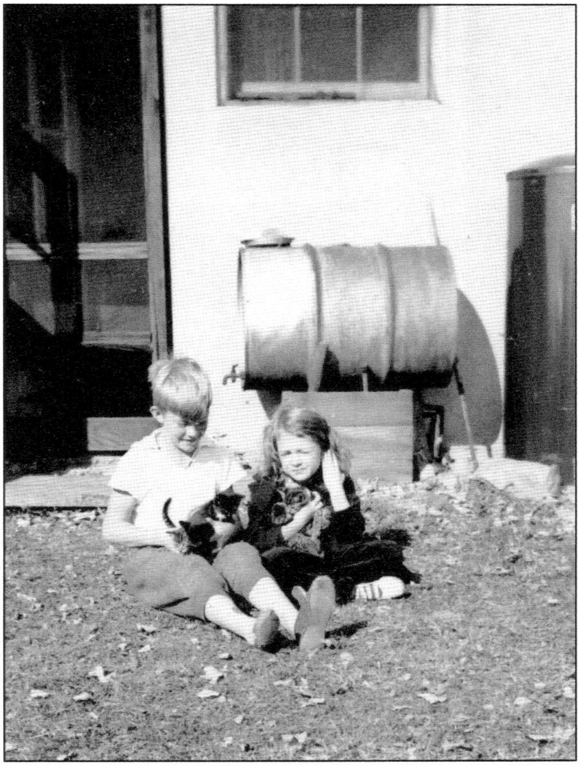

Richard and Lois Poffley play with kittens in front of the family kerosene barrel in 1935. Before electricity, kerosene fueled oil lamps, and kerosene stoves heated some homes even after electricity was available. Children were tasked with cleaning the lamp chimneys of soot. Those whose homes were still heated by kerosene might be teased by classmates because they bore the faint odor of kerosene with them. (POF.)

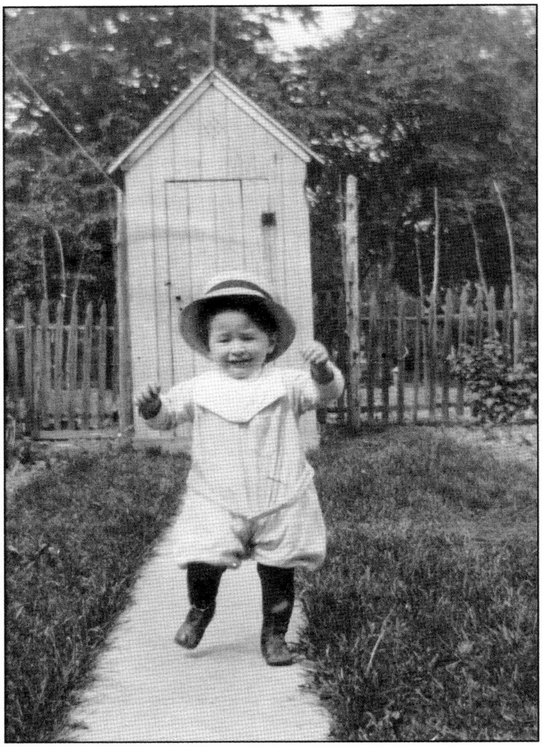

Young Lester Roberts toddles down the path from the family privy in 1915. The outhouse, also known as the necessary or the privy, was an essential fixture in every backyard before the installation of indoor plumbing. It might be considered an occupational hazard for teachers, judging by stories of schoolboy pranks that linger in many parts of the country, including Martinsville. (RBT.)

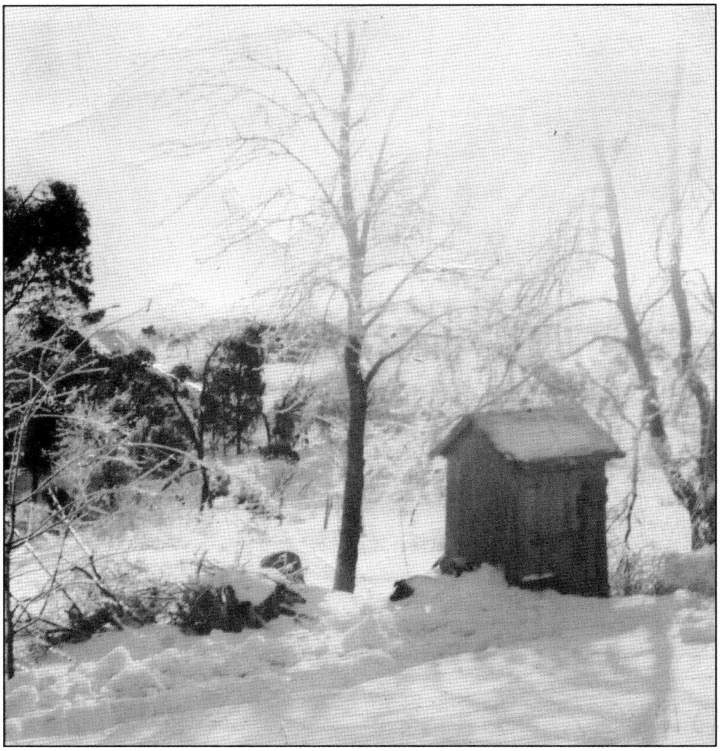

Daylilies were so commonly planted beside the outhouse in summer that they were sometimes called "privy lilies." Fragrant honeysuckle vines also helped to make the visit more pleasant. A trip to the outhouse in winter, however, was especially *un*pleasant. The path has been shoveled through deep snow in this photograph. None of the outhouses that have appeared in Martinsville photographs feature the traditional crescent moon cutout on the door. (JCD.)

Three

BUSINESSES IN THE COMMUNITY

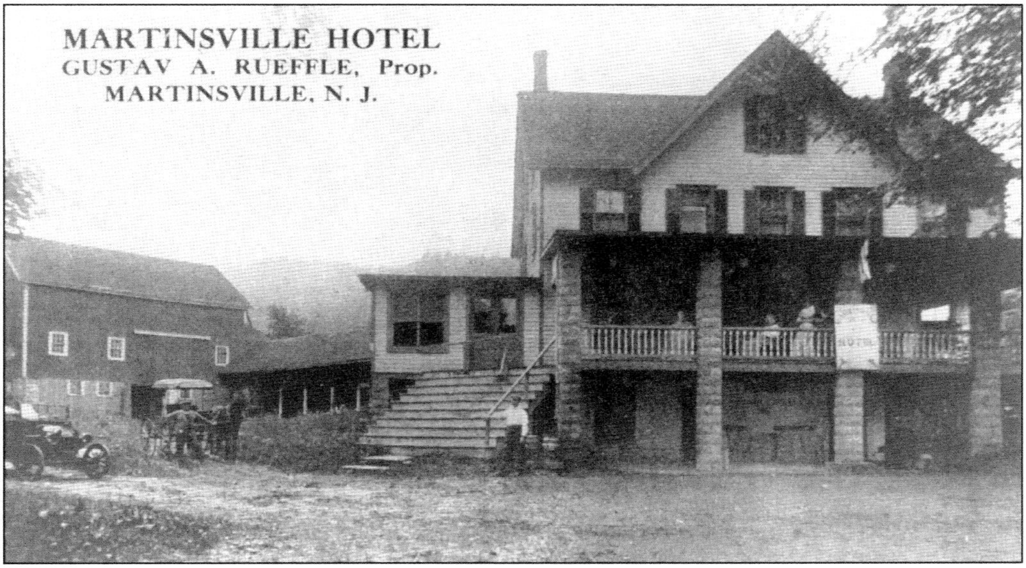

The Martinsville Hotel, pictured in 1917, began as a stagecoach stop between Liberty Corner and Bound Brook. It occupied the northeast corner of Mount Horeb and Washington Valley Roads where a bank now stands. Known previously as Jackson's Hotel, it was a popular watering hole until Prohibition seriously hampered business. With the repeal of Prohibition, business improved, and it continued as the Hoffman House for many years. There were also several summer boardinghouses in the area. The Baist farm on the edge of Middle Brook at the end of Quarry Lane hosted summer guests before the site was purchased for the construction of the reservoir. (IKE.)

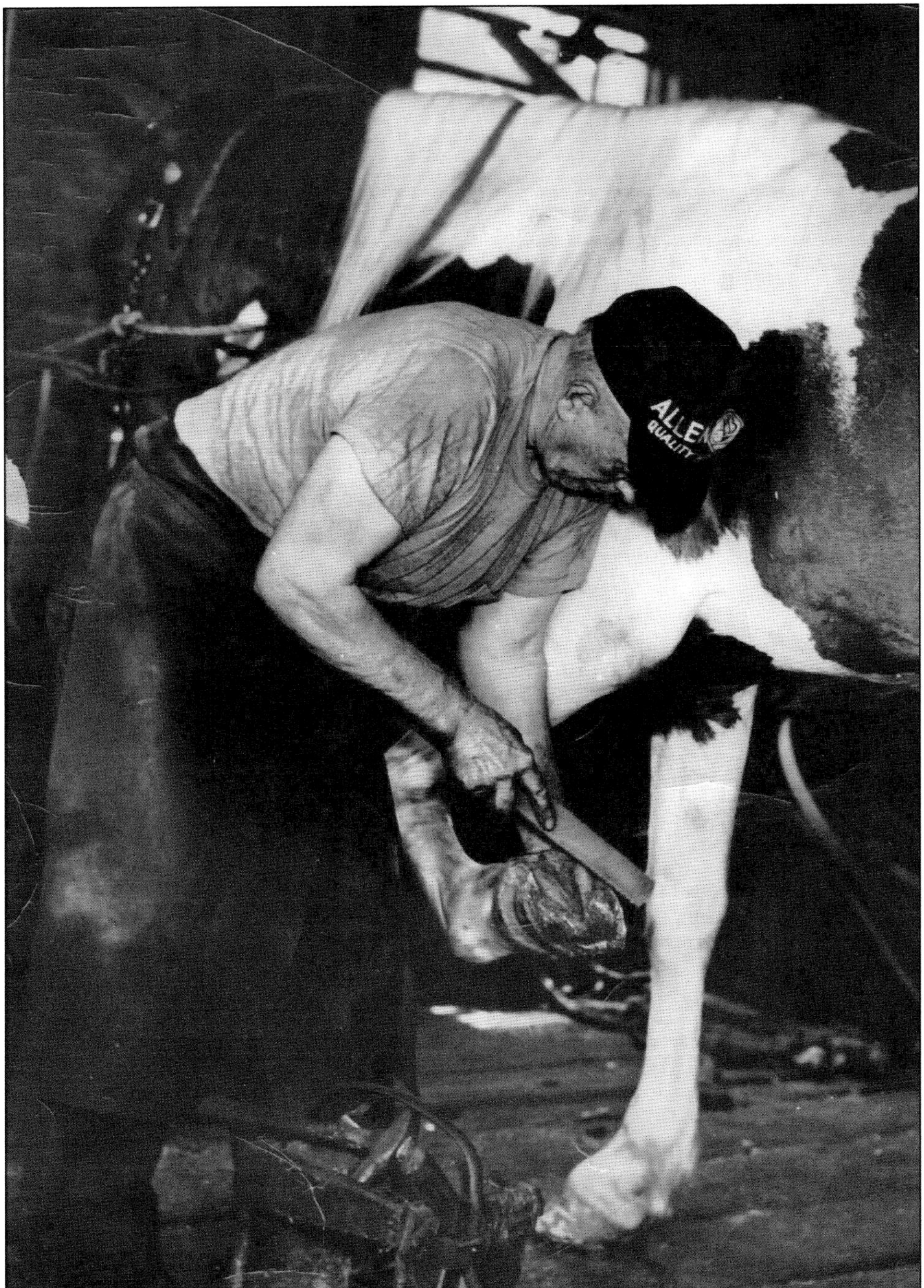

The village blacksmith ran an essential business in earlier times. His skills included crafting hardware and household items, sharpening and repairing farm machinery, and shoeing horses. The ring of the anvil from Fred Bartle's shop, which was across the road from the Hoffman House, invited young and old to stop and watch him work. Fred, pictured around 1940, was also a talented musician, entertaining with his banjo and fiddle and whistling catchy tunes. (DOC.)

When Fred Bartle retired in 1960 after 55 years, his sturdy concrete block building was reincarnated as Martinsville's first bank, which opened in 1965 while the Somerset Trust Company's permanent home was being constructed. The building later housed a beauty salon and then an art studio before being demolished for the construction of Blacksmith Commons Shopping Center. (SMR.)

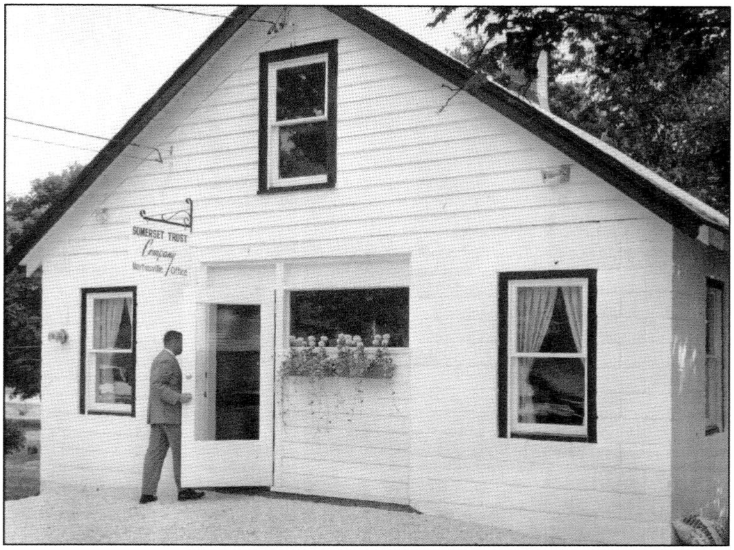

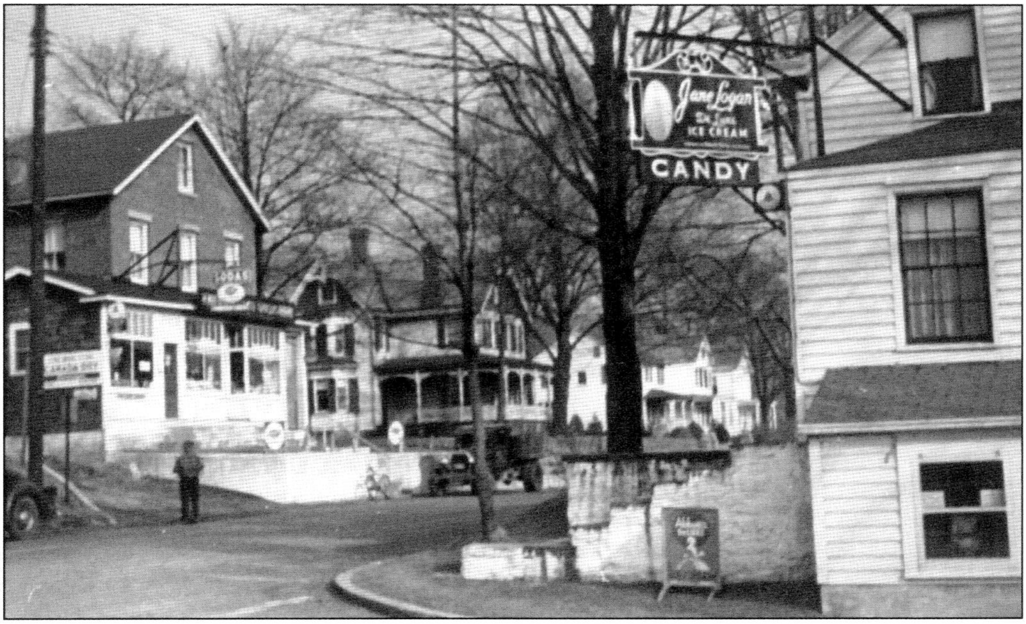

The intersection of Chimney Rock and Washington Valley Roads where the schoolhouse stood later became the hub of village commerce. Lyng's General Store was on the north side, beside the school and to the left in this 1930s photograph, and the Waldron Stationery Store and Post Office stood opposite. Both stores also sold ice cream, penny candy, and soft drinks. (POF.)

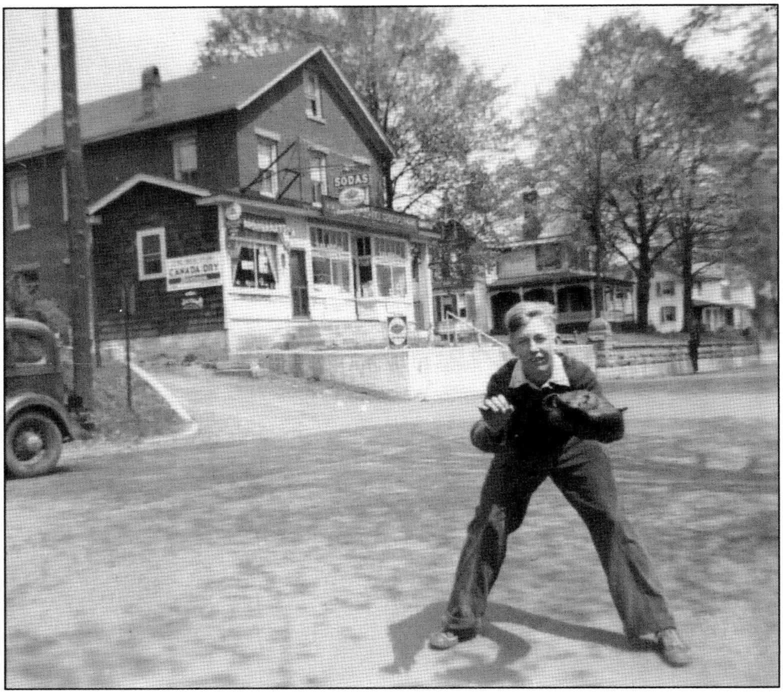

A youngster who had 10¢ to spend at Lyng's (later Wagner's) recalled, "It was the first time I ever bought anything by myself. I bought a Coca-Cola for 10¢, drank it, and returned the bottle for the 2¢ deposit. So then I bought a pretzel for a penny and wisely saved the other penny to take home." In 1938, Richard Poffley is ready to catch a baseball at the intersection. (ECD.)

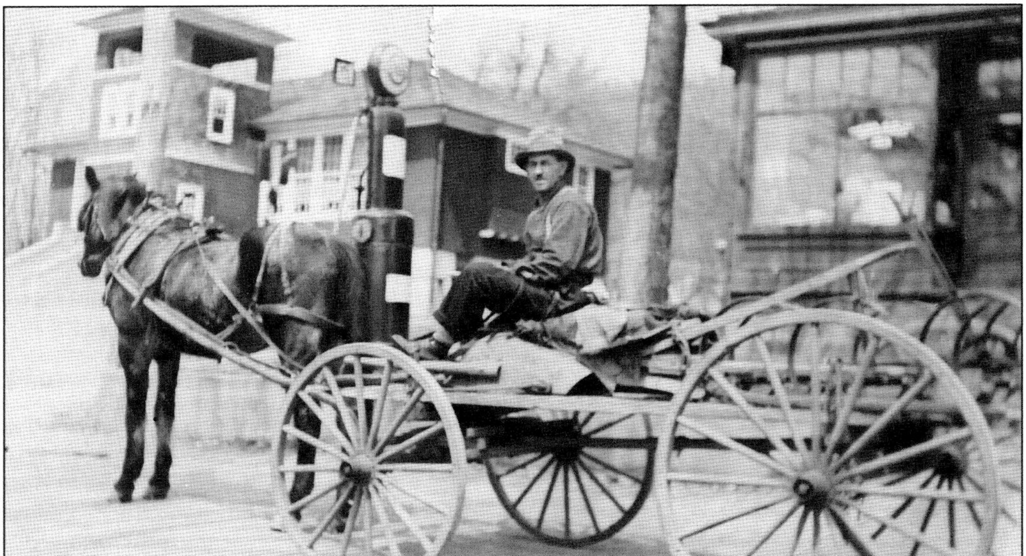

In this photograph of Raymond Haines from about 1925, a gasoline pump appears in front of Lyng's store. When several girls on their way to the swimming hole stopped for penny candy one day, a large black automobile was parked in front, and three large men in black fedoras were inside the store. One man told William Lyng, "Give the kids some candy, whatever they want," and they each received a bag of candy. (HNS.)

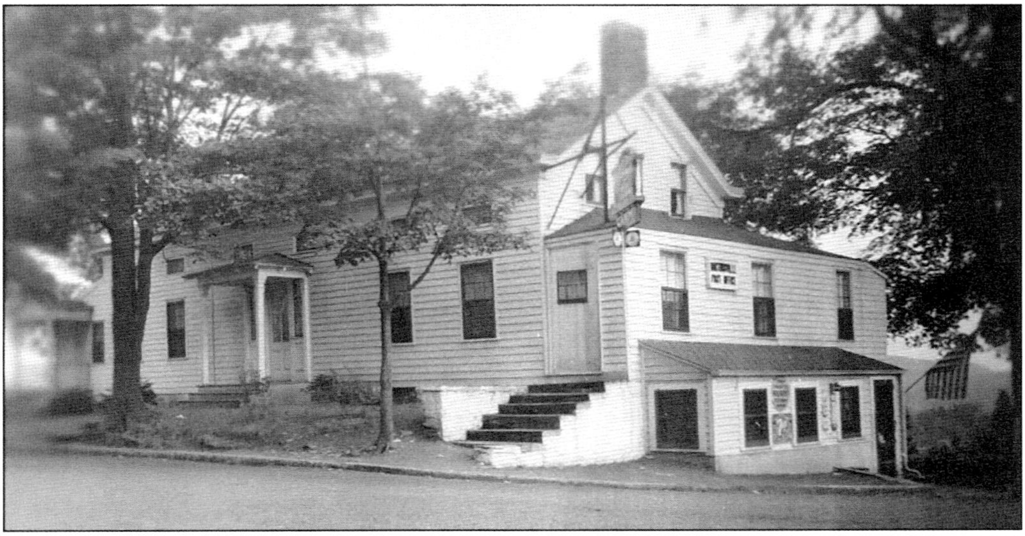

The Waldron house, built about 1775, is pictured around 1940. Arthur Waldron, blinded by a 1930 accident at the stone crusher, managed his small stationery store here for many years. It housed the post office from 1938, when Valentina Waldron succeeded William Lyng as postmaster, until a new post office was built in the adjacent shopping center in 1960. Other former postmasters were Henry Zimmerman and Harriet Smalley, sister of Edwin Smalley. (POF.)

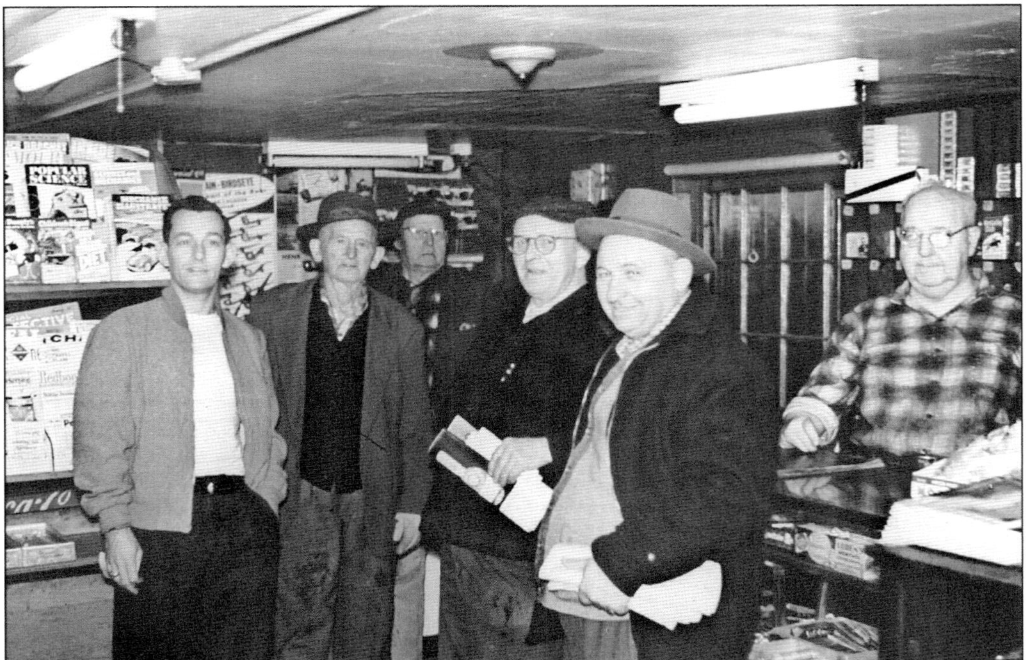

In this 1950s photograph of Arthur Waldron behind the counter of his store, visitors include, from left to right, pastor of the Methodist church Kenneth Fowler, John Nees, unidentified, Chick Bartle, and ? Kaiser. When notorious New York gangster Dutch Schultz visited the store and realized that Waldron was blind, he bought the entire supply of cigars. He was also the man who bought the penny candy for the girls in Lyng's store. (IKE.)

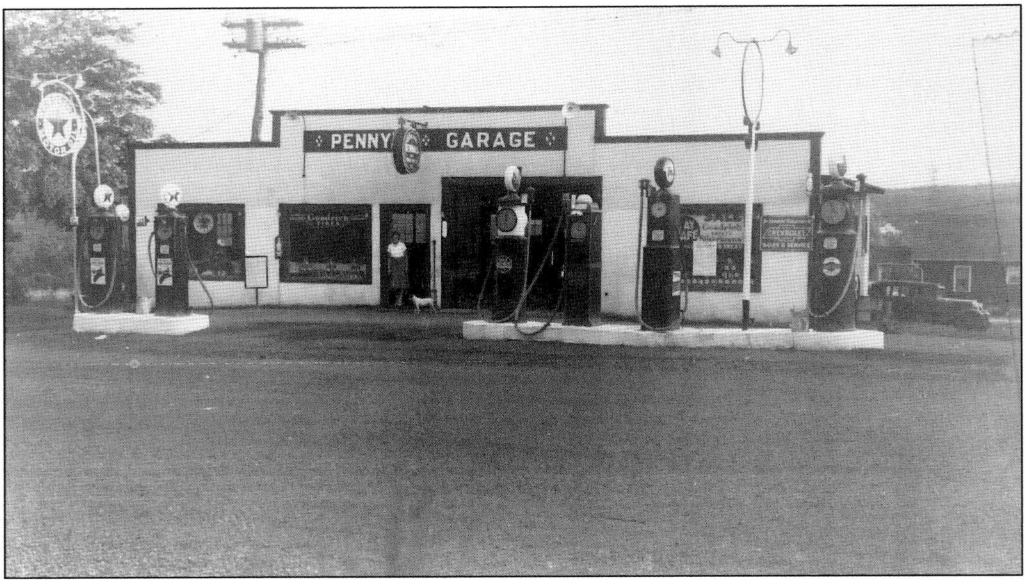

As automobiles became more popular, two repair and filling stations were established. Penny's Garage was at the corner of Chimney Rock and Washington Valley Roads, where a gasoline station operates to the present time. The Texaco station was originally operated by Grayland Penny, then his son Curtis, and later Donald Waldron and subsequent owners. The automobile parked behind the garage suggests that this photograph dates to the 1930s. (FBR.)

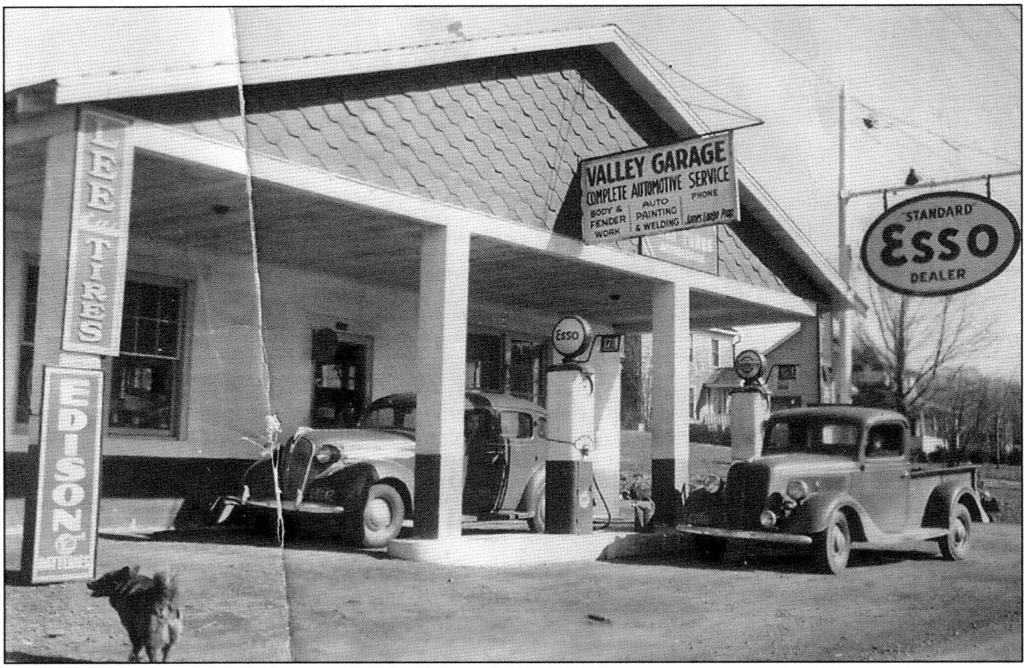

At the head of Quarry Lane, James Longo operated an Esso station known as the Valley Garage in 1938. His dog Beauty liked to ride on the fender of his truck (shown parked). In 1951, Jim and other local fathers organized Boy Scout Troop 46. They took the boys swimming, fishing, hiking, and camping and taught them to appreciate and protect the natural environment. (SAL.)

When Chester Coddington stopped for gasoline at the Esso station, the price was 17.9¢ a gallon. Chester and his brother Elmer, avid hunters, were the sons of David Coddington, one of the many branches of the Coddington family, some of whom spelled their name Codington. Their home is featured in the final chapter of this book. (SAL.)

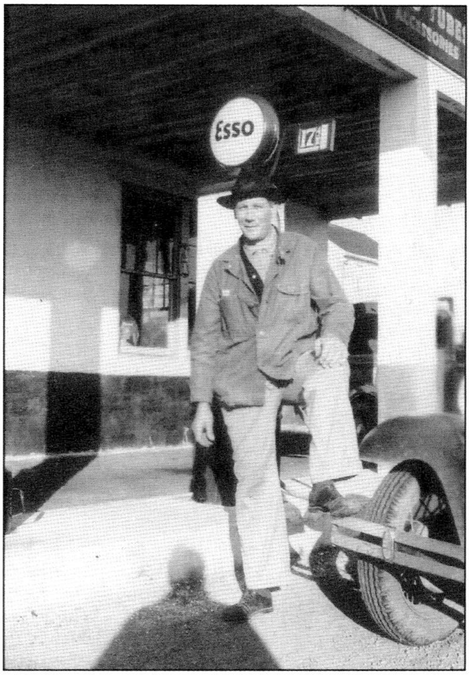

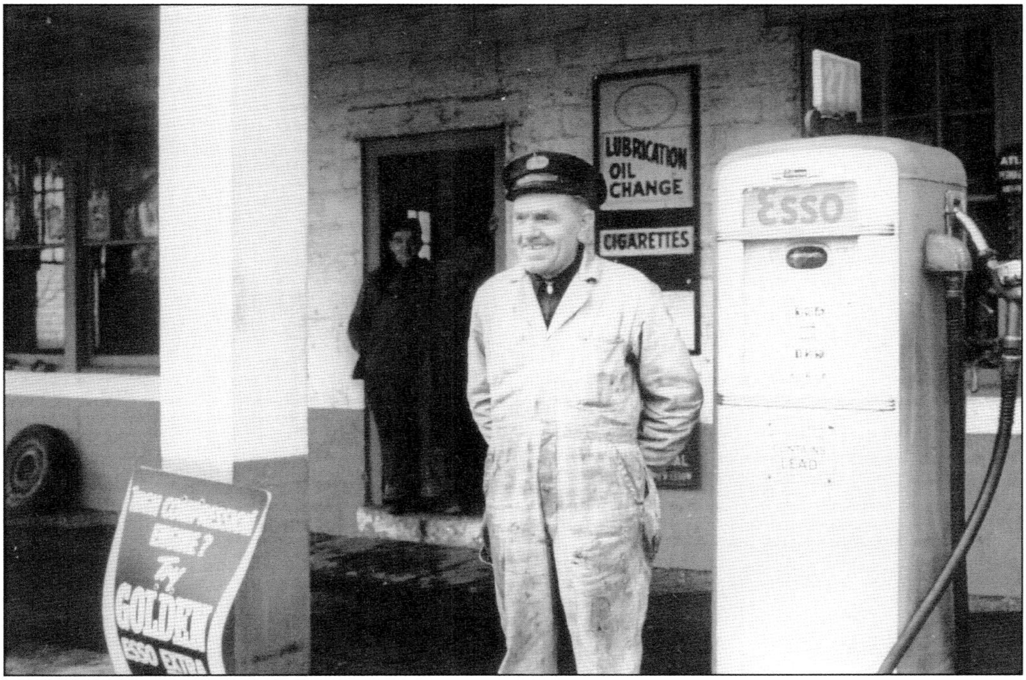

Bud Baldwin succeeded Longo as proprietor of the Esso station in 1940. The price of gasoline had increased to 27.9¢ a gallon at the time of this photograph. During World War II when gasoline was rationed, all vehicles had to have the top half of their headlights painted black to reduce the light in the sky above New Jersey, thereby lessening the visibility of land targets for German submarines lurking off the coast. (IKE.)

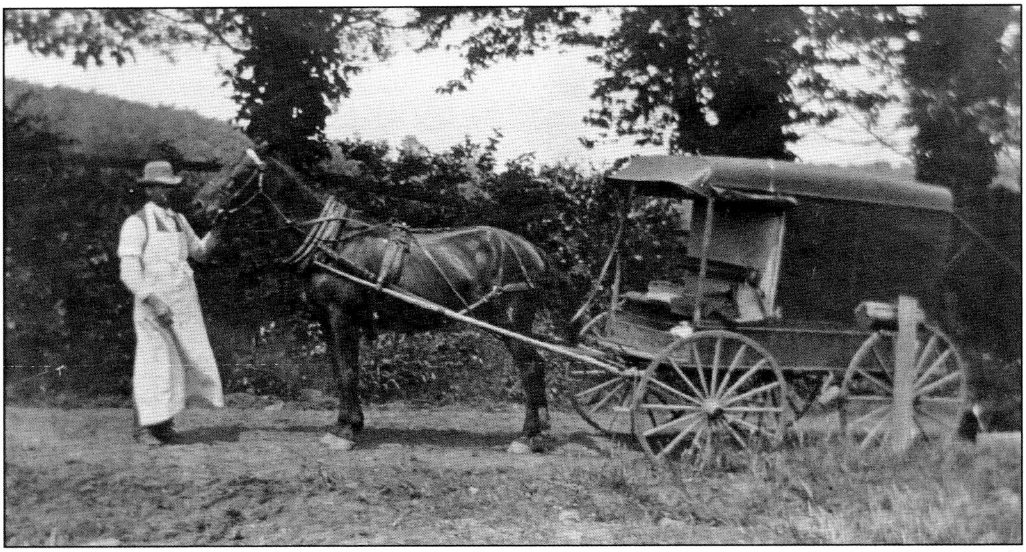

John Mundy, an itinerant butcher, is pictured around 1920 as he makes his rounds of area homes with fresh meat as well as a variety of sausages and smoked meats. Farmers preserved their own meats, especially pork, in barnyard smokehouses, and housewives canned meats as well. Mundy always had a slice of salami for each of the children who eagerly gathered around his wagon. (RBT.)

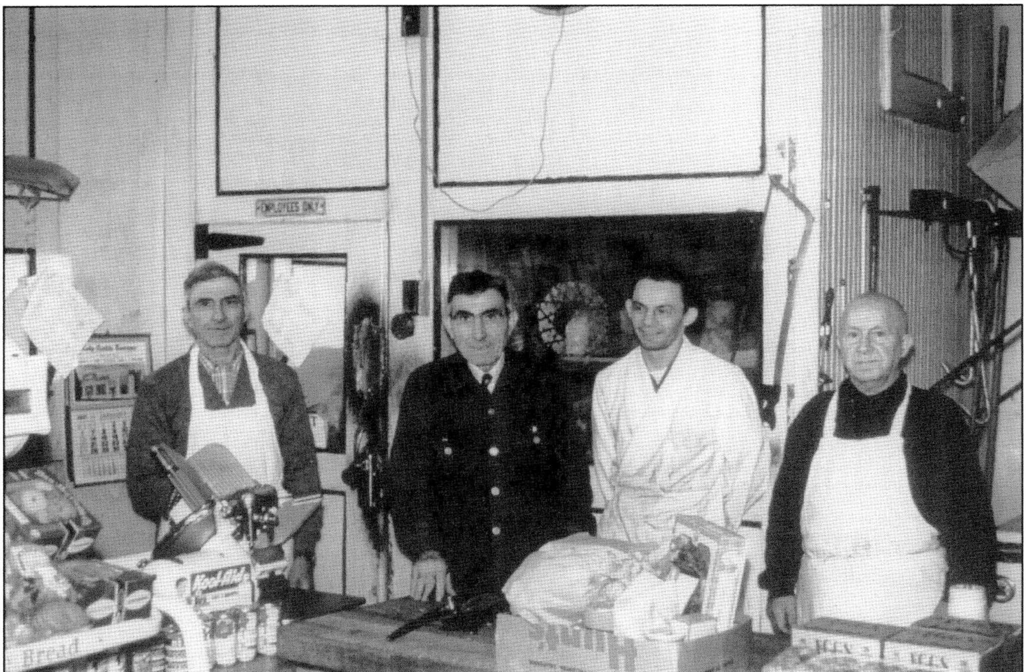

Frank Buono's butcher shop was on the corner of Quarry Lane. During wartime when meat was rationed, he insisted that "we must be sure those little kids are fed," and he carefully managed his meat supply to accommodate as many residents as possible. He also gave a slice of salami to customers' children. Frank is second from left in this photograph from about 1960. The others are unidentified. (IKE.)

Around 1875, William Bartle and his son William Ellis began quarrying a sandstone deposit in the valley, for which they imported skilled Italian stonemasons. The fine sandstone had to be shaped while freshly exposed; the hardened blocks were then shipped for buildings as distant as Trinity Church in lower Manhattan. In this c. 1910 photograph, William Ellis stands among the workers. From left to right are unidentified, Bartle in business suit, Frank Wahl, and unidentified. (JCD.)

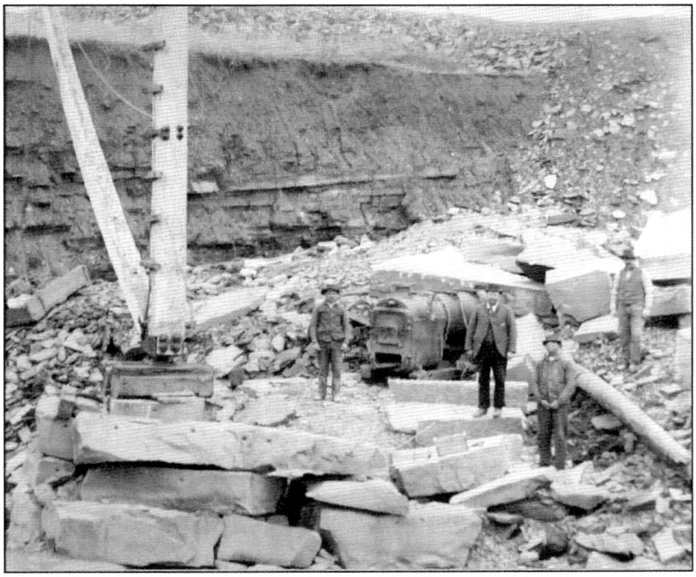

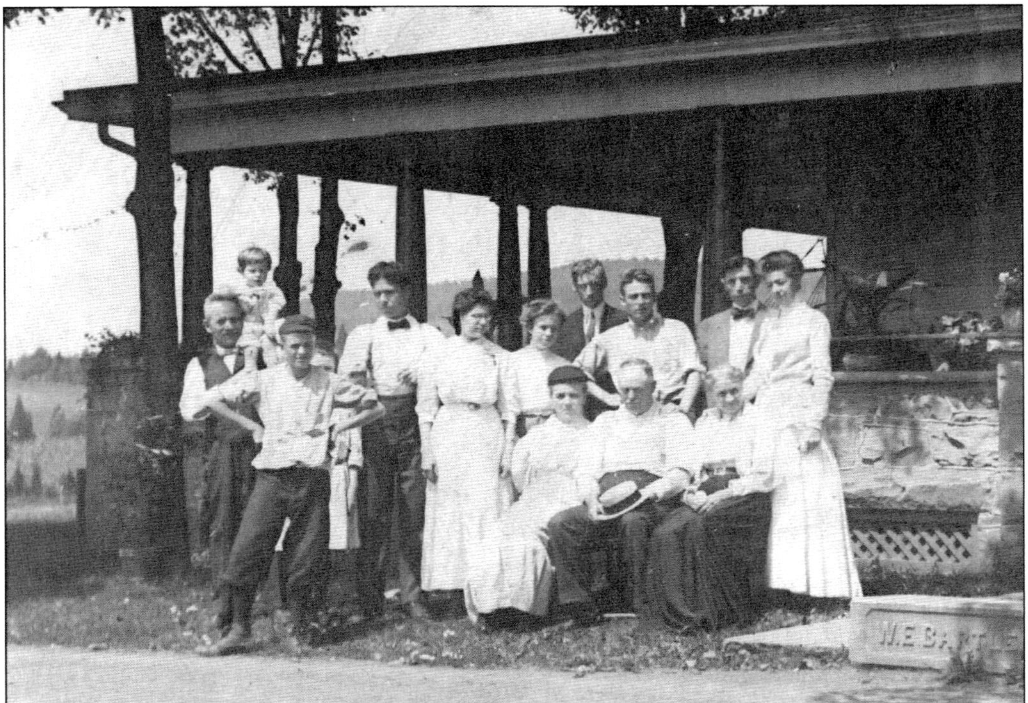

Bartle family members placed stones carved with the homeowner's name in front of their homes, as seen in this photograph of the family assembled in front of the W.E. Bartle home in 1910. In this image are, from left to right, (first row, seated) Elizabeth Zimmerman Bartle, William Ellis Bartle, and unidentified; (second row) Franklin "Chick" (with hands on hips), unidentified, Jessie Bartle, Stanley Bartle, and unidentified. No others are identified. (JCD.)

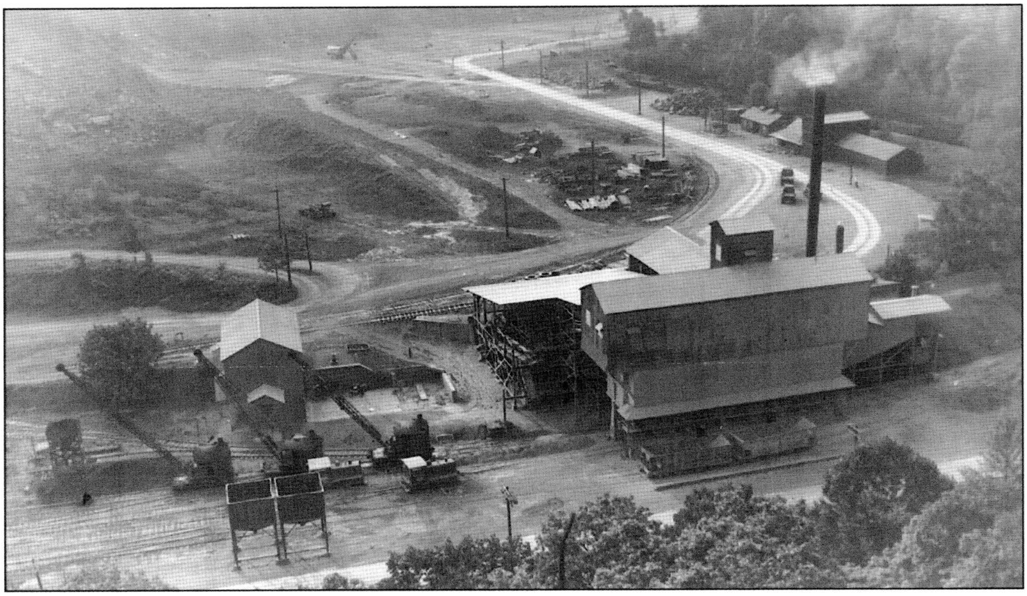

The volcanic basalt that formed the Watchung Mountains contains small deposits of copper, which was mined without much profit. The basalt itself, however, has been producing crushed stone in the Chimney Rock Gorge since about 1886. US Census reports list many residents as employees of this and the Bartle quarry operation over the years. (JWG.)

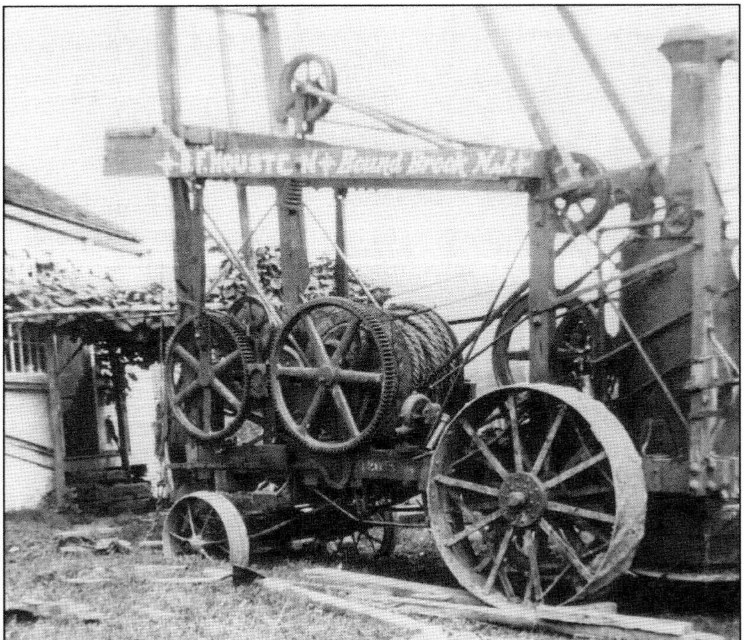

James Housten, a grandson of John Peter Roberts and son of Minerva Roberts and David Housten, operated this well-drilling rig, at work on the corner of Newmans Lane in 1913. The Assante brothers, who started as drillers in the quarry, later became the primary well-drillers throughout the area. (HST.)

Four

A VILLAGE UP IN FLAMES

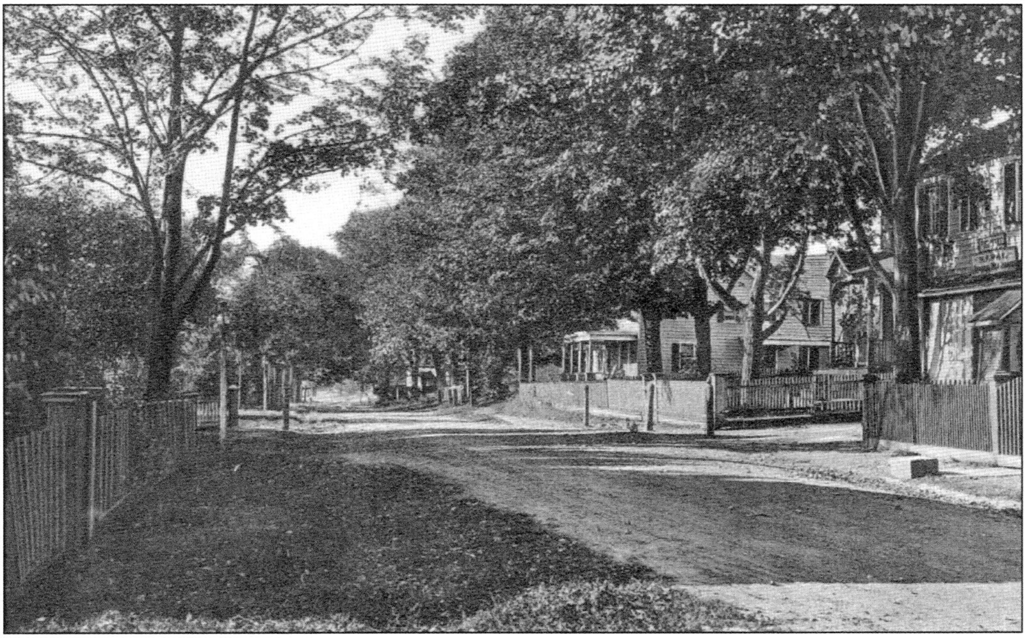

By 1911, the date on this postcard, picturesque Washington Valley Road was lined with Civil War–period houses behind picket fences, with mature shade trees arching over the street. Hitching posts stood in front of each home to accommodate horse-and-carriage visitors. An illegible sign beneath the upper windows of the house on the far right indicates that a business was located here. (KCD.)

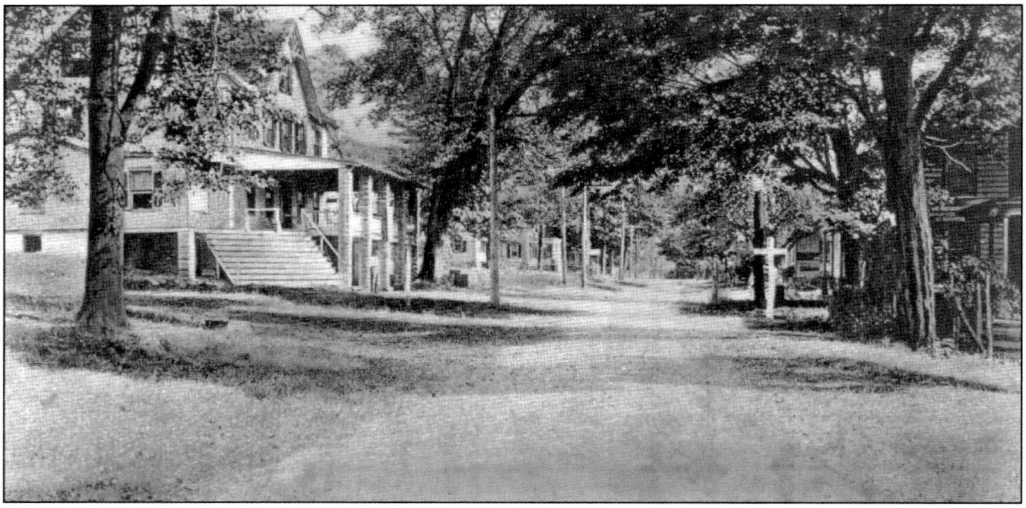

This view east from the intersection of Mount Horeb Road shows Agnes Jackson's Jackson Hotel, on the left. Her son, "Stonewall" Jackson, conducted a lively horse auction business, which can be seen beyond the hotel, followed by the John King home, the Azariah Mundy home, the post office, and the store. On the right are the S. Brown home and Fred Bartle's home, next to his blacksmith shop. (IKE.)

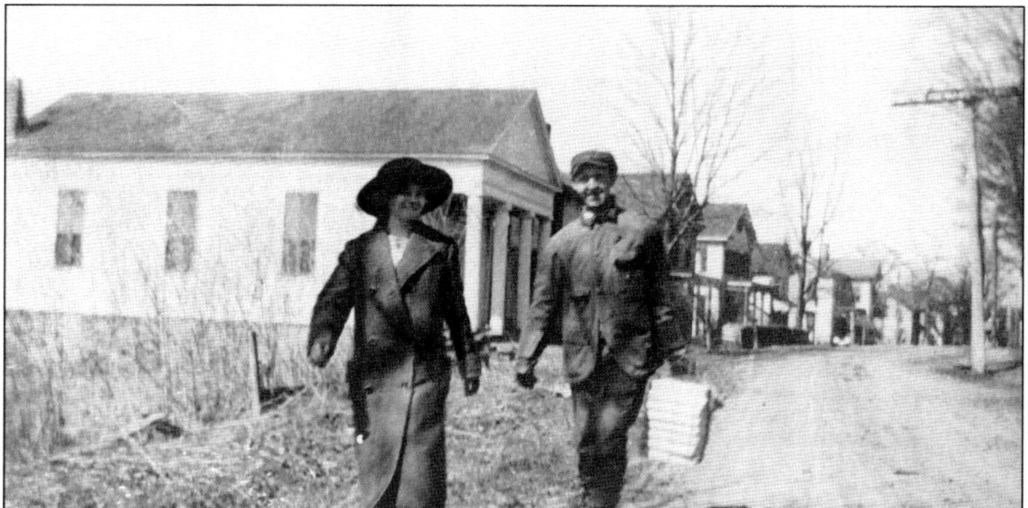

The village featured a mixture of residences and public buildings, including the columned former Presbyterian church, visible in this photograph of Art Waldron and his sister Sarah from about 1920. The building housed a lodge of the Junior Order of American Mechanics. During World War I, ladies met here to knit socks for the soldiers. The upper grades of the school held classes here while a new school was being built. (IKE.)

On the windy afternoon of March 29, 1923, several men were heating varnish to paint a canvas-top Buick touring car in Fred Bartle's garage beside the blacksmith shop. The varnish caught fire, which was fanned by the winds and quickly spread beyond the building. Within a few hours, 11 homes and seven other buildings had been reduced to ashes before fire companies from as far away as Plainfield and Somerville contained the flames. Bartle, the blacksmith, is pictured here. (DOC.)

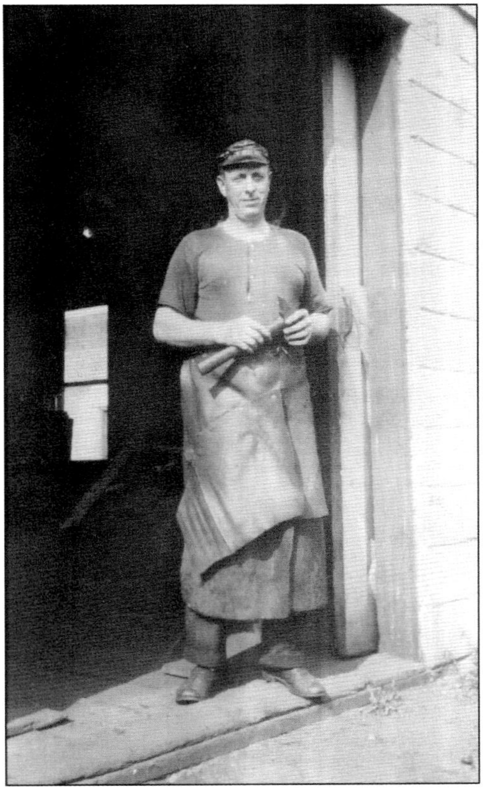

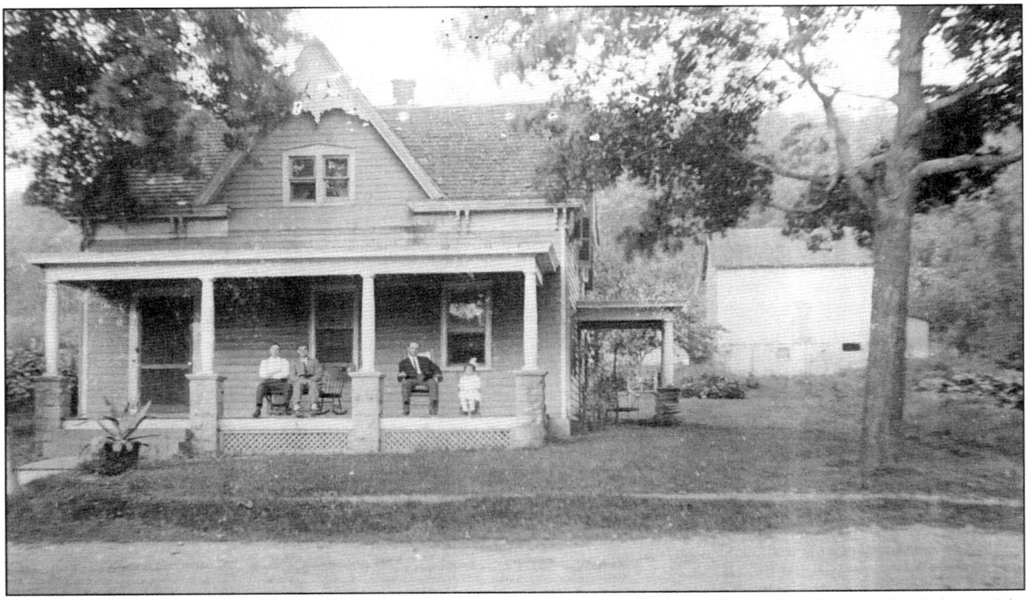

Albert and Lillian Bartle's Victorian-style home with the gingerbread trim at the peak of the gable stood beside the Martinsville Hotel across from the blacksmith shop. As seen here, the porch pillars are supported by blocks from the Bartle stone quarry. Before the fire, Albert, third from left, relaxes on the porch with his daughter Dorothy. The other two people are unidentified. (IKE.)

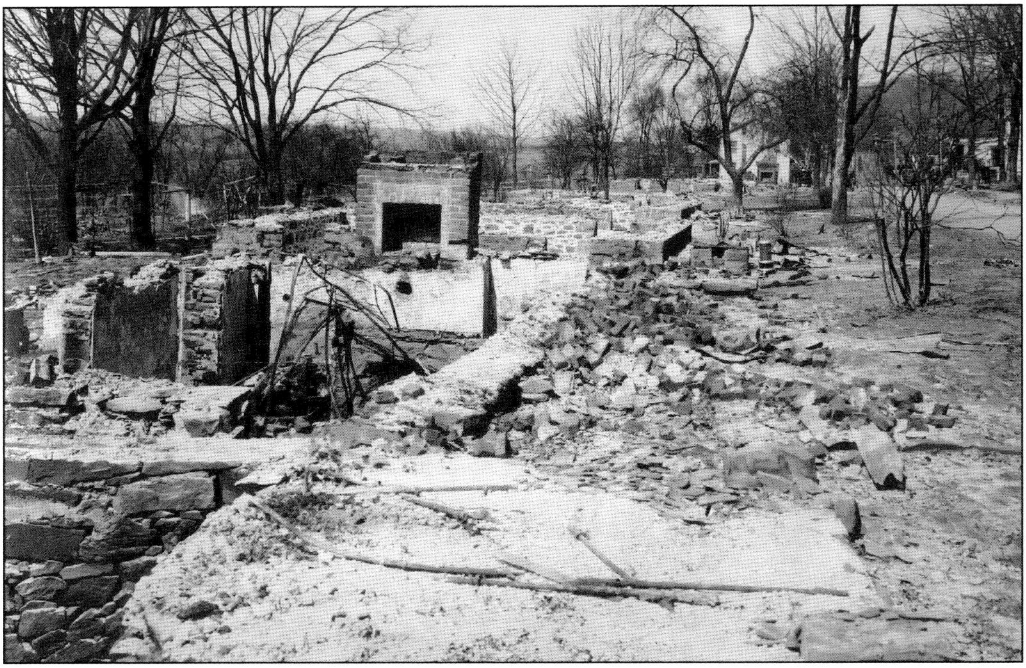

When Lillian Bartle saw the blacksmith shop in flames, she rushed down the road to spread the alarm to her neighbors. She returned to find her own home completely destroyed. The losses, besides her own, included the Bartle garage and blacksmith shop, houses belonging to Joseph Campbell, Eugene Davis, Robert Doty, John Mastapeter, Raymond Vactor, William Way, John Van Nest, John Thum, and Frank Hartman, the former Presbyterian chapel, and several barns. (MFD.)

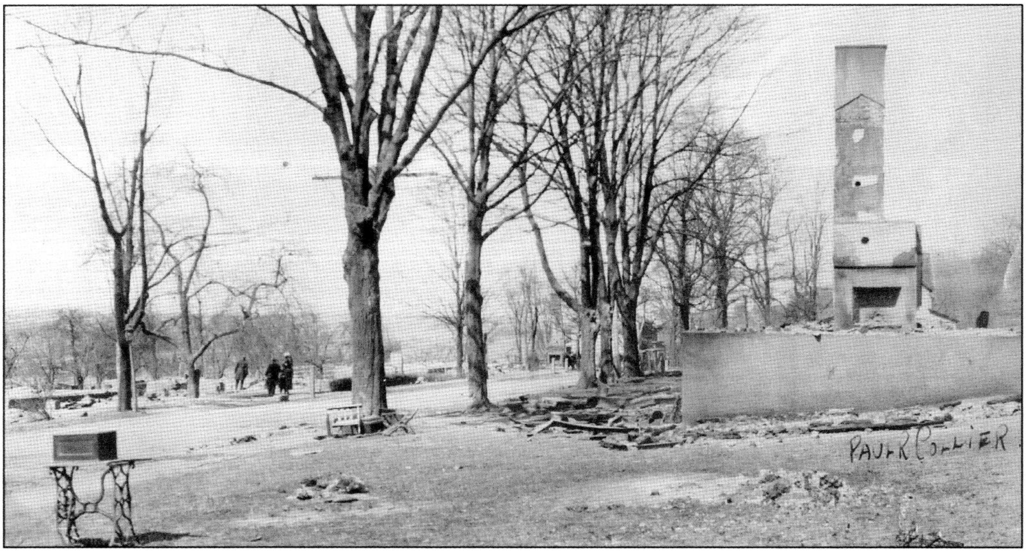

The dazed residents, who had escaped with only the clothes on their backs, were sheltered in the homes of friends and neighbors, while constable John Thum and deputies stood guard against looters during the night, warming their hands over the piles of burning embers. Most victims planned to rebuild and would perhaps live in small garages while their larger homes were erected. Jennie Vactor's sewing machine appears in the lower left. (MFD.)

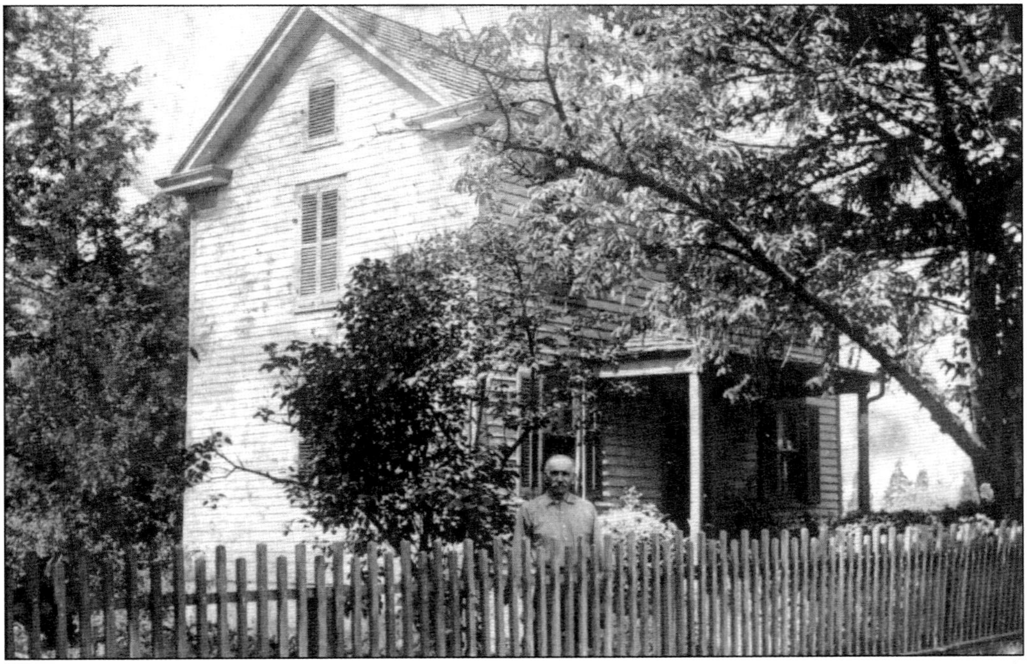

Pictured around 1925 tucked behind its picket fence, the home of boot and shoemaker Jacob Schlenz survived as a reminder of the charm that had been destroyed by the fire. Steve Grandner, grandson of Schlenz, amassed a collection of Indian artifacts during his lifetime of roaming freshly plowed fields. He later donated these valuable objects to the Somerset County Historical Society. (IKE.)

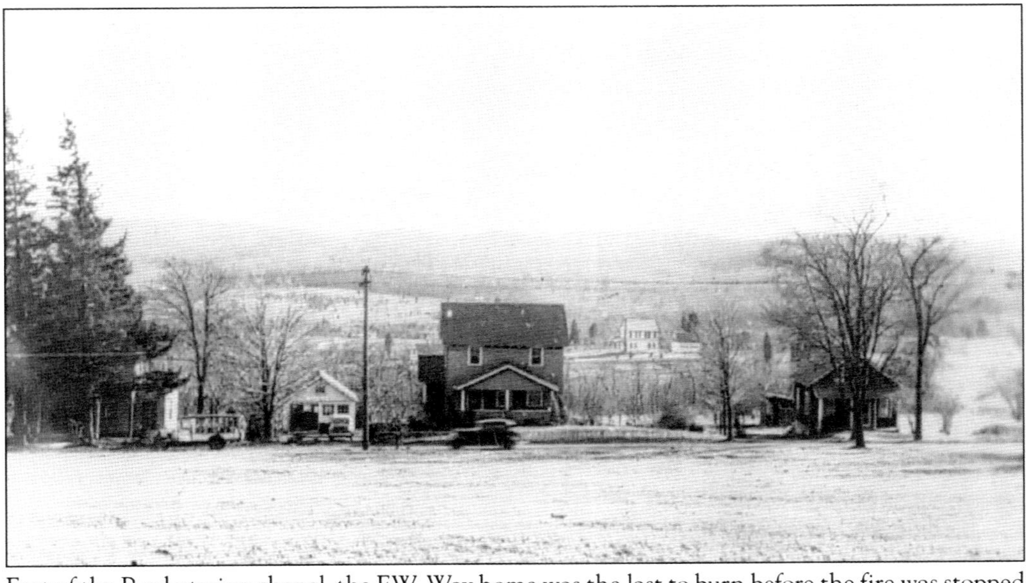

East of the Presbyterian chapel, the F.W. Way home was the last to burn before the fire was stopped at the Schlenz home, hidden by the tall spruce trees in the left of this photograph. After the fire, the widowed Sarah Coddington built the home in the center of this image on the former site of the Way home. Today, this is the location of Gabriel's Fountain restaurant. (BCD.)

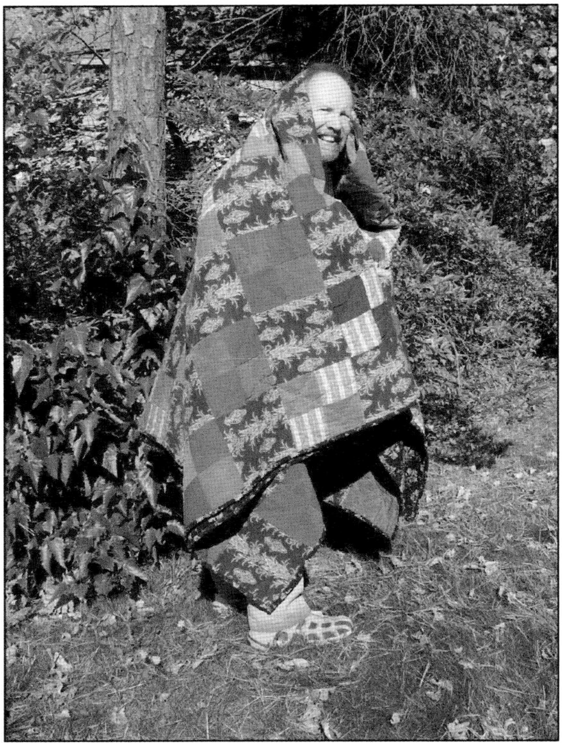

As Mary Todd Van Nest, wife of John Van Nest and mother of Hattie Roberts, fled her burning home with an armload of valuables, she grabbed a quilt off the bed to wrap around herself as sparks flew everywhere. This quilt, with burn holes from sparks, was inherited by her great-grandson John D. Roberts, who models her protective shield. (PVW.)

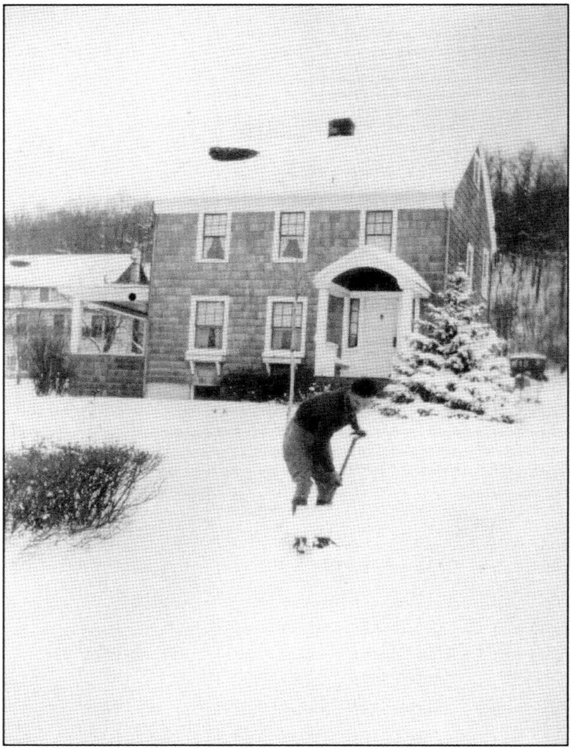

At the height of the fire, Edwin Smalley grabbed a heavy extinguisher from one of the fire trucks and climbed to the roof of Robert Doty's burning house. Finding himself trapped in a firestorm with sparks igniting his clothing, he edged his way to the front porch roof and slid down a pillar to the ground—minutes before the building collapsed. The Doty family then built this home. (DOC.)

George Davis manufactured wagon wheels and brooms in a shop beside the blacksmith forge. His son Eugene was a wagon painter and stage driver who carried mail between Martinsville and Bound Brook. Eugene's son Earl returned from Bound Brook High School the afternoon of the fire to discover the family home at the corner of Quarry Lane burned to the ground. The Davises then built this house. (DOC.)

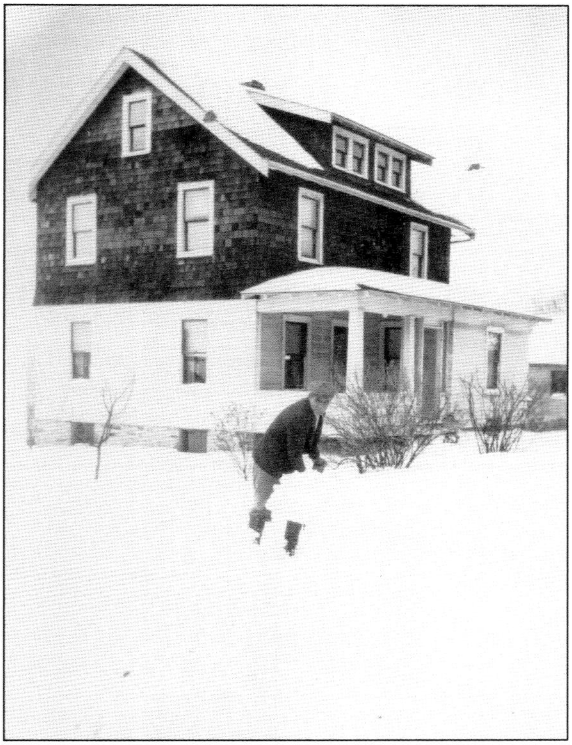

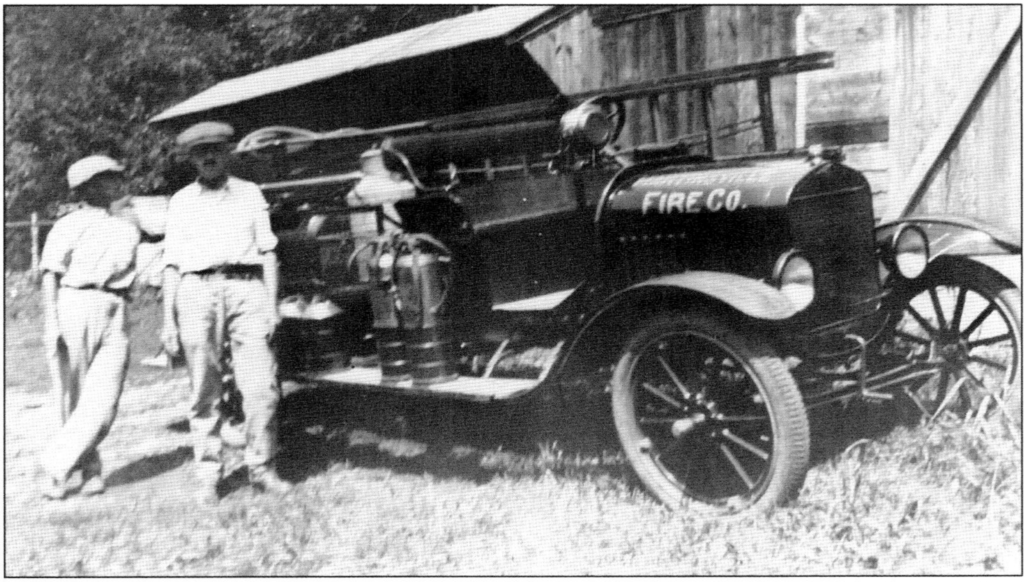

The Martinsville Engine Company formed in December 1923. The first members were chief Arthur Waldron, Leon Abbott, William Van Nest, John Thum, John Nees, Edwin Smalley, John Mastapeter, Joseph Seunderhaft, Grayland Penny, Chick Bartle, Stanley Bartle, Robert Doty, and William Lyng, who was president. They promptly ordered a fire truck, which arrived in a number of shipping crates with some assembly required. The men in this photograph are not identified. (IKE.)

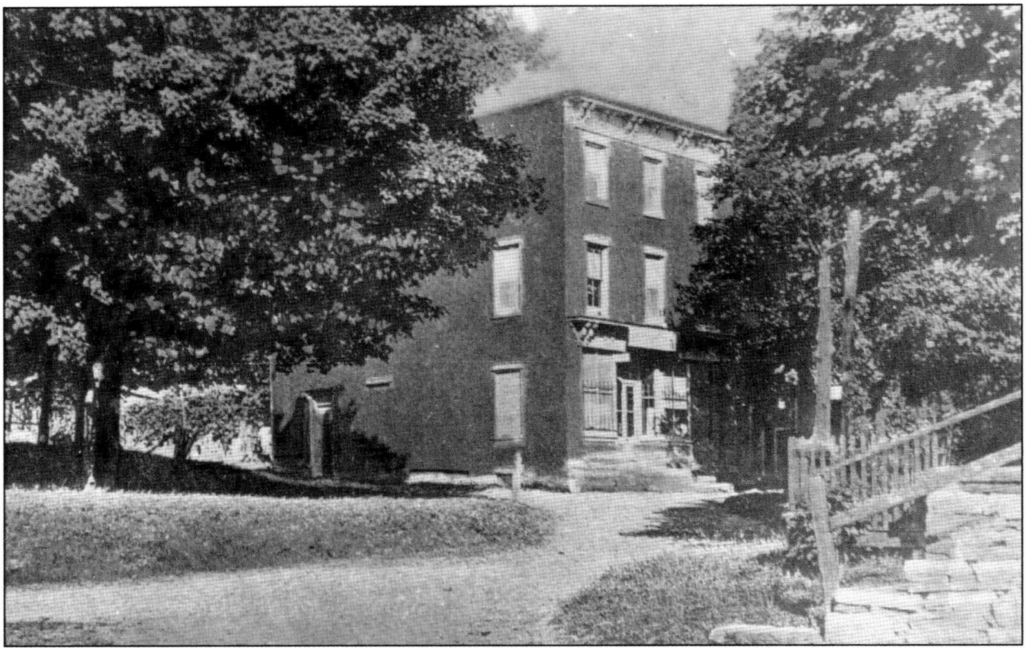

The Model T chemical truck was operated by adding sulfuric acid to the water in two 30-gallon storage tanks. The truck was housed in a barn behind Lyng's store at the intersection of Chimney Rock and Washington Valley Roads. The steep driveway was convenient for getting the hard-to-start Model T running as it rolled down to the road in gear. (IKE.)

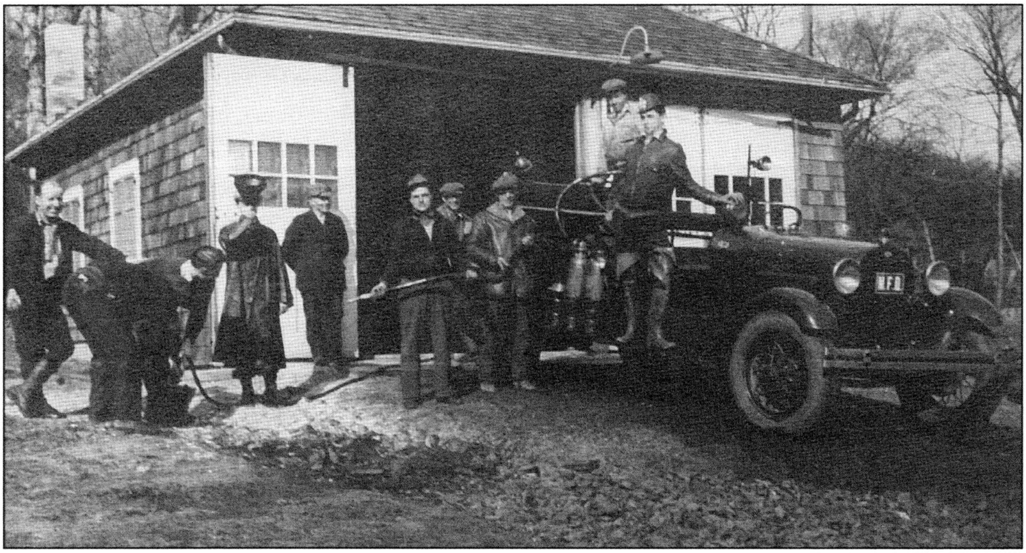

In 1928, residents built the first firehouse, which later became the Washington Valley Library. They then purchased a 1930 Model A Ford truck chassis, which they outfitted with the equipment from the older truck. In 1933, the men clown a bit as they wash their truck. The only identified man in this photograph is Floyd Valentine (far right), standing on the running board and clad in hip boots. (MFD.)

The first fire alarm was a split ring hanging in front of Lyng's store. Later, the adjacent school's bell was called to duty. By 1940, an electric siren was mounted in front of the firehouse, and calls for help came to the Clifford Hall house across the street. The firemen then dropped whatever they had been doing and responded from all directions. Here, they roar down Chimney Rock Road. (DOC.)

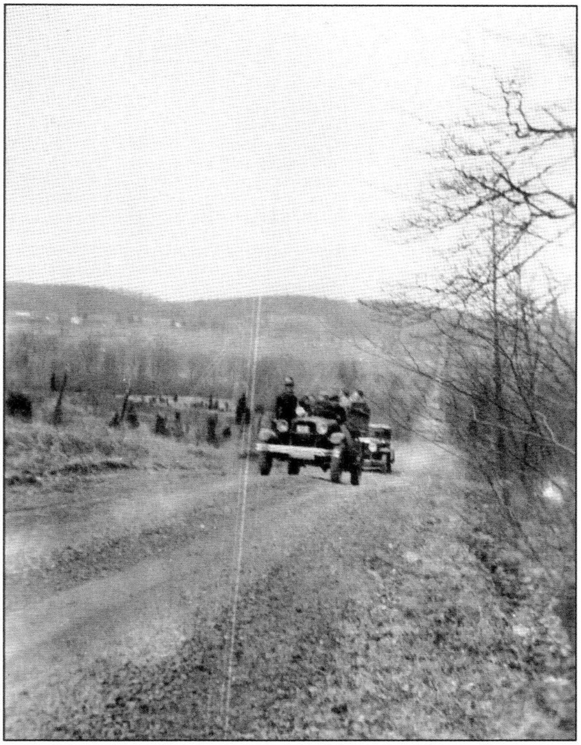

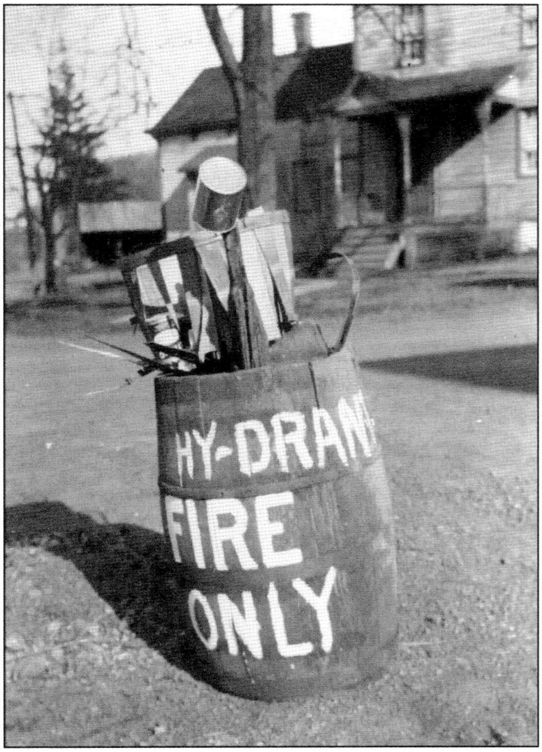

Although some skeptics joked about the village's fire preparedness by erecting a mock fire hydrant, residents were haunted by memories of the dreadful blaze. Jennie Thum had barely escaped with her life as she led her horses and cows out of the barn and a burning beam fell where she had stood moments before. (DOC.)

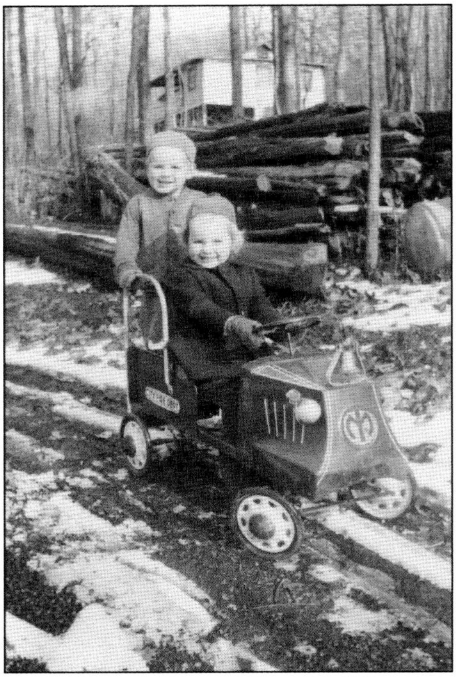

What child has not dreamed of becoming a fireman one day, as they have witnessed the spectacle of the shiny, red truck rushing off to fight a blaze with sirens roaring? Don (left) and Pat Valentine, pictured in 1942, recall their fireman father, Doug, laying out his clothes each evening so that he could dress quickly if the siren echoed across the valley during the night. (PVW.)

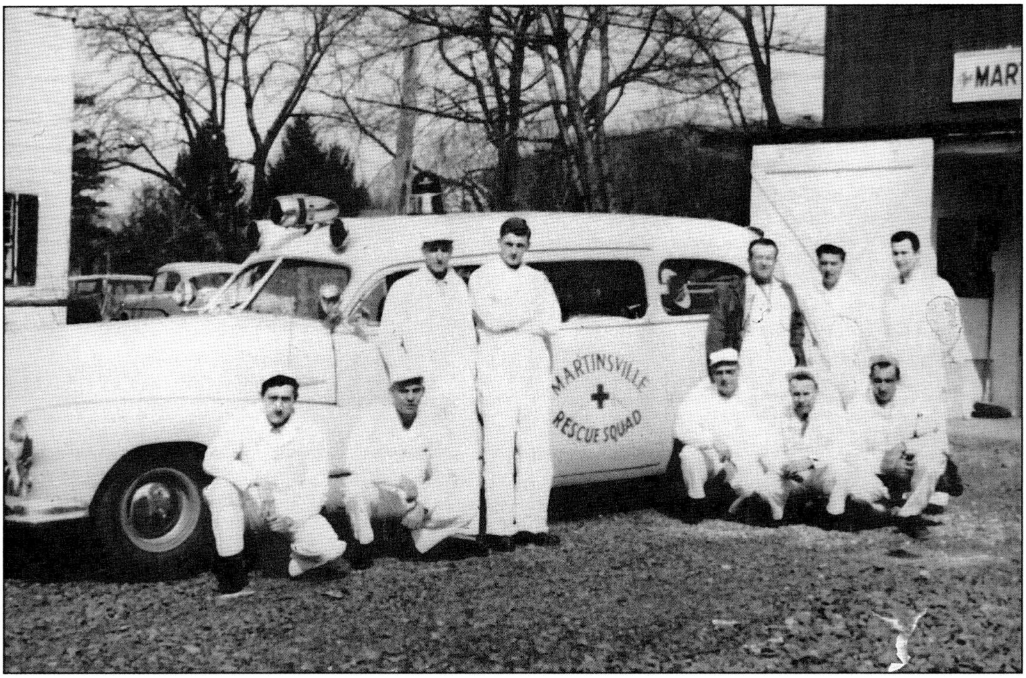

In 1957, residents organized a rescue squad to provide emergency medical service to the area. The first ambulance, a used 1953 Cadillac, was housed in the barn behind the Hoffman House on the corner of Mount Horeb Road. From left to right are (kneeling) David Housten, Ken Peterson, unidentified, James Housten, and Doug Huff; (standing) Otto Klein, Erwin "Sonny" Van Allen, Bill Obszanski, Ed Frazer, and unidentified. (BIX.)

Five

Wartimes Over the Years

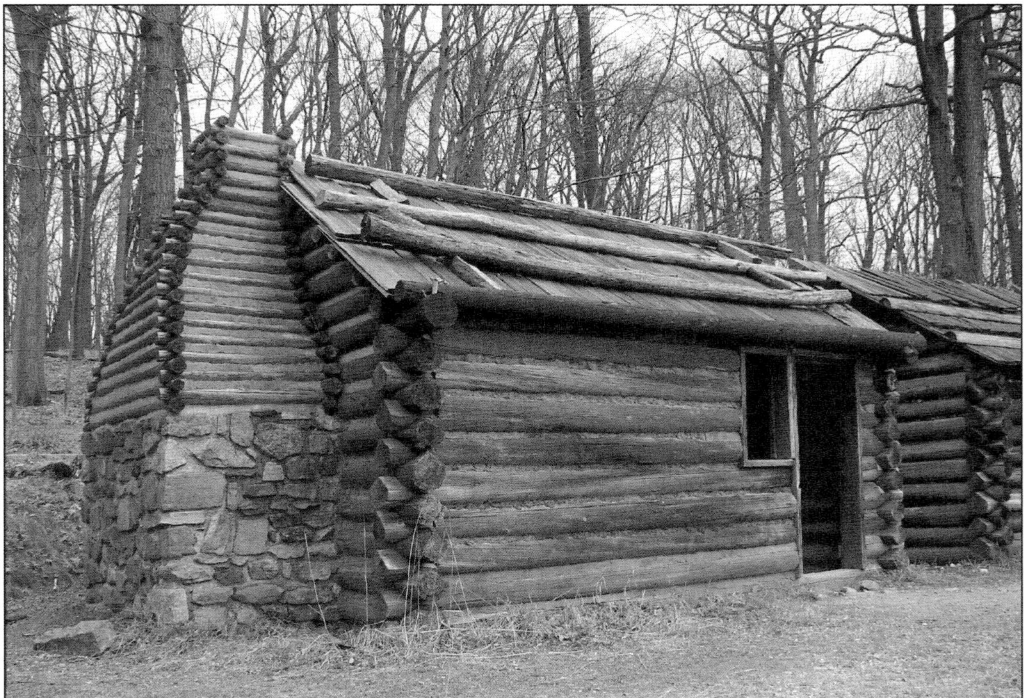

George Washington discovered the strategic location of the Middle Brook Valley when he camped here in June 1777. While secure from invasion through the narrow Chimney Rock Gorge, Washington observed the movements of the British in the plains of New Brunswick to the south from lookout points on the First Watchung Mountain. He chose this valley as winter quarters for part of his army in 1779–1780, ordering the construction of log huts like these reproductions at Jockey Hollow National Park, in Morristown, New Jersey, where they had spent the previous winter. (PVW.)

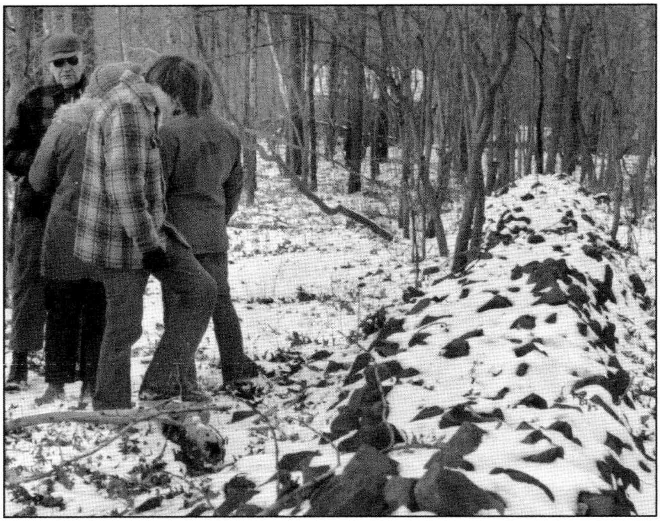

The remains of Washington's earthworks, indicated on an 1873 atlas map, survive in the Spring Run area (pictured) and on the mountain behind Chimney Rock. Residents were sympathetic to the soldiers and their meager supplies, sharing food and clothing with them and surreptitiously providing applejack on occasion, although Washington had forbidden alcohol in or near the camps. These unidentified people are members of the team that wrote the 1975 book *North of the Rariton Lotts*. (IKE.)

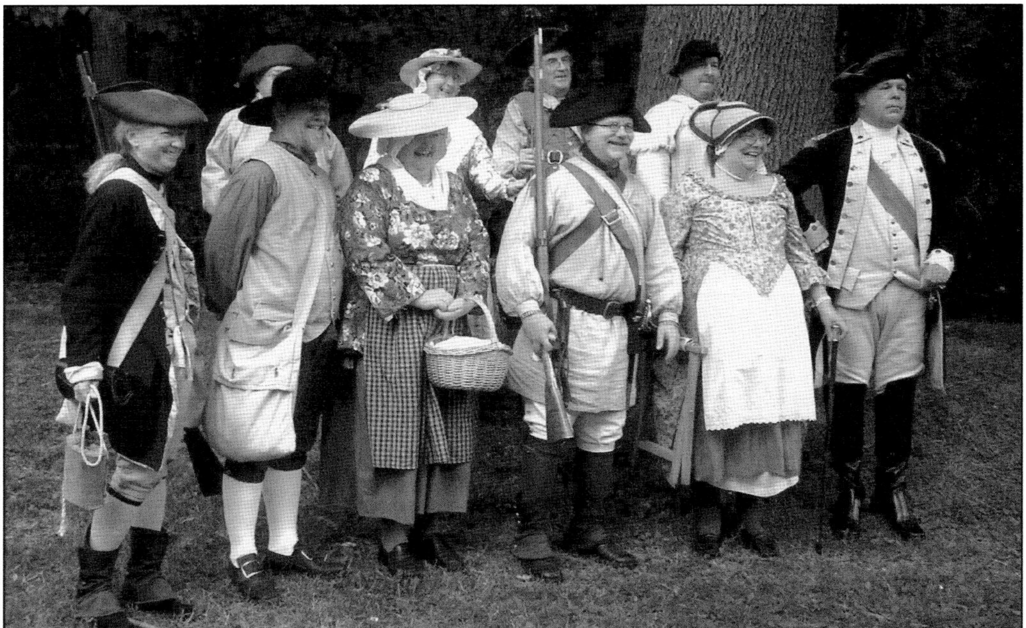

Washington's campground atop the First Watchung Mountain above Bound Brook is generally recognized as the first place where the 13-star so-called Betsy Ross flag was flown. In 1890, George LaMonte donated the hallowed ground to the Washington Camp Ground Association with the proviso that on every July Fourth, the Declaration of Independence be read there. In 2007, this group of reenactors adds historical context to the annual ceremony at which a new flag is raised. (BER.)

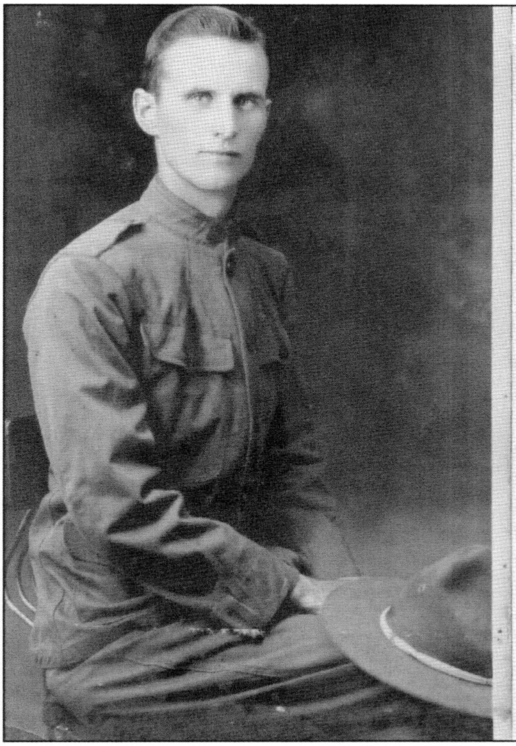

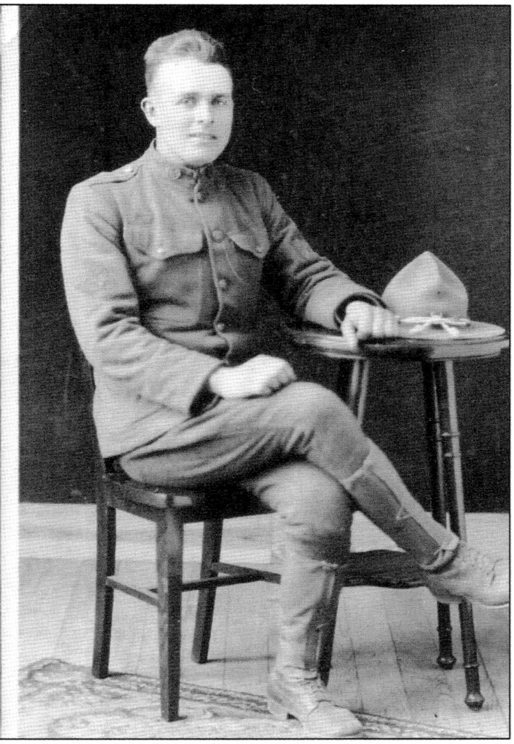

Several of Martinsville's young men served in World War I. Brothers-in-law Edwin Smalley (left) and Franklin Chick Bartle later built houses side by side on Chimney Rock Road and remained friends and neighbors for life. After the war, Smalley planted a circular garden of Peace roses on his lawn to commemorate the signing of the Treaty of Versailles, which he had witnessed. (JCD.)

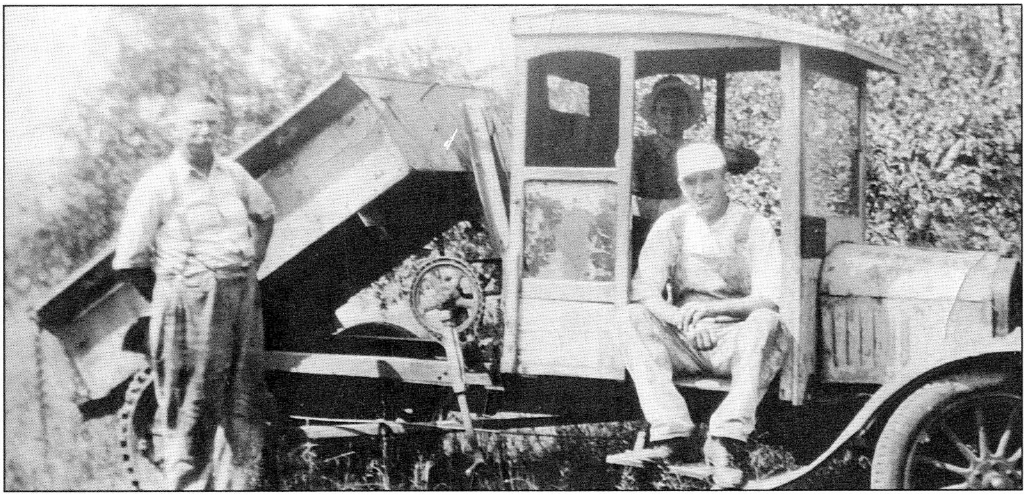

As the nation recovered from the Great Depression, new housing lots were needed. In 1936, Frank Wahl (left), Edwin Smalley (center), and William Zimmerman worked with this vintage dump truck to build Fieldstone Road. Neighbors had no problem communicating with Wahl, a deaf mute who had been severely injured by a bull in his youth. Wahl attended church each Sunday, took up the collection, and participated in other community activities. (JCD.)

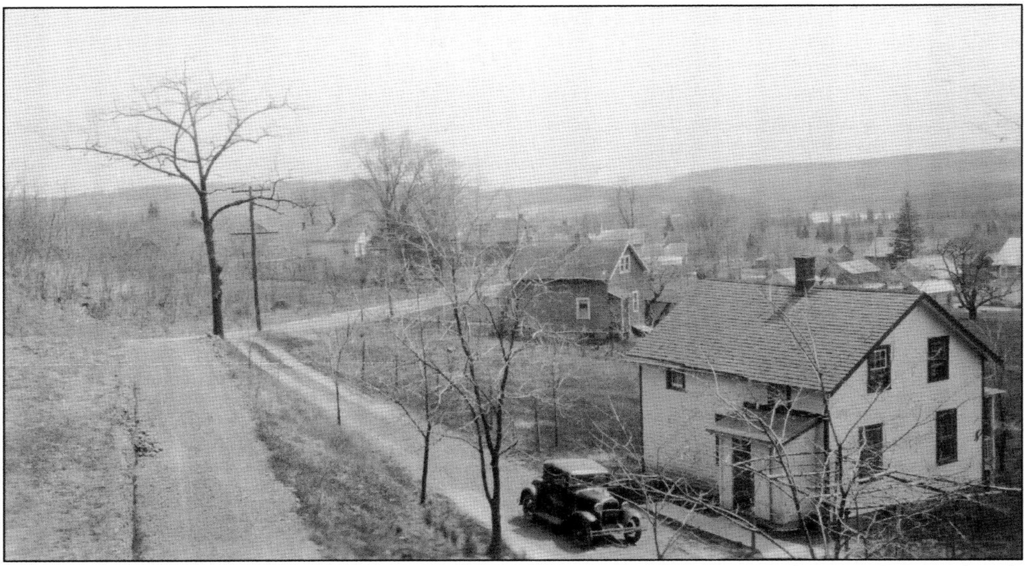

While Leonard Reudiger served in the US Navy in the 1930s, his German-born wife moved with their three children to Germany to be near her family. When son Leonard Jr. was repeatedly struck by his schoolteacher for refusing to salute "Heil Hitler," the family returned to their home on Mount Horeb Road, shown in the foreground in this 1938 view. His father was killed in the war, and young Leonard entered the service after high school graduation. (JVC.)

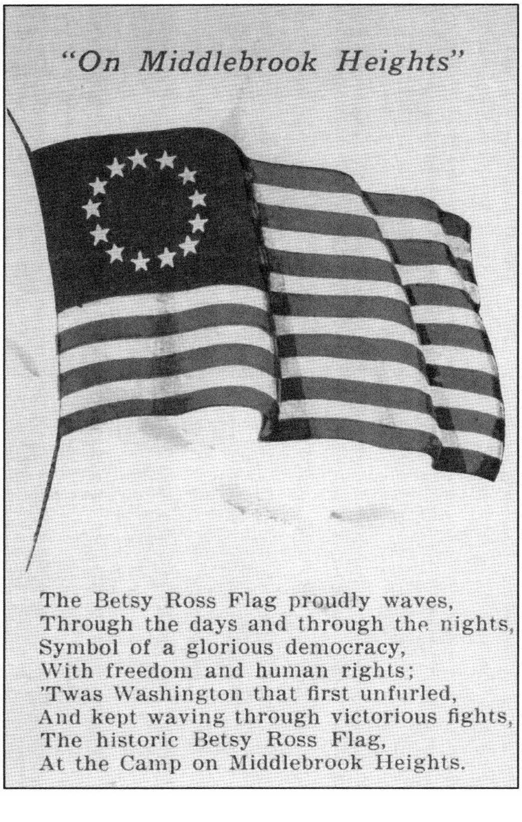

In February 1941, naturalized citizen Dominick Beronio, concerned about the Nazi advances in Europe, completed his poem "On Middlebrook Heights" with these verses: "A great free nation was then built, / On a foundation of equal rights / Where men and women from all lands, / Found a haven of greater lights. / Many years have passed since then, / And there have been many dark nights, / But the Betsy Ross Flag still waves, / At the Camp on Middlebrook Heights. / In this troubled world of ours, / Where some flags fall over night, / There's one flag that waves serenely, / With peace, liberty, and freedom's light; / And may God help to protect her, / And lead her to greater heights, / The Betsy Ross Flag that waves, / At the Camp on Middlebrook Heights." (BER.)

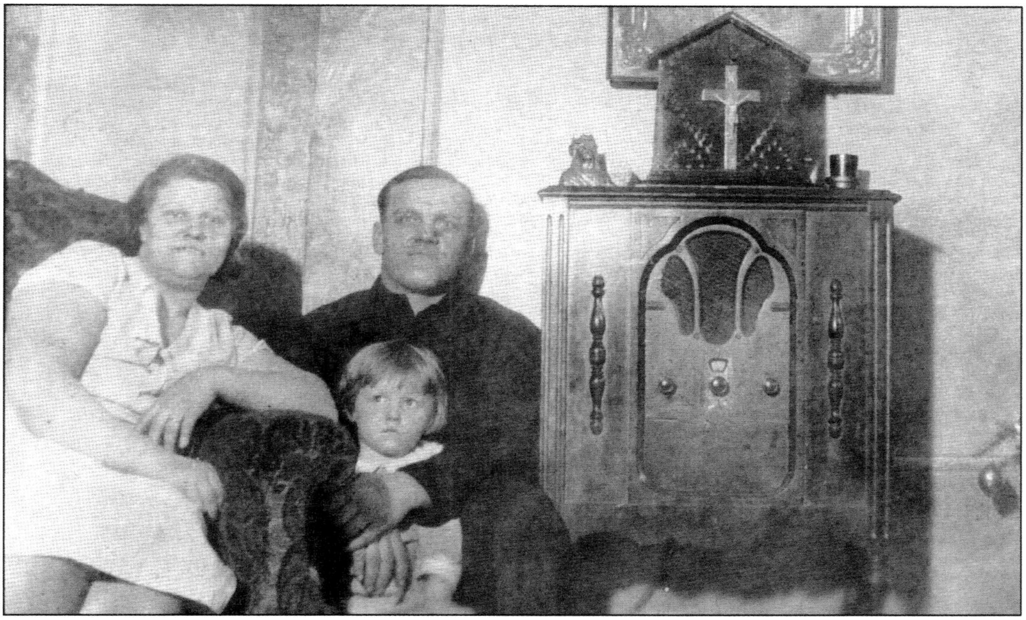

Senior citizens today vividly recall listening to the family radio on Sunday afternoon, December 7, 1941, as Pres. Franklin D. Roosevelt announced the Japanese attack on Pearl Harbor, which he later described as "a date which will live in infamy." Radios were such a novelty that the 1930 US Census recorded whether a family owned one. Dolores Geschwindner is with her mother, Martha, and her uncle Chester Bonowicz in 1934. (EGS.)

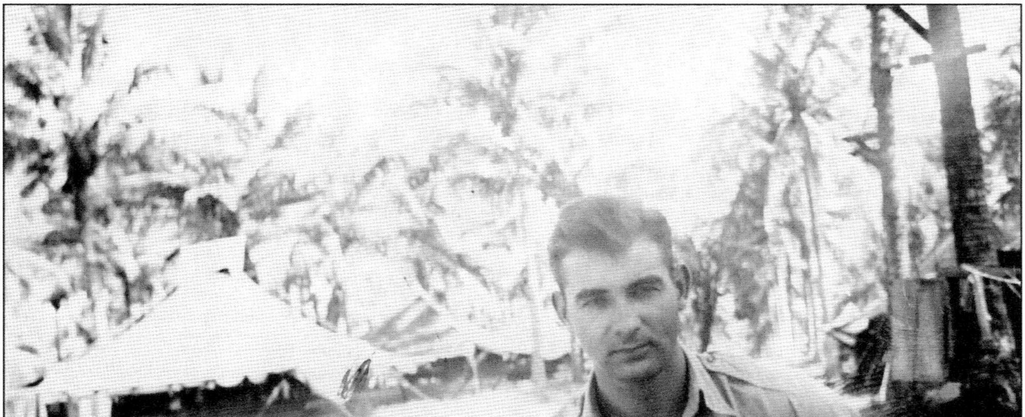

While the young men and women served in the military, the folks at home were busy supporting the war effort in numerous ways. With gasoline rationing, Joe Van Nest returned to delivering milk with a horse and wagon. Women revised recipes to use fewer of the ingredients that were rationed to help feed the troops and European allies. Girl Scouts volunteered to babysit for mothers who were helping the Red Cross. Bob Byrne, pictured on Guadalcanal, was a B-24 bombardier. (PVW.)

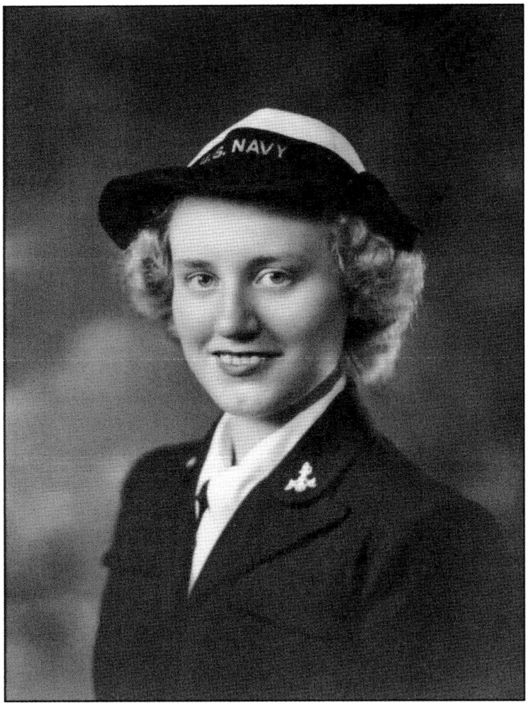

The Van Nests have a long history of serving their country in wartime, beginning with Jeromys Van Nest in the Revolutionary War. His 1776 letter reports, "The regurals have landed at Powelshock [Paulus Hook]," and, "Whe expect an actac every day." Another Van Nest died in the Civil War. William Van Nest served in World War I, and his daughter Irene (seen here) volunteered for the Navy WAVES in World War II. (IVN.)

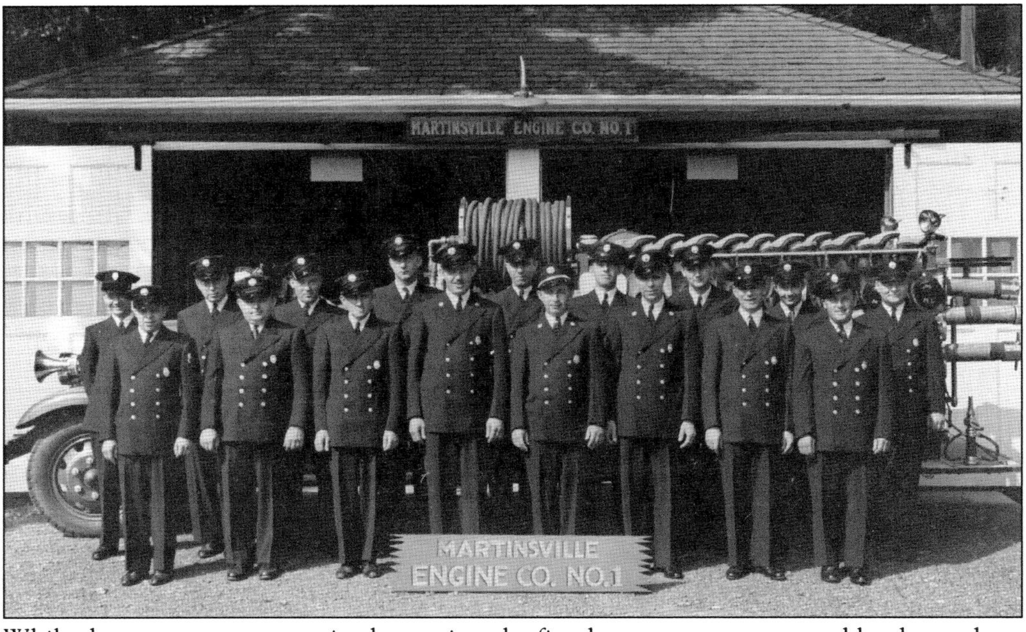

While the younger men were in the service, the fire department was manned by those whose civilian occupations were critical to the war effort. They also served as air raid wardens. In this August 1942 photograph, they are, from left to right, (first row) Arthur Hoyt, William Hettle, Carl Franz, Albert Mason, Earl Davis, Harold Howarth, Peter Peterson, and Robert Zingler; (second row) Theodore Bartlett, Doc Bartle, John Brarens, Walter Uken, Ken Koshoffer, Todd Harrison, Doug Valentine, Harold Coddington, and Joseph Musialowski. (JCD.)

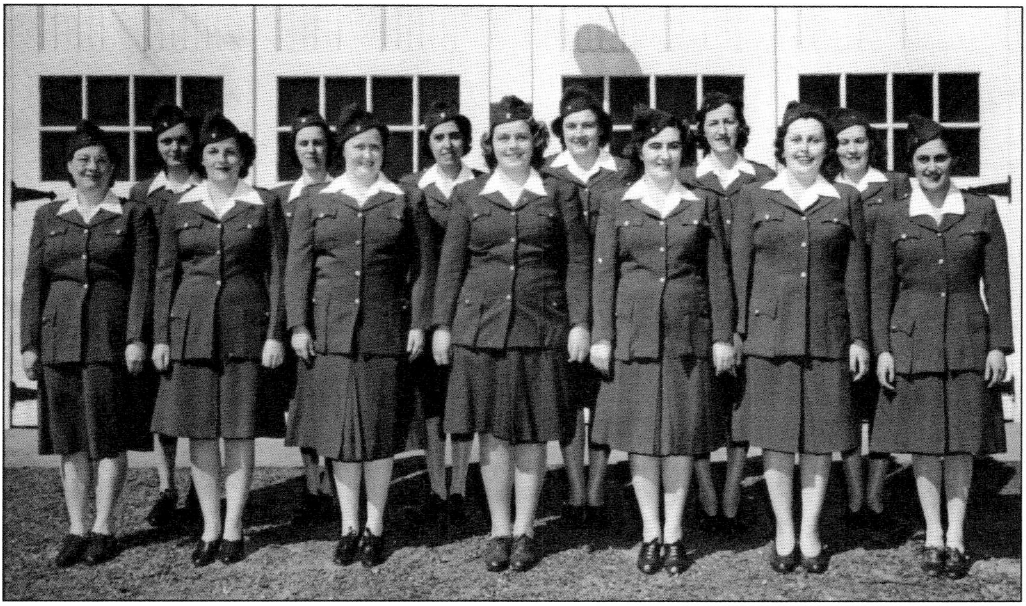

Mildred Musialowski was part of a team of women who were trained to identify both friendly and enemy aircraft. They rotated shifts to monitor the skies during daylight hours. Mildred and others were also members of the Ladies' Auxiliary of the fire department, which stood proudly for this photograph. From left to right are two unidentified members, Beatrice Hoyt, unidentified, Isabel Mason, ? Buono, Irene Davis, Mae Goddard, unidentified, Mildred Musialowski, Clara Davis, Julia Thum, and unidentified. (MUS.)

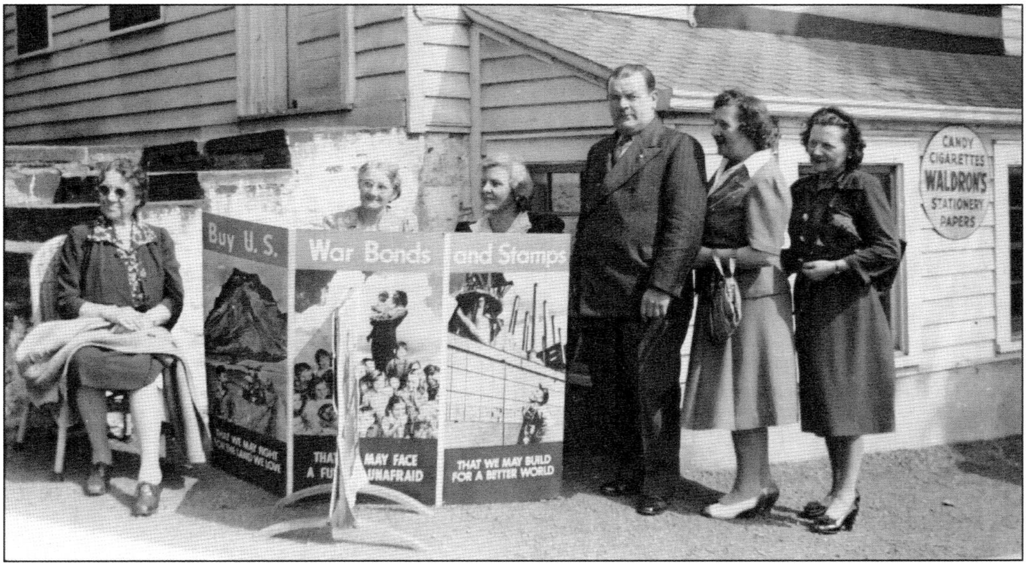

Sarah Coddington (left) and postmistress Vala Waldron sell war bonds outside the Waldron store. From left to right are unidentified (seated) and William Dryburgh, Sophia Dryburgh, and Ruth Lessing lined up to purchase their bonds. Children brought dimes to school on Fridays to purchase stamps to paste in their war bond books. When the books were full, they were issued a war bond. Coddington, Waldron, and Dryburgh sons were in the service. (DOC.)

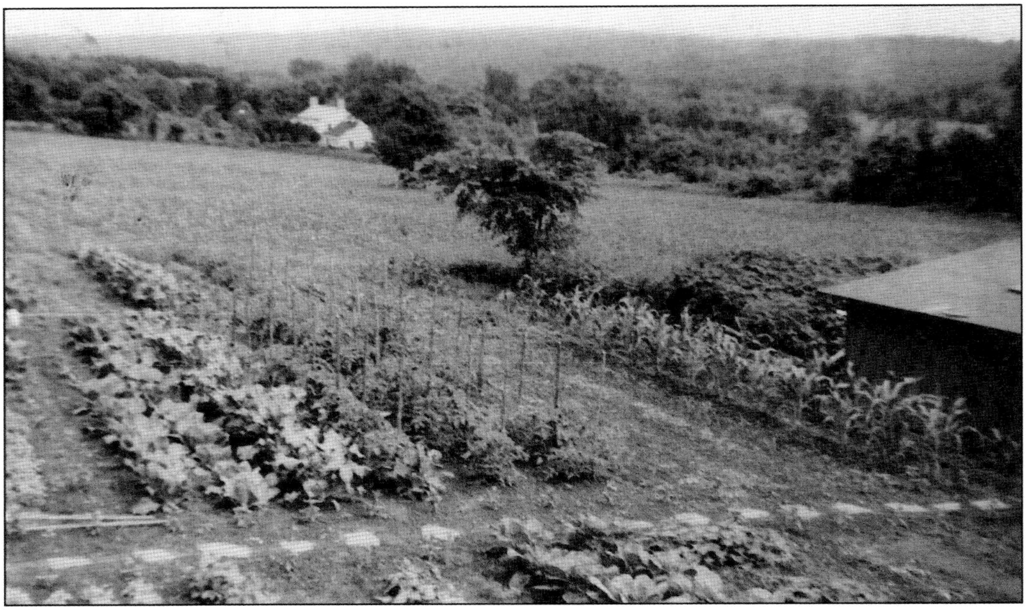

Everyone planted victory gardens to augment food supplies. Harry Poffley's neatly tended garden is now the site of the Martinsville Shopping Center and the post office. This field is thought to be the approximate location of George Washington's June 1777 encampment. The soldiers were said to have drawn water from the well at the former Waldron-Cramer-Fais house visible in the distance. (DOC.)

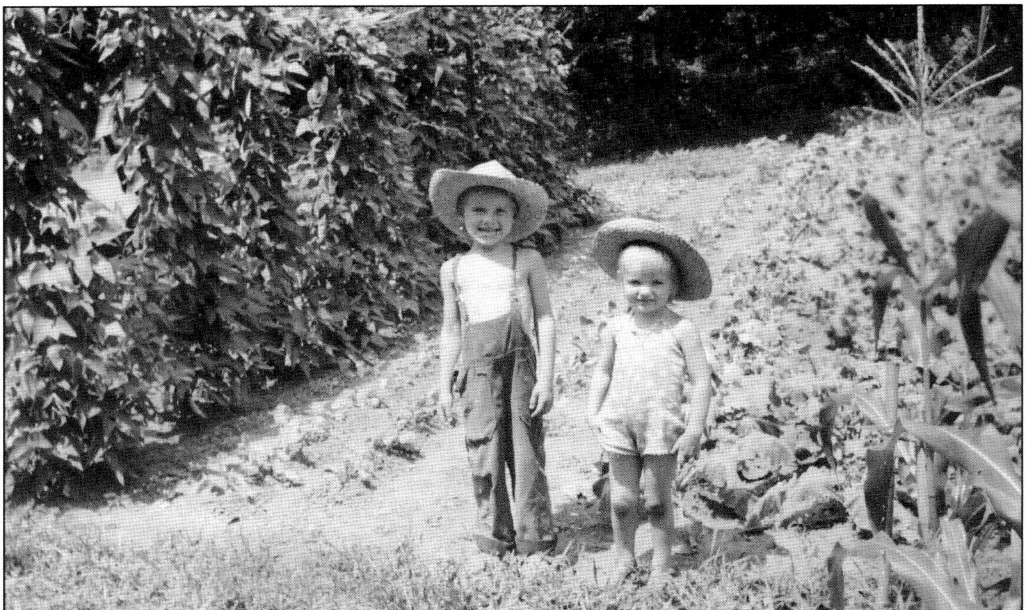

The entire family often worked in the victory garden. Don and Suzy Valentine are pictured. Women were so inspired by all the gardening techniques they had learned during the war that they formed the Washington Valley Garden Club in 1946. (PVW.)

In 1942, schoolmates, from left to right, Carol Howarth, Sally Richards, Lois Poffley, and Glenn ? collected scrap iron on the Poffley lawn across from Lyng's store. To show the children what their donation had helped to build, the military drove a Jeep to the Martinsville School and gave them all a ride. Children sang, "Whistle while you work. Hitler is a jerk. Mussolini is a meanie, but the Japs are worse!" (POF.)

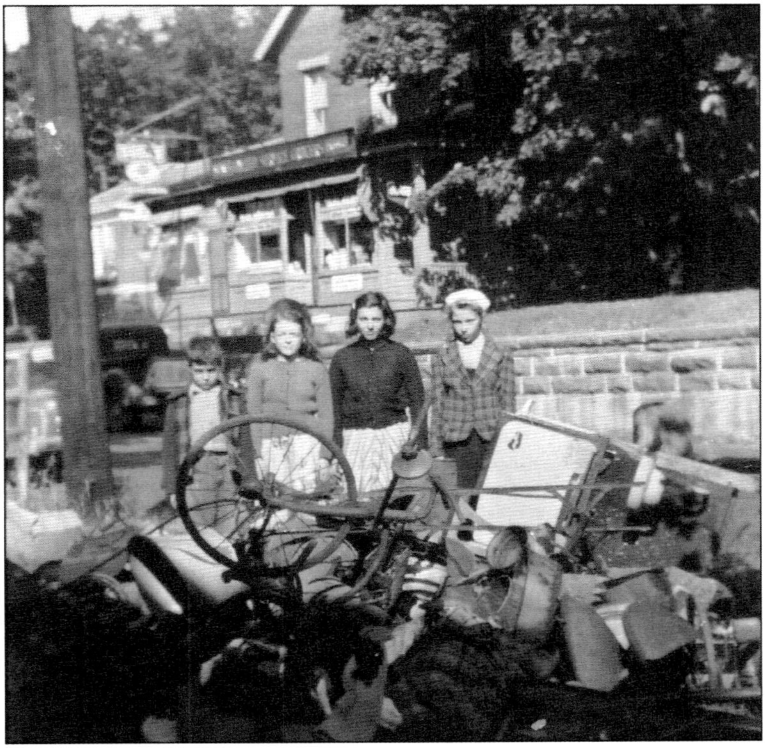

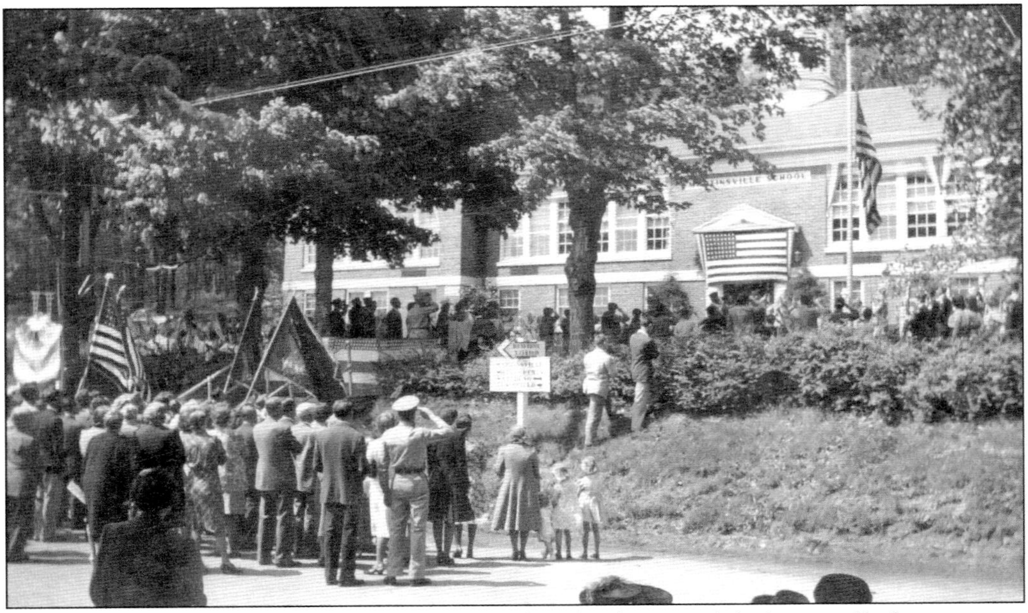

In May 1943, the community gathered in front of the school to unveil the honor roll of servicemen, including Michael Ackerman; Jack Allaire; Leonard and Samuel Assante; Paul, Willard, and Dorothea Bartlett; Thomas Bean; Russell Brarens; Louis Buono; William Burrell; Robert Byrne; Donald Case; Harold and William Coddington; George and William Cunningham; Franklin Dexter; Kenneth Dryburgh; John Eckert; Leonard Eddy; and Stephen Estochen. (IVN.)

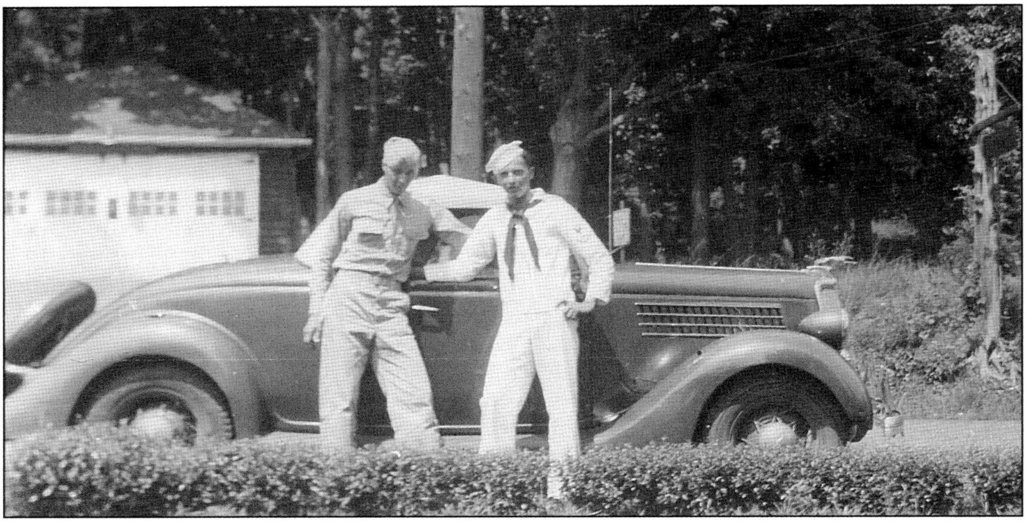

Edwin Coddington (left) and Otto Klein swap war stories beside this 1935 Ford DeLuxe roadster, in front of the firehouse. Friends occasionally came home on leave at the same time. Others were fortunate to cross paths while serving elsewhere. Additional local servicemen included Clyde, George, and Walter Ferris; Raymond and William Frazer; Charles and Frank Gianotti; Fred Goddard; Wilmer Haines; Robert Hamblin; Andrew Harcarick; and Douglas Hill. (ECD.)

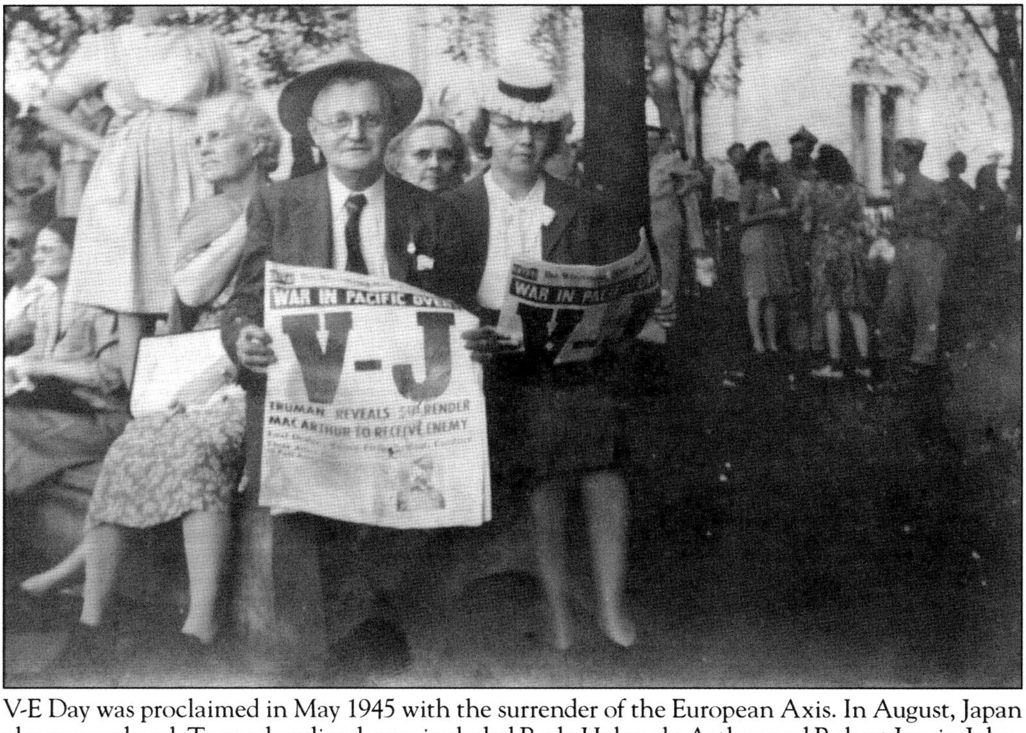

V-E Day was proclaimed in May 1945 with the surrender of the European Axis. In August, Japan also surrendered. Troops heading home included Rudy Hubacek; Arthur and Robert Jarvis; John, Joseph and Thomas Kozic; Erwin Langfeldt; Ralph Lyng; Robert and William Mason; George and Theodore Mastapeter; George and John Meyer; Howard, Robert, and William Moody; Joseph Mondak; William Morecraft; Arnold Napoleon; Stanley Norkovich; and John Ogilvie. (JWG.)

By the June 1946 wedding of Irene Van Nest to Navy seaman Robert Hall, Irene had been discharged, and Hall arranged for a two-week leave, as he continued with his Navy service. Many of their friends were able to return home in time to witness the happy event at the Martinsville Methodist Church. (JWG.)

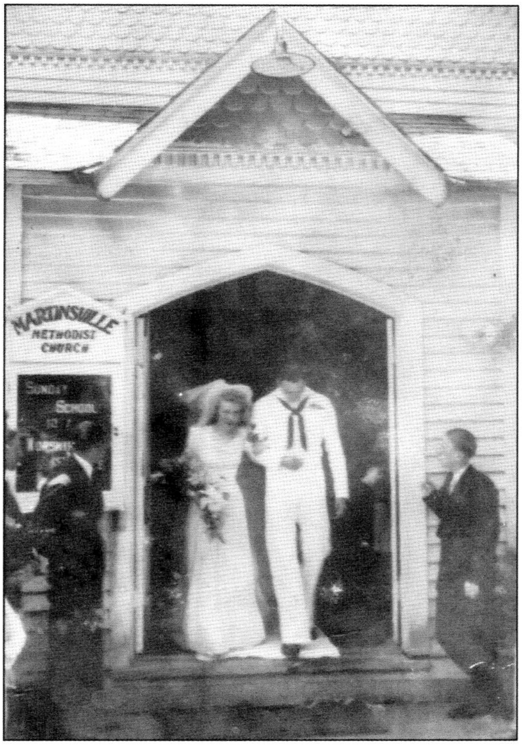

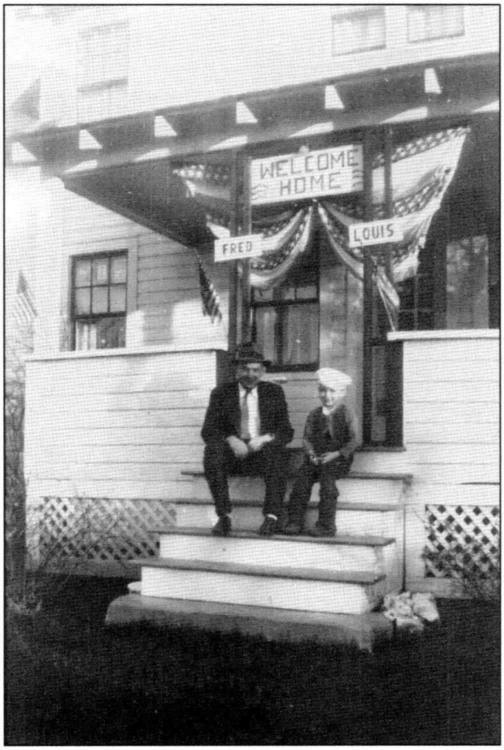

Henry Geschwindner (left) and neighbor Bobby Gluck await the arrival of Henry's sons Louis, Frederick, and Richard. Others looked forward to the returns of Ralph Papen; Curtis Penny; Ken and Lawrence Peterson; Frank, Harry, and Richard Poffley; Leonard Reudiger; Albert and John Roberts; C. Schmeltzer; John Schweitzer; William Shrewsbury; Andrew and Joseph Sopko; Benjamin Stein; and Frank and Douglas Totten. (GSH.)

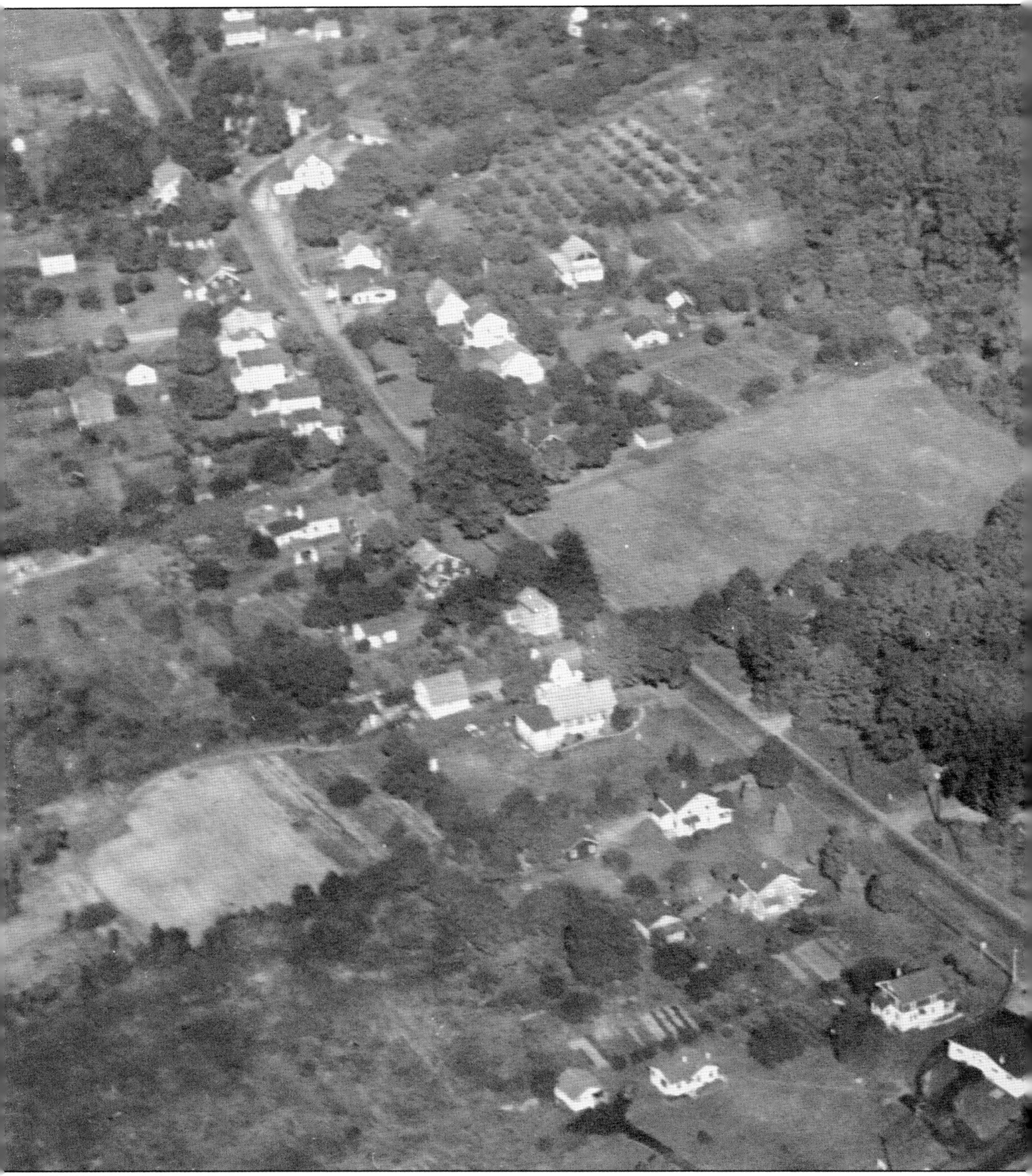

Taken after the war, this aerial photograph records the center of the village. Beginning in the upper left, Mount Horeb Road meets Washington Valley Road. The large, white Hoffman House Hotel is on the corner. Following Washington Valley Road east, toward the lower right corner, the Davis home is on the corner of Quarry Lane, opposite the Esso station. The large field in center right is the site of the present Methodist church. Opposite this field is the original Methodist

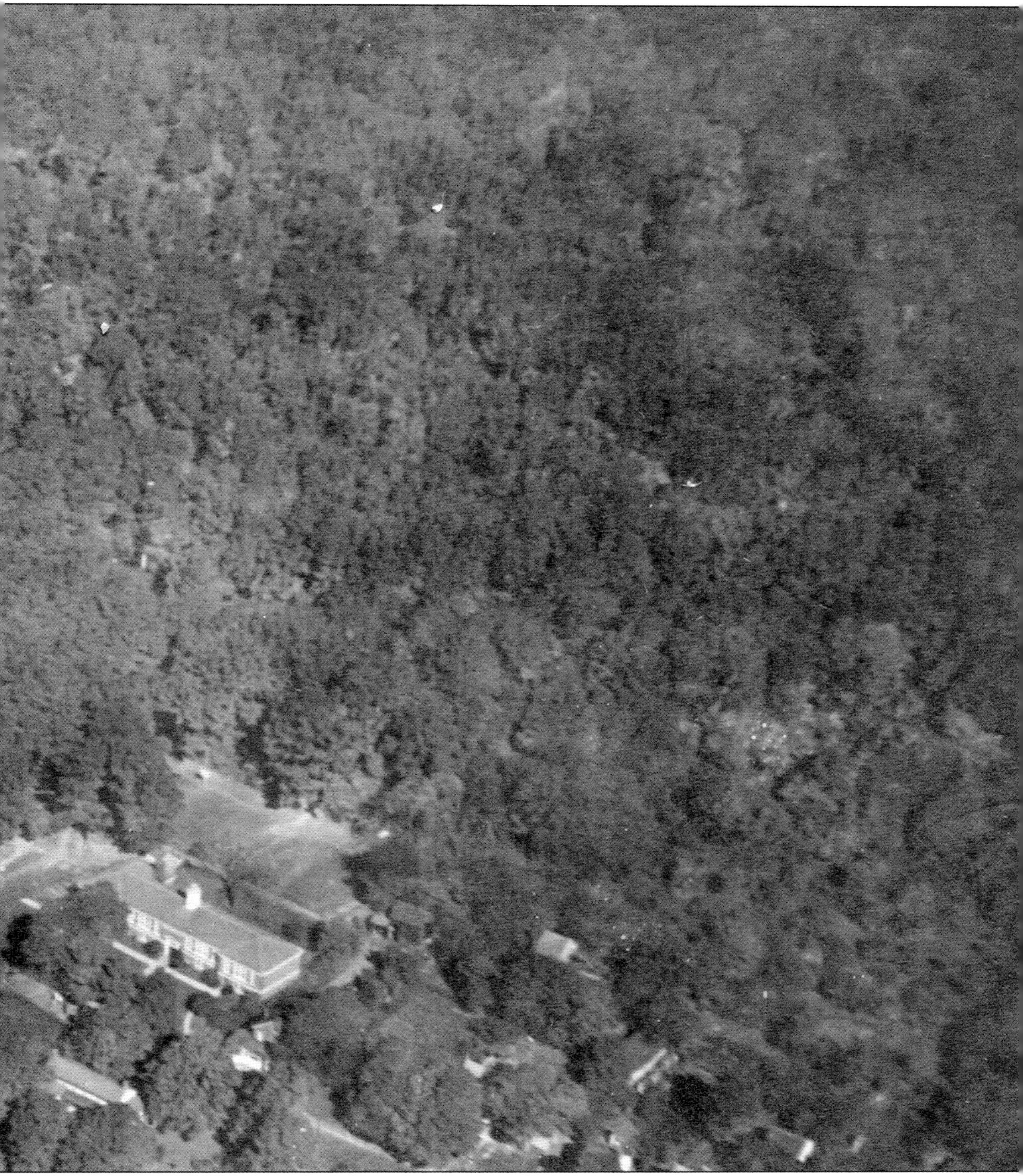

church, with lawn on the right. Penny's Garage is in the lower right corner. Near the fold of the right page, at the head of Chimney Rock Road, the Martinsville School is very prominent. The cluster of trees on the lower left corner conceals the former Waldron store and home. This area and the field to the east, out of the photograph, are now the sites of two shopping centers. (JWG.)

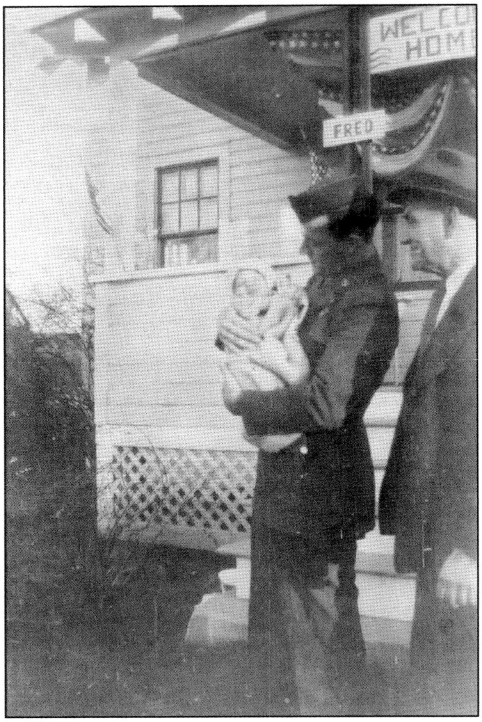

As proud grandfather Henry Nicholas Geschwindner beams, Louis Geschwindner meets his new son, Louis Jr., who represents the generation of postwar baby boomers. Other servicemen soon to return were John, Pasquale, and Dominick Tullo; Harmon and Robert Tunison; Walter Uken; Donald and John Waldron; Robert Wilde; Kenneth Wilson; and John Wojnar. (GSH.)

After the war, the GI Bill helped to send several veterans to college or night school as they returned to their prewar occupations, while others started in new ventures. Longtime friends Albert Roberts (left) and Robert Byrne launched an excavating business as the postwar building boom began to change the landscape of Martinsville. (KBN.)

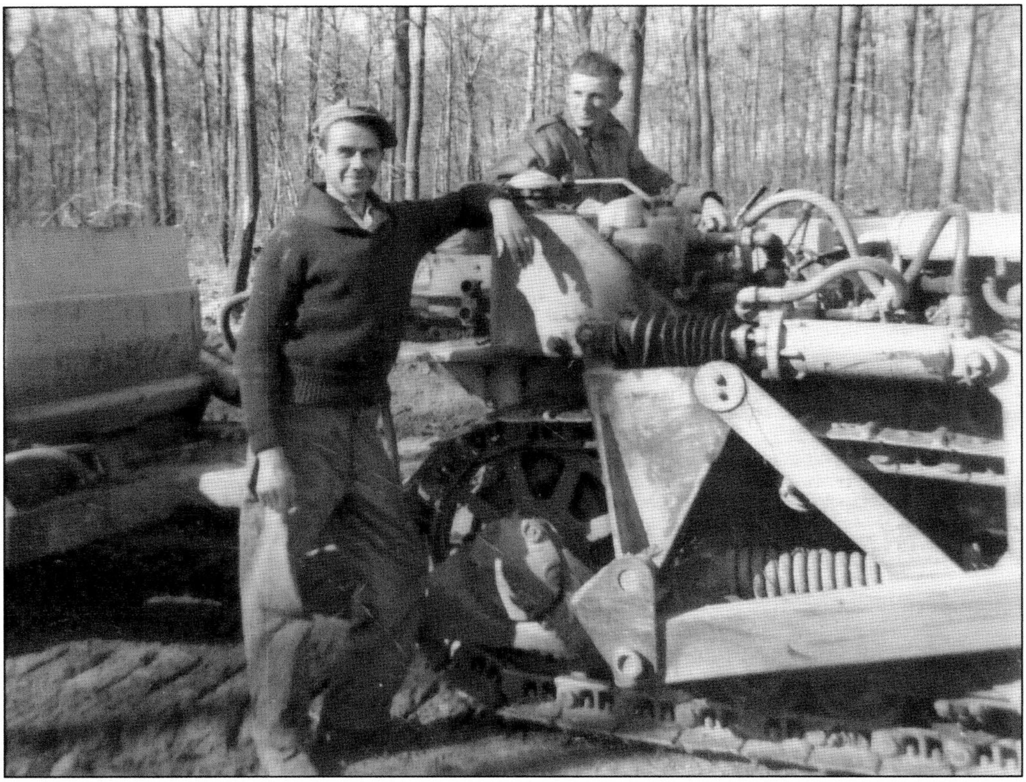

Six

Leisure Activities for All Ages

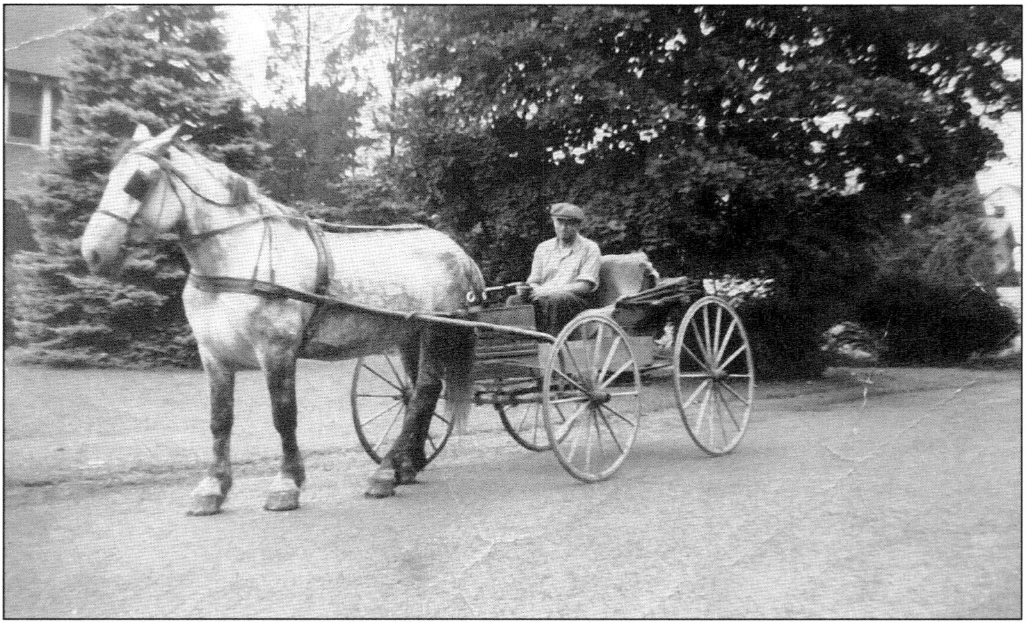

Before the 20th century, a horse-drawn wagon, a carriage, or simply a horse were the only alternatives to traveling by foot in the area. William Van Middlesworth, whose Swiss father had settled in Martinsville in 1855, drives down Washington Valley Road around 1929. A few years earlier, his brother Thomas was struck by a truck while crossing Route 22 with his wagon on his way to Bound Brook. (IKE.)

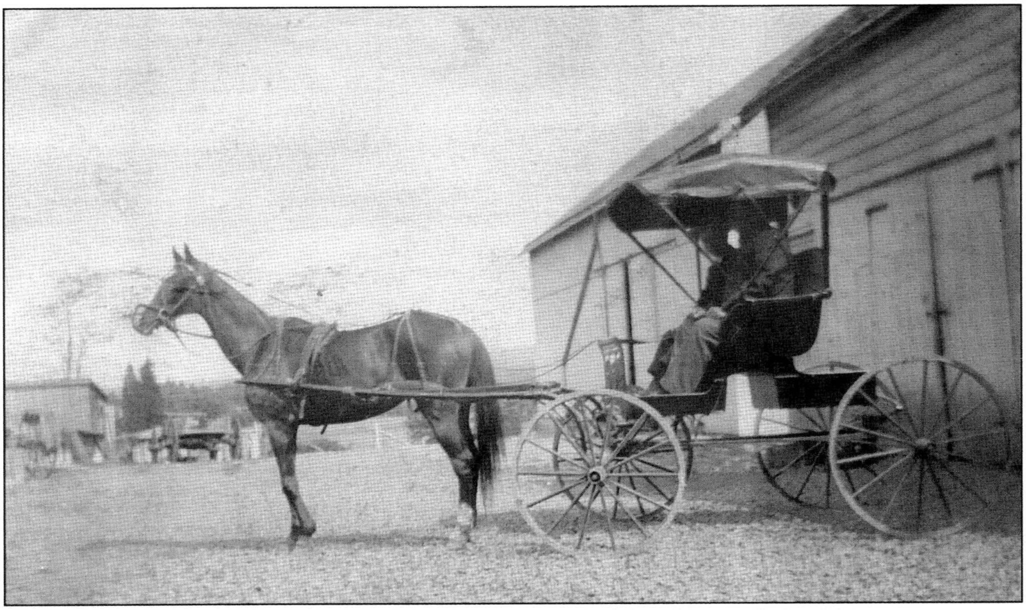

Stagecoaches on the route from Liberty Corner to Bound Brook provided public transportation through Martinsville from early times. Families relied on the horse and buggy for personal transport; the roof protected passengers in inclement weather better than an open wagon could. This buggy on the Bartle farm could only accommodate two people and was a favorite of courting couples. (JCD.)

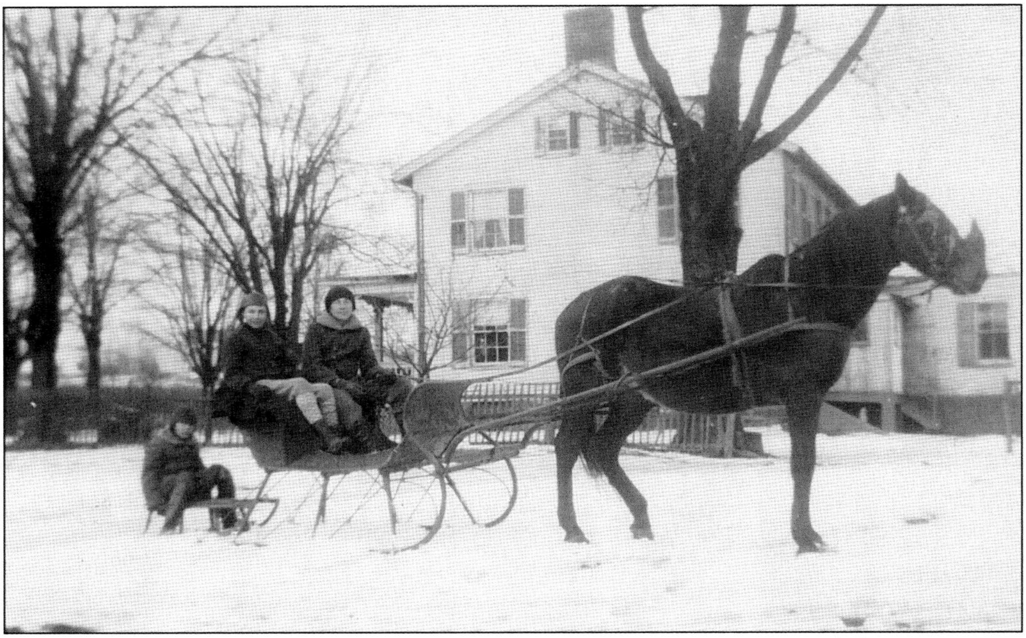

In winter, this one-horse open sleigh with passengers bundled in warm robes provided entertainment, even when no particular destination was in mind. In 1930, Harold (left) and William Coddington, sons of Reuben Coddington, hitched a small sled behind the family sleigh to tow brother Edwin for a joyride about the countryside surrounding the family farm. (KCD.)

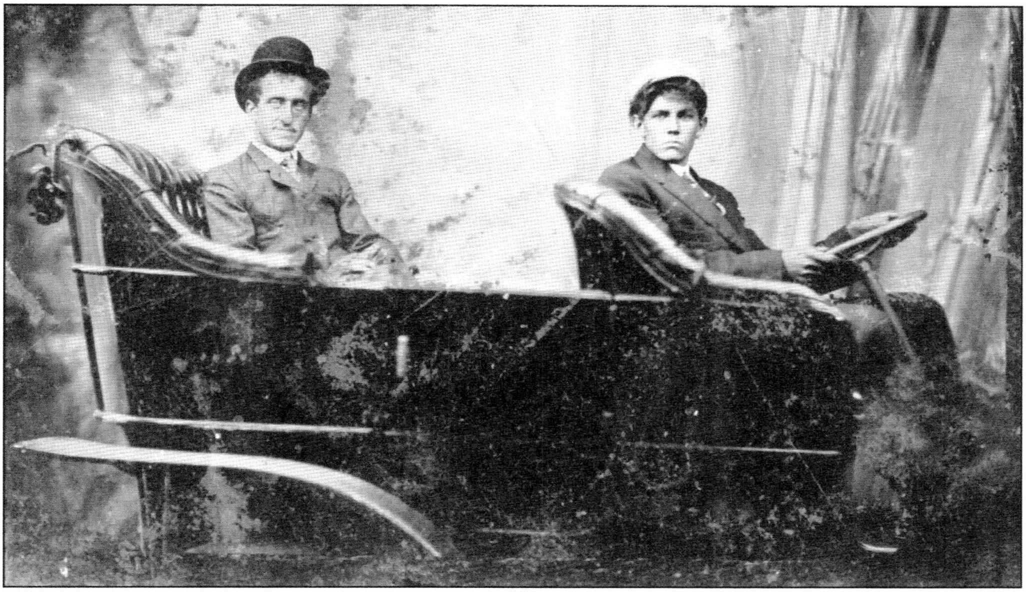

This tintype of William Van Nest (left) and Fred Bartle was taken before an artificial background. The owner of the vehicle is unknown. Fred's age in 1900 was 19, which may help to date the photograph and the new horseless carriage in which they sit. A lamp appears to hang from the back seat, and a fender has been designed to protect passengers from mud kicked up by the wheel. (IKE.)

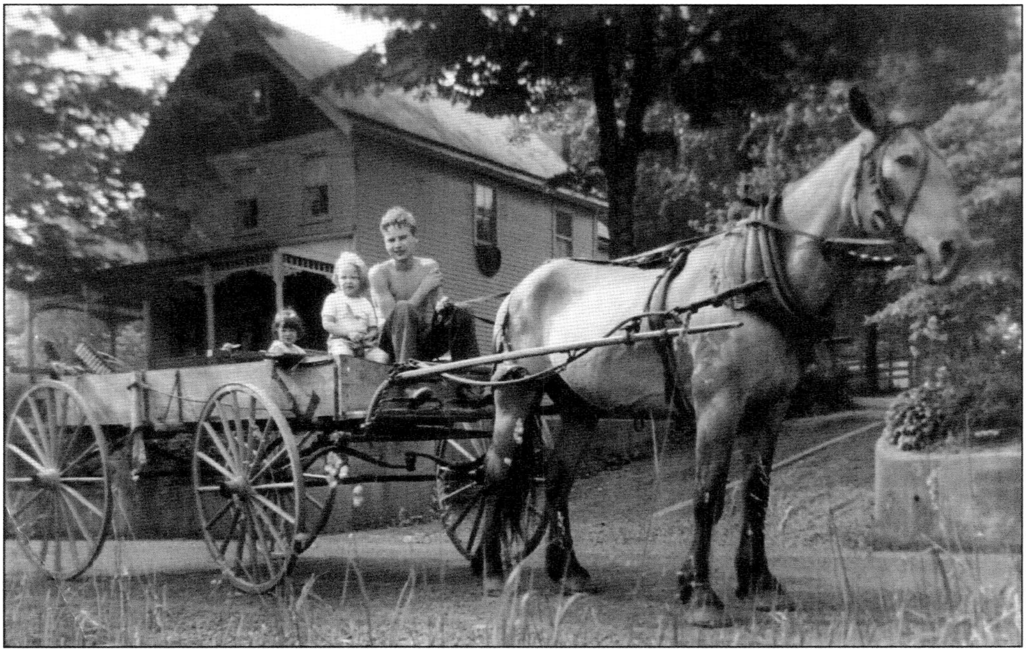

Although people were generally eager to embrace the automobile, some romantics enjoyed reliving the horse-and-buggy days. In 1955, Don Valentine takes his cousins Nora (left) and Tracey Waldron for a ride. The house in the background was built by William Ellis Bartle and owned by the Morecraft family at the time of this photograph. William Morecraft, better known as "Stretch," served in World War II. (HZW.)

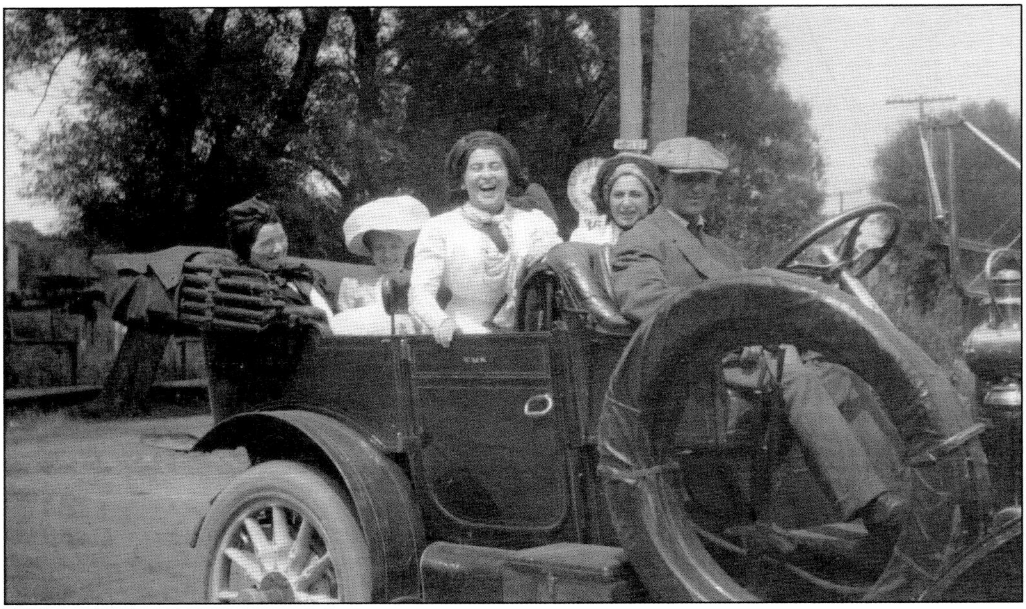

This party, including Elizabeth Bartle (left) and daughter Jessie behind in the rear seat, must be hoping for an uneventful ride, but are prepared for the worst. The car is equipped with a spare tire, encased to protect it from road dirt and stones, and two tool boxes in case the engine starts to miss and the driver has to "get out and get under," in the words of a 1913 song portraying the challenges of early automobile ownership. (JCD.)

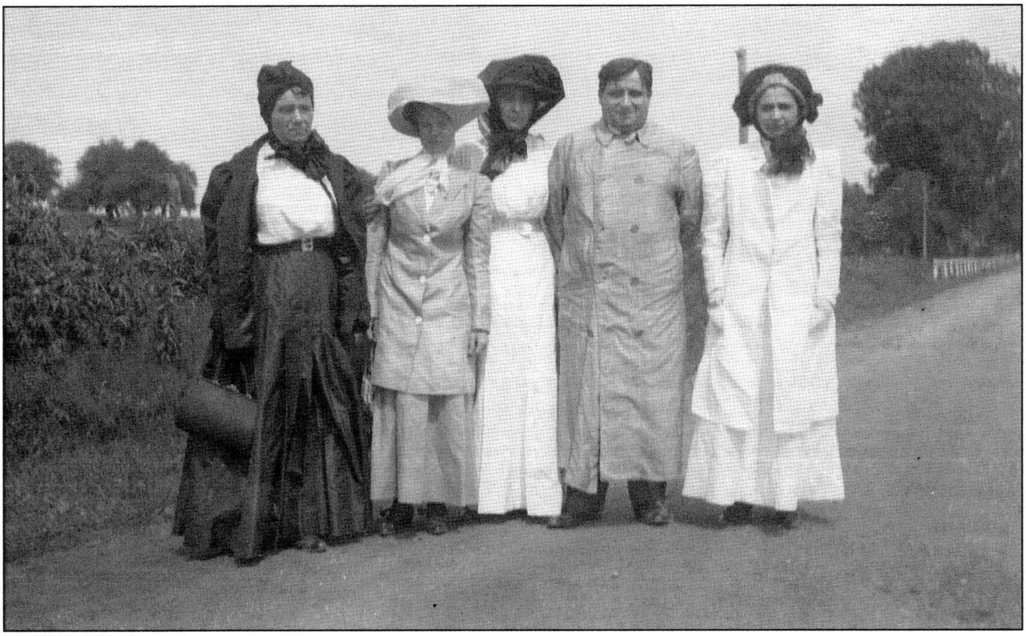

Protective clothing was needed for passengers in open cars as they rambled along the dusty, unpaved roads. The group from the previous photograph posed for a full view of their outfits in 1917, except that the photographer had apparently exchanged places with the driver in the first view. From left to right are Elizabeth Bartle, her daughter Jessie, and unidentified friends. (JCD.)

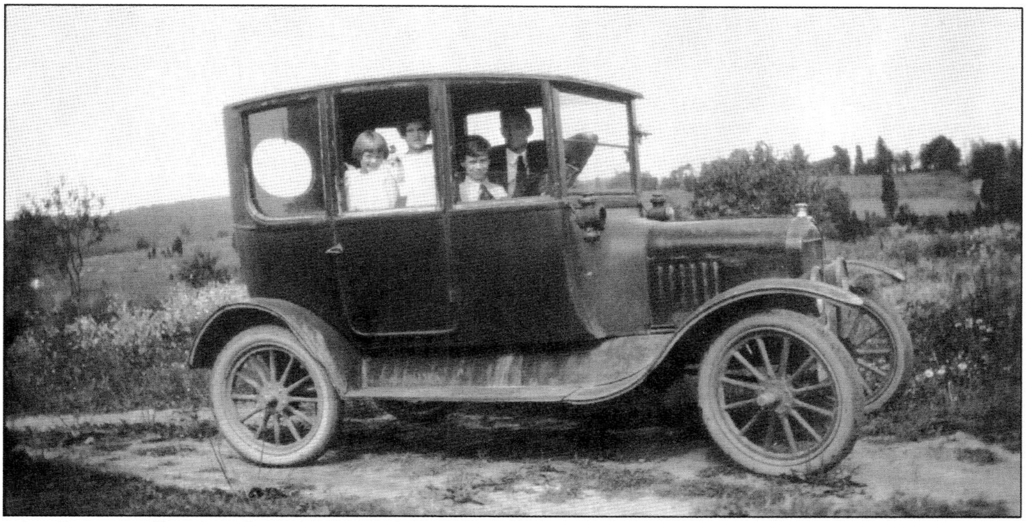

The first Smalley family sedan was this 1917 Ford Model T, often referred to as a "center door." The driver had to enter the door and crawl between the two front seats. The windshield was divided to permit partial ventilation. The vehicle appears to have a dented fender and a missing lens in the headlamp, indications that the driver had experienced some teachable moments in the transition from horse and buggy. (JCD.)

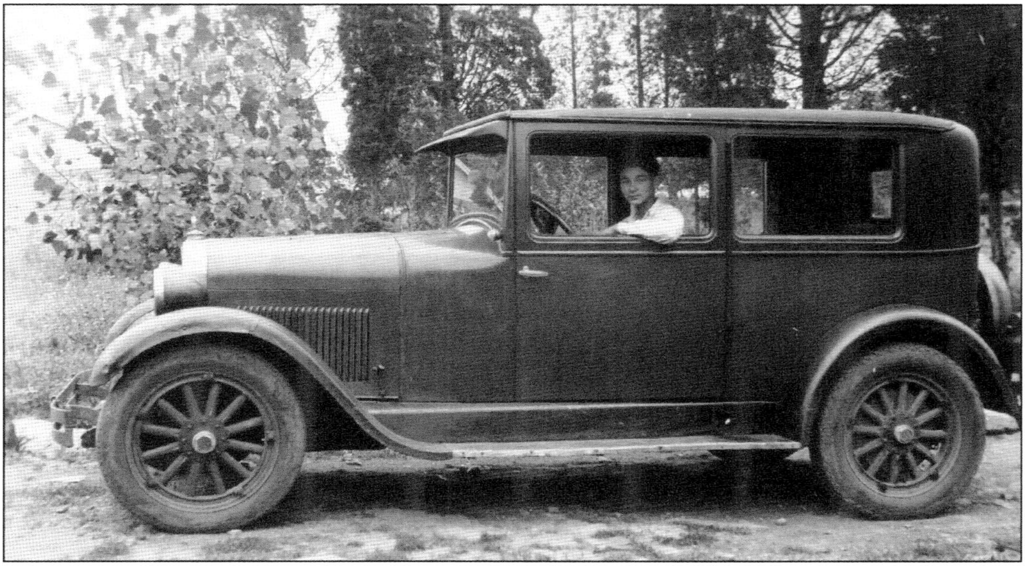

Ed Byrne owned a succession of touring cars, beginning with a 1916 Model T, which had no fuel pump. Drivers learned to back up a hill so fuel could flow towards the engine, or to get a good running start and hope to get to the top of the hill before it stalled. By 1930, Ed had progressed to this two-door 1927 Essex sedan. His son Bob is at the wheel. (PVW.)

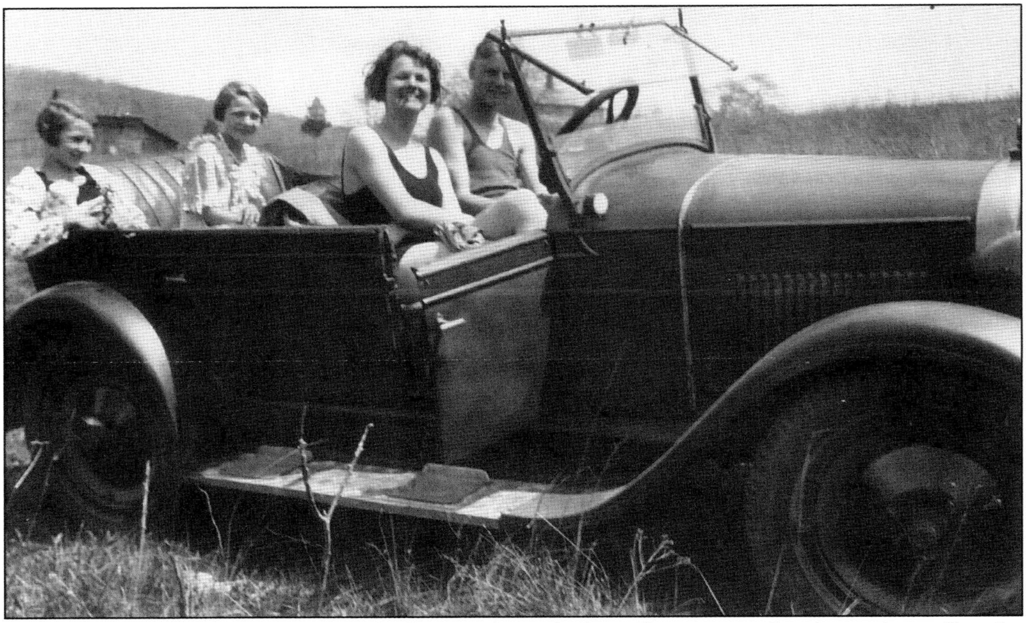

Several swimming holes in the brooks flowing through the valley were perfect for cooling off in the summer. But if they had to make a lengthy hike, the swimmers might be overheated again by the time they returned home. A car solved that drawback in 1934 as Doug Valentine drives (from left to right) Hazel, Ruth, and Eleanor Byrne, all clad in their stylish wool bathing suits. (PVW.)

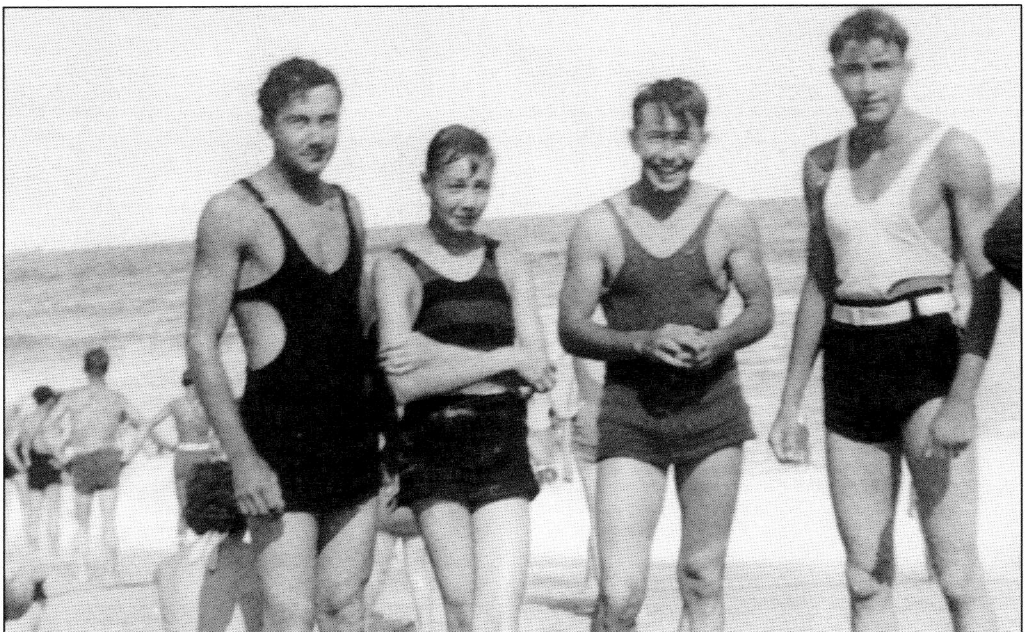

As automobile speeds increased and roads improved, a trip to the Jersey shore for the day was possible. From left to right, William and Edwin Coddington, Wilmer "Chub" Haines, and Harold Coddington enjoy at day at the beach in 1937. Chub was another grandson of John P. Roberts, a son of Raymond Haines, and a cousin of the Coddingtons through their Van Nest roots. (KCD.)

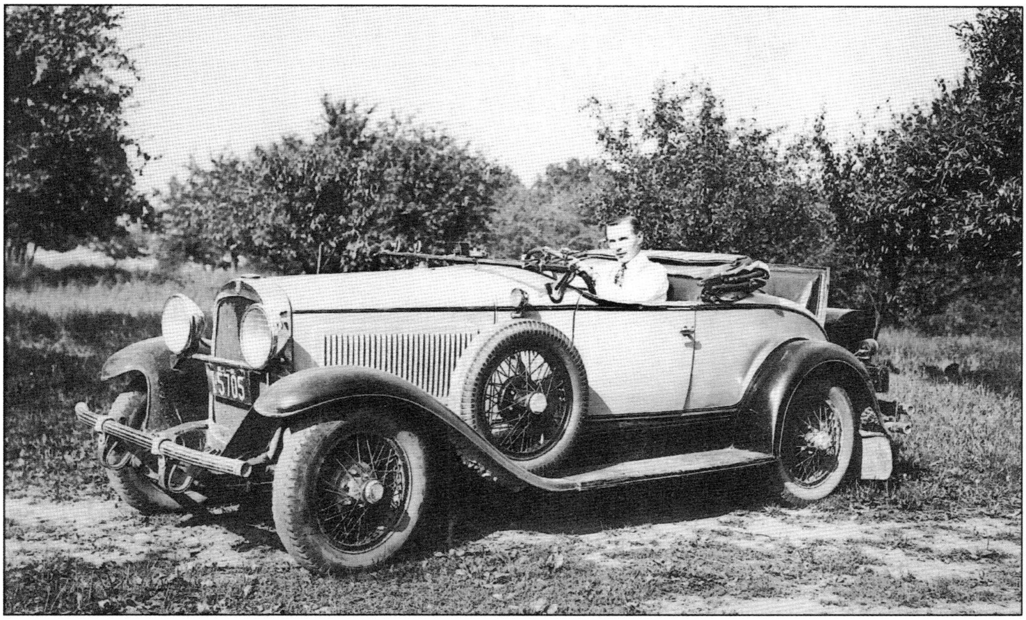

John Brarens' sister Frances recalls that John won this Whippet roadster with rumble seat, but she does not know how he won it. He was the envy of all the young men of Martinsville. Whippets were produced from 1926 to 1930. Rumble seats, which folded away into the trunk area when not in use, exposed passengers to chilling breezes while those in the front seat were protected by the windshield. (FBR.)

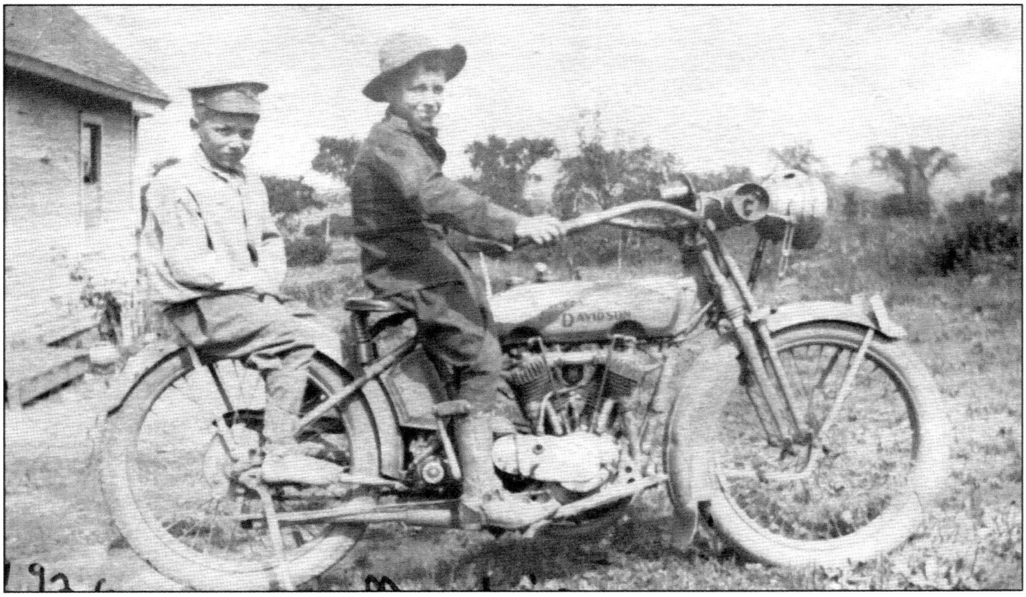

Motorbikes (motorcycles) were another means of getting around the countryside. In 1926, brothers Paul (left) and Robert Moody sit astride this Harley-Davidson motorcycle. Their older brothers, John and Theodore, were more likely the actual operators of this vehicle. The boys' father, John Moody, the son of Irish immigrants James and Susan Moody, listed his occupation as copper miner in 1910. (EGS.)

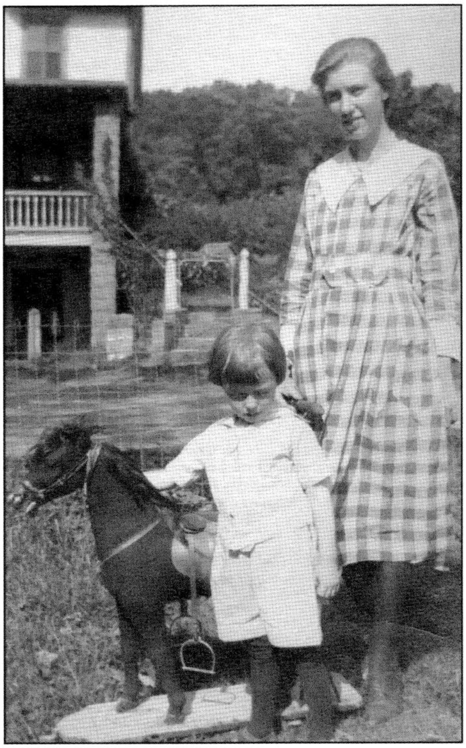

A rocking horse, also known as a hobbyhorse or a toy pony, had long been a cherished possession of children. In 1920, young Franklin Bartle, son of blacksmith Fred Bartle, stands with his aunt Evelyn Way beside his deluxe-model toy pony, complete with realistic stirrups and fur. The Martinsville Hotel is visible behind them. (DOC.)

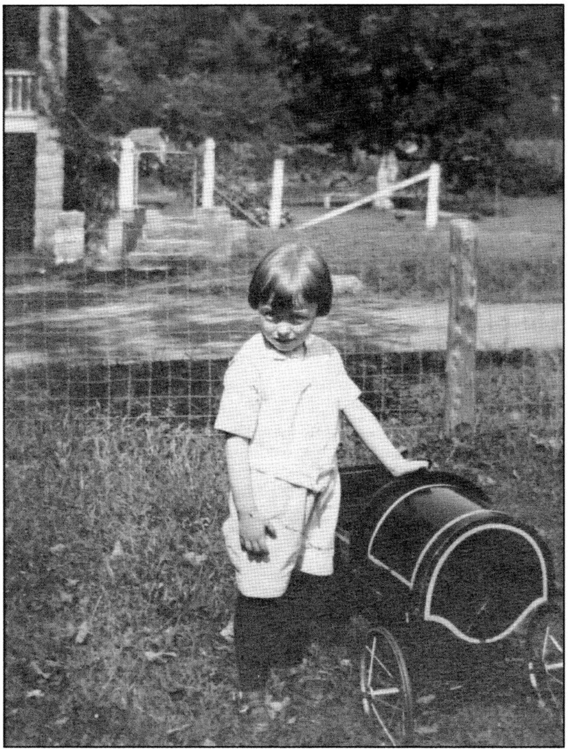

As cars became more popular, children began to crave toy cars to keep up with modern times. Franklin Bartle followed the trend in 1920 as his parents gave him the luxury of choosing between the old ways and the new. Horses, however, continued to require the services of his blacksmith father for another 40 years. (DOC.)

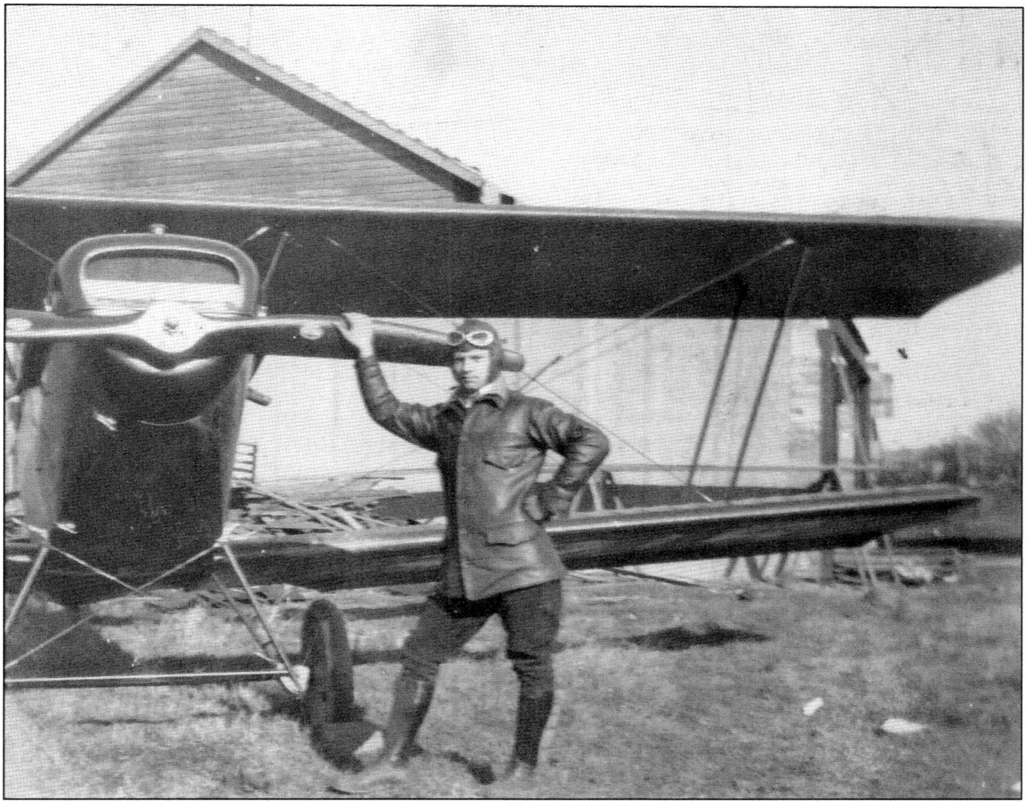

Stanley Musialowski was the first in the valley to buy an airplane. In the late 1920s, friends gathered outside the Hoffman House to watch Stanley's stepson, Elari "Larry" Tarangul (pictured), pilot this Waco Wright Whirlwind–motored biplane down the valley to land in Stanley's pasture. Several other Martinsville residents were fascinated by aviation. Floyd Valentine, whose first pilot's license in 1929 was signed by Orville Wright, became a TWA pilot. (MUS.)

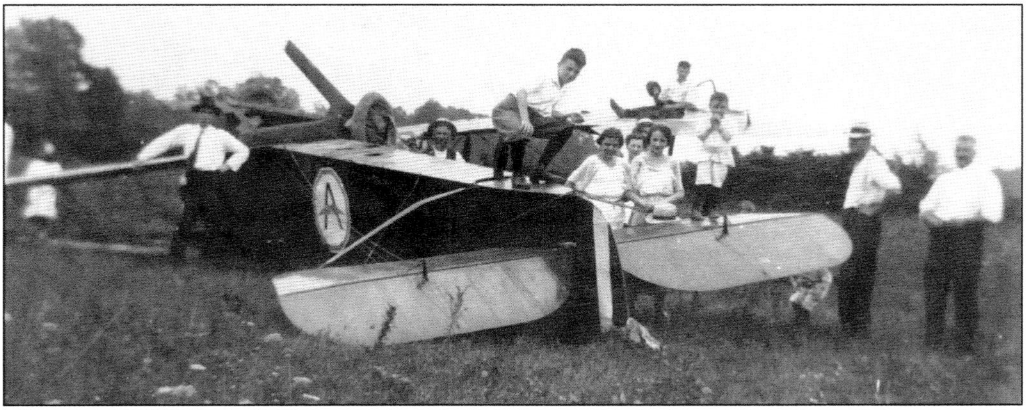

Attempts at piloting early planes sometimes resulted in emergency landings in farm fields. This plane set down in Horace Coddington's field in 1921 and drew a crowd of curious observers. The Bicknell sisters stand behind the tail, while Bill Coddington perches on the tail. Atop the fuselage is John Bicknell. Will Van Nest, Reuben Coddington, and Harold Coddington are also present, but cannot be specifically identified among the others. (KCD.)

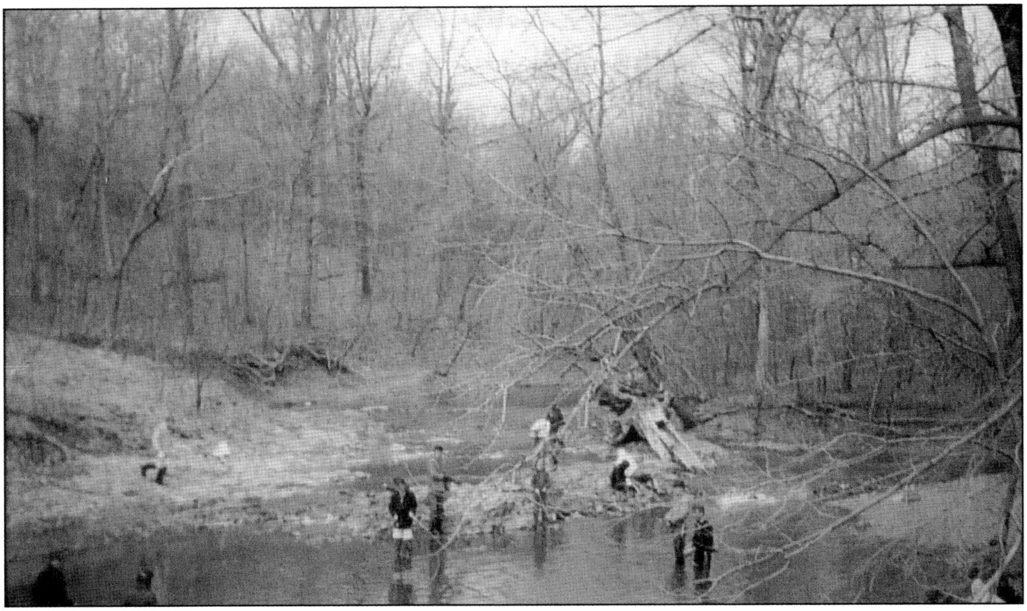

As spring approached with the emergence of skunk cabbages, and spring peepers filled the evenings with their sleigh-bell-like chirping, fishermen looked forward to opening day of trout season. School absences were excused if a child's parents sent a note explaining that the child had been absent for trout fishing. A crowd has gathered in 1965 to fish the deep pools above Bender's Bridge. (PEP.)

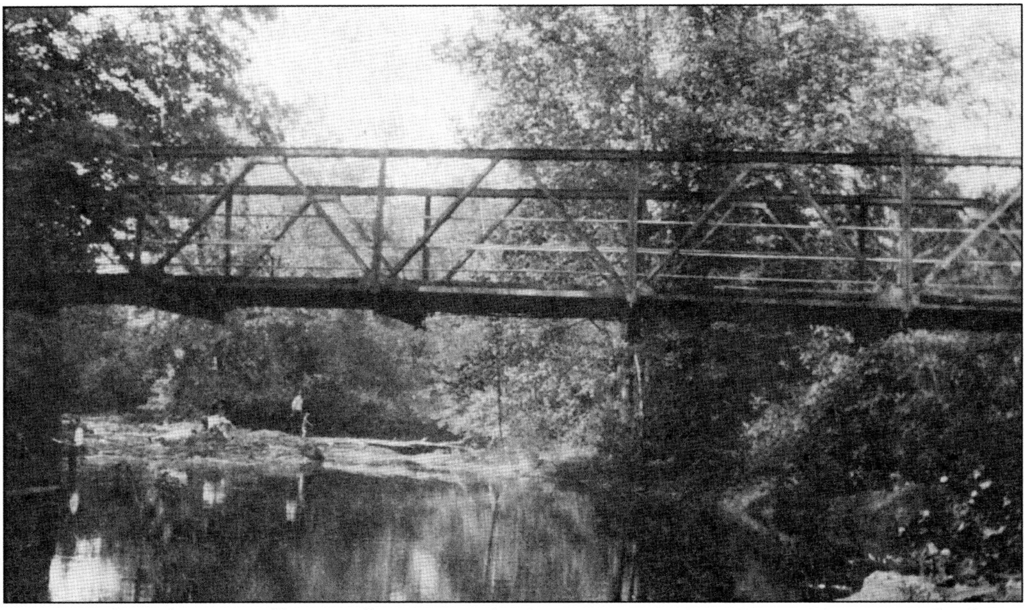

A gristmill and a sawmill, owned over time by Jeromys Van Nest, James Martin, and others, stood in the Bender's Bridge area on Gilbride Road until being swept away in a flash flood in the 1830s. On hot summer days, youths converged on the area with lunch bags to spend hours alternately swimming and sunning on the flat rocks visible beyond the bridge in this 1930s photograph. (KCD.)

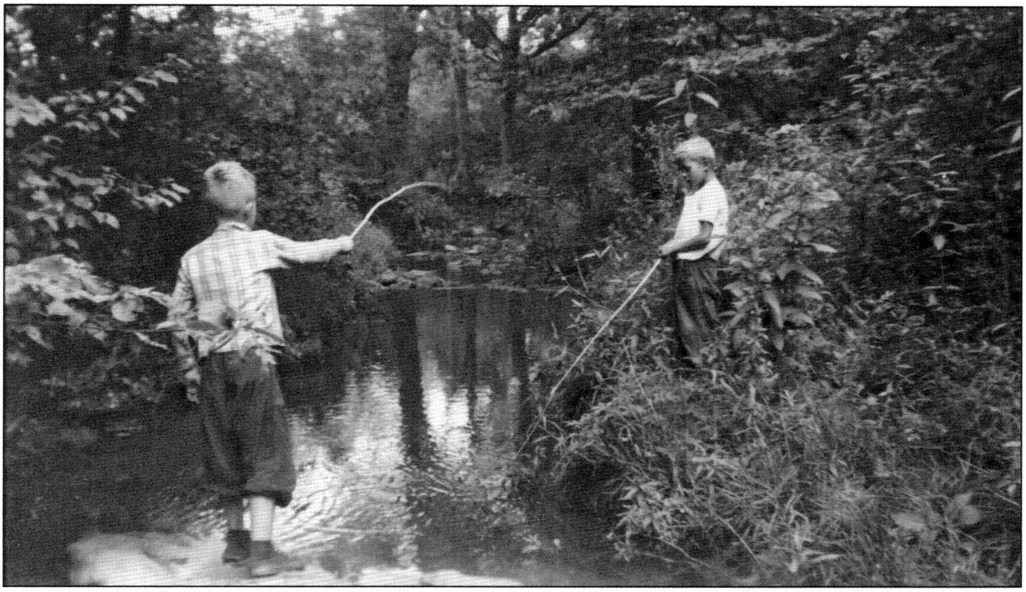

After farm chores were done, the Brarens boys had time for some fishing in the brook that flowed behind their farm down to Dock Watch Hollow. During haying season, their sister Frances Brarens Toleno remembers, riding on the load of hay was fun but made them quite itchy. A jump in the cool brook brought welcome relief. (FBR.)

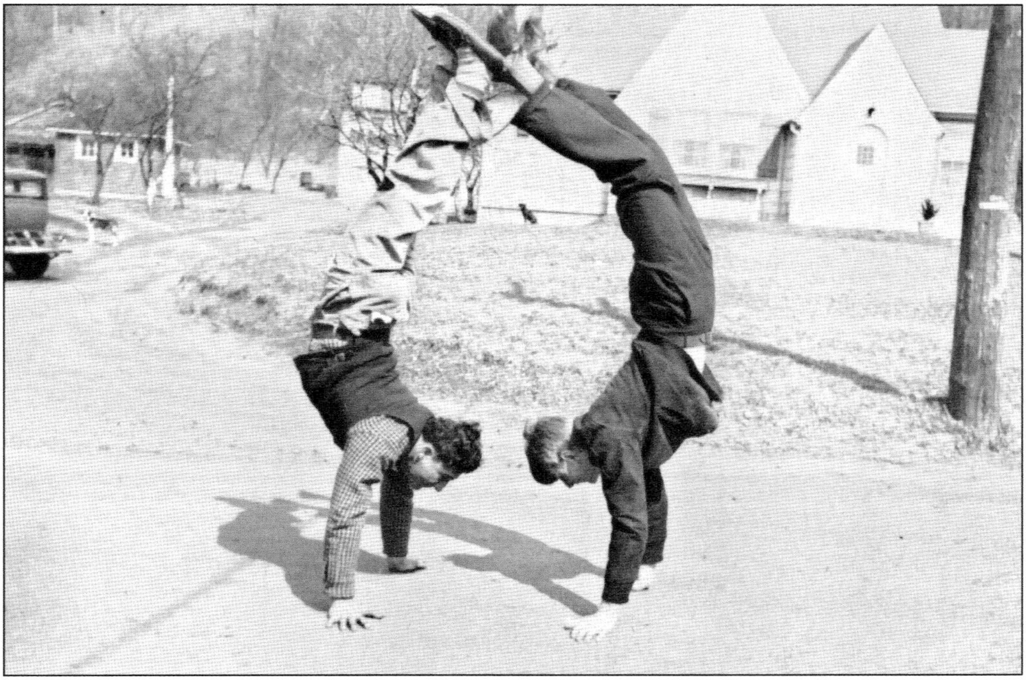

Acrobatic stunts were another way of whiling away leisure hours. Mario Torta (left) and Doug Valentine performed handstands in 1933 in front of the Torta home, which was next to the Valley Garage. Doug continued to do handstands over the years, encouraged by his grandchildren, who were permitted to keep the change that fell out of his pockets. (DOC.)

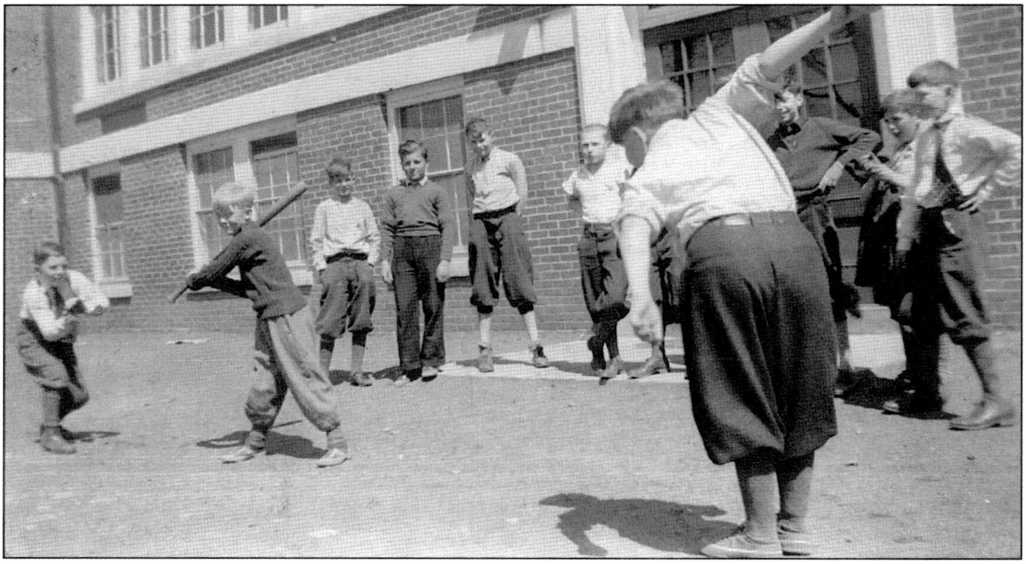

Martinsville had few level areas not under cultivation where boys might play baseball. This gang has gathered in front of the school in 1935, possibly assuming that a foul ball will not smash a window. From left to right, are unidentified, batter Richard Poffley, unidentified, Frank Totten, Bob Hall, Dickie Moore, pitcher Donald Waldron, and three other unidentified boys. (JWG.)

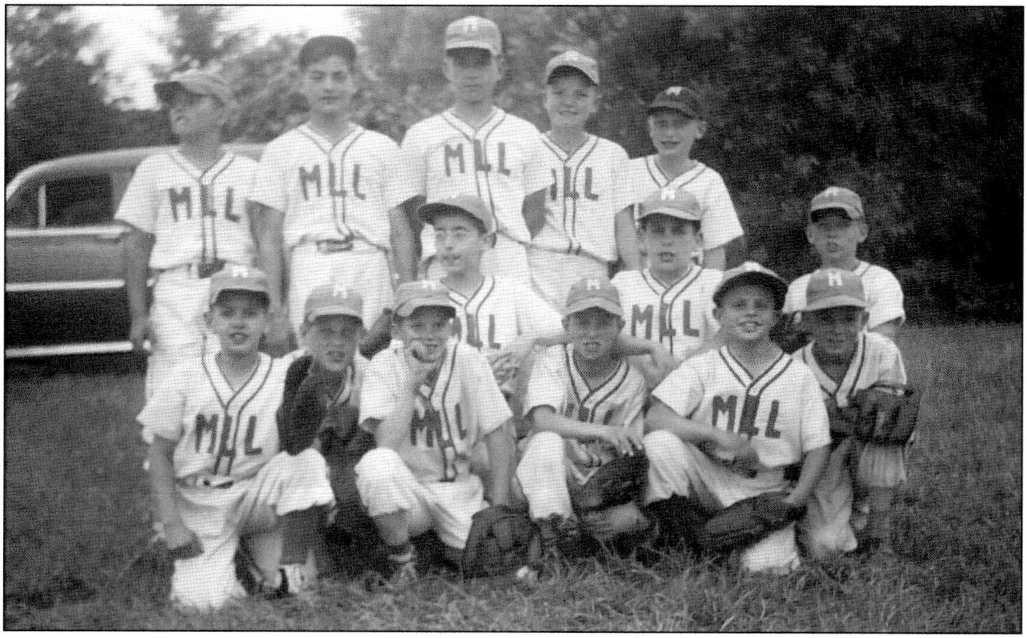

A generation later in 1953, the Martinsville Little League team includes (first row) George Newman (far left), Charles Clark (third from left), and James "Chip" Longo (third from right); (second row) Lenny Assante, Russell Roth (second and third from left), and Kenny Lessing (far right). The team was coached by Clark Waage, who also volunteered with the fire department and rescue squad. (SIS.)

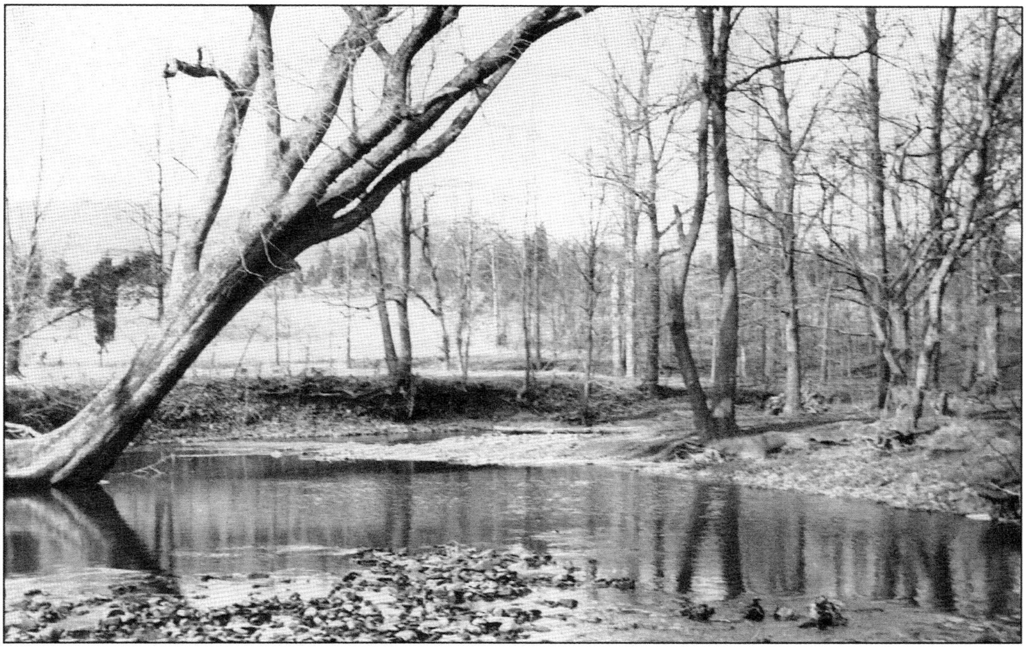

The pool known as the Deep Hole was near the Vosseller Avenue bridge over Middle Brook, where swimmers had constructed a dam to increase the depth. Unfortunately, the deeper stagnant water became a breeding pool for leeches, but this drawback did not discourage the swimmers. (DOC.)

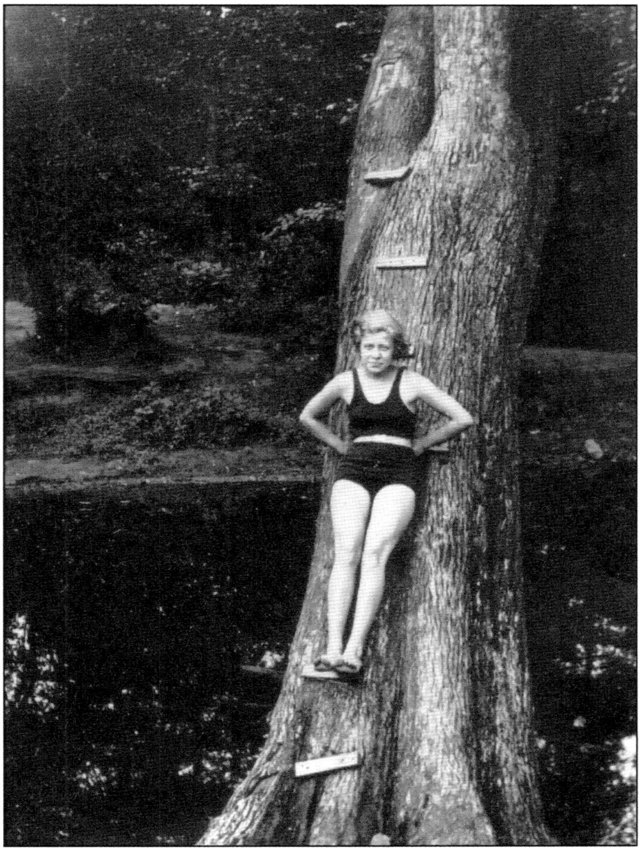

Youngsters sometimes wore their itchy woolen bathing suits to school beneath their clothes so they could go swimming directly after dismissal without having to go home to change. Ladder rungs were nailed to the large tree that leaned out over the water so that swimmers could jump from high in the tree into the deep water. Ethel Vactor rests on the tree in 1933. (DOC.)

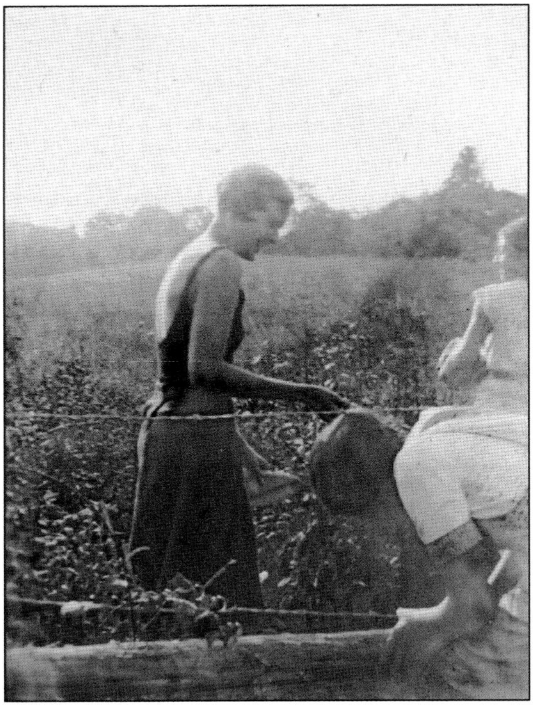

Passing through a barbed-wire fence to get to a swimming spot required caution. After confirming that the farmer's bull was at a safe distance, swimmers had to squeeze between strands of barbed wire and quickly pass to the other side of the pasture and through the opposite fence before being spotted by the bull. In 1931, Sis Van Allen (left) and Eleanor Byrne pass cautiously. (DOC.)

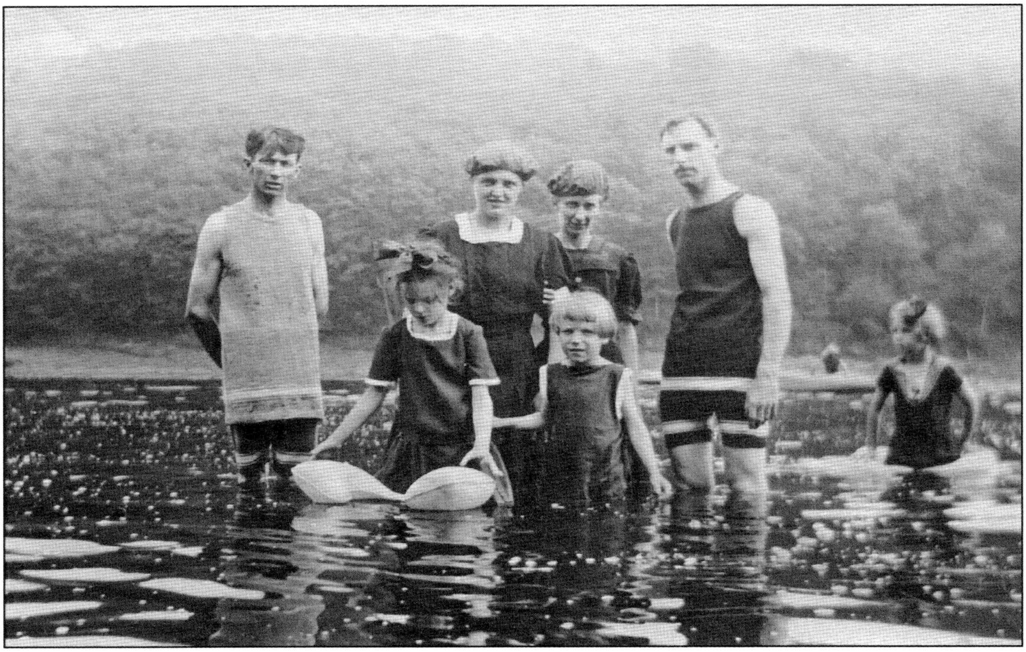

The evolution of swimsuit fashions is interesting to observe, as Victorian ways gradually gave way to revealing more and more of the body. In the 1920s, these knitted wool suits for the men and cotton outfits for the ladies are considered properly modest as this group bathes in the pond that was part of the West Branch of Middle Brook before the reservoir covered that section of the valley. John D. Roberts is on the far left. (RBT.)

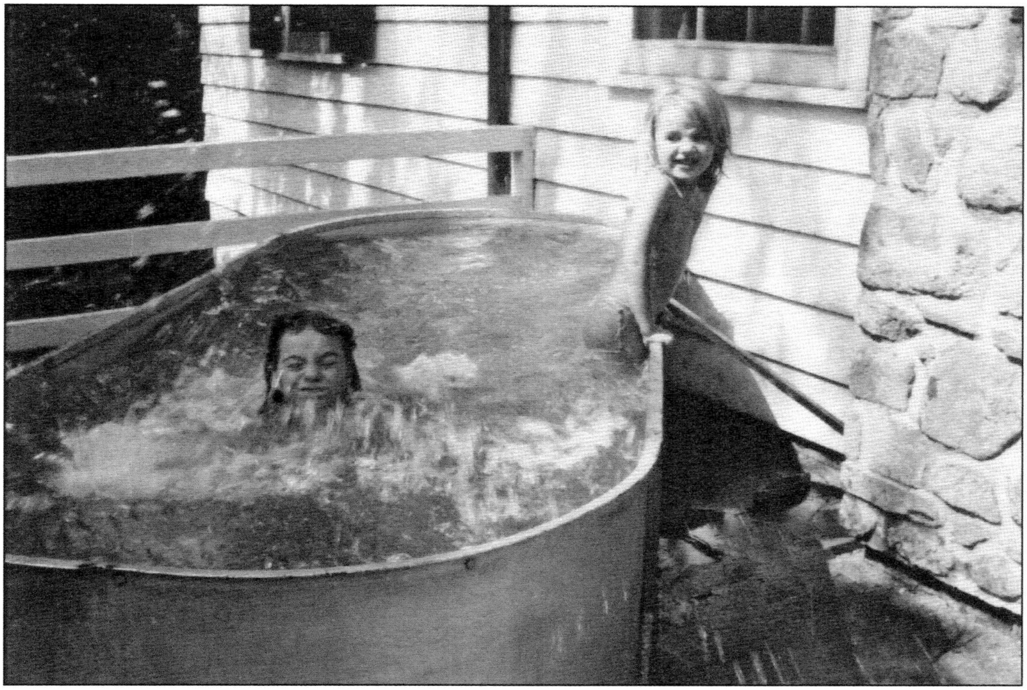

Prior to the advent of plastic wading pools (so-called kiddie pools) and before backyard swimming pools became popular, Doug Valentine filled this large livestock-watering trough on his terrace. While his three children splashed happily on hot summer days, they also learned to swim. Pictured in 1943 are Pat (left) and Suzy Valentine. (PVW.)

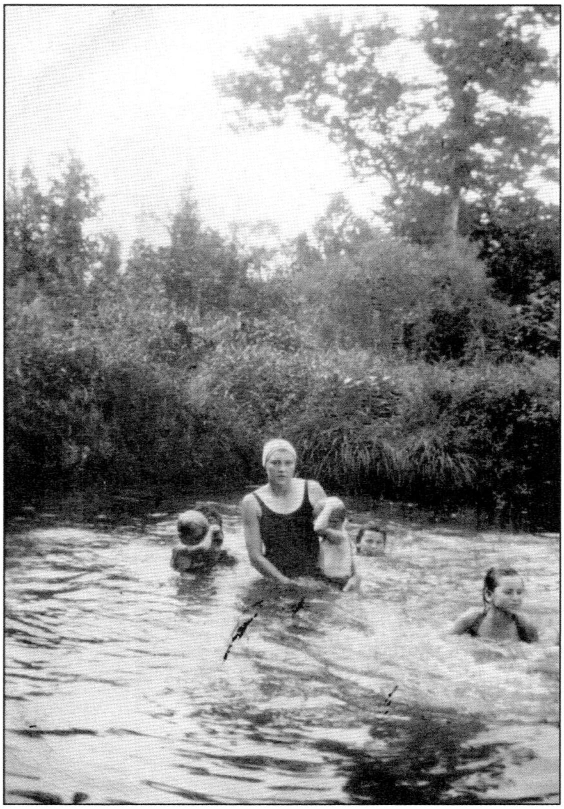

When Bartle's quarrying operations halted because they were no longer profitable, the pit filled with water. Parts were shallow enough for safe swimming, while other sections were 40 feet deep. According to local stories, an old Whippet automobile and a brass bed were discarded into the pit on top of the old quarrying machinery. In 1930, Marie Geschwindner and unidentified children enjoyed swimming, despite the leeches that would cling to swimmers' legs. (EGS.)

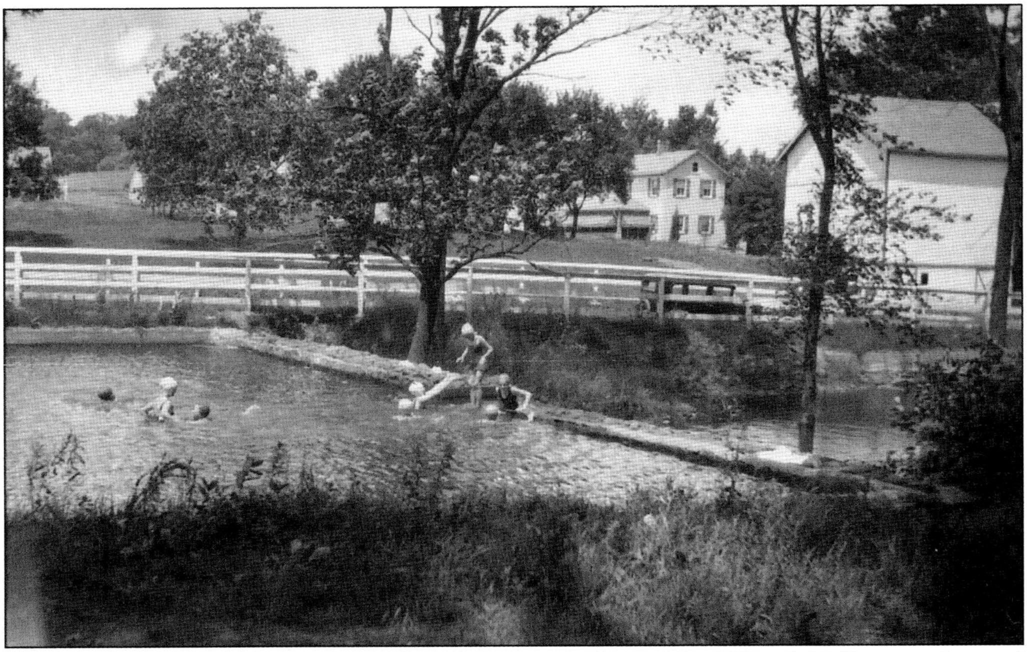

On the Schultz farm in Warren Township, the stream leading to Dock Watch Hollow was dammed to form a swimming pool for boardinghouse guests, and local youths were welcome. The dam is still visible, although cattails have taken over the pond. The owner is reported to have been related to gangster Dutch Schultz, which would explain the latter's occasional visits to Martinsville, but these reports have been disputed by others. (DOC.)

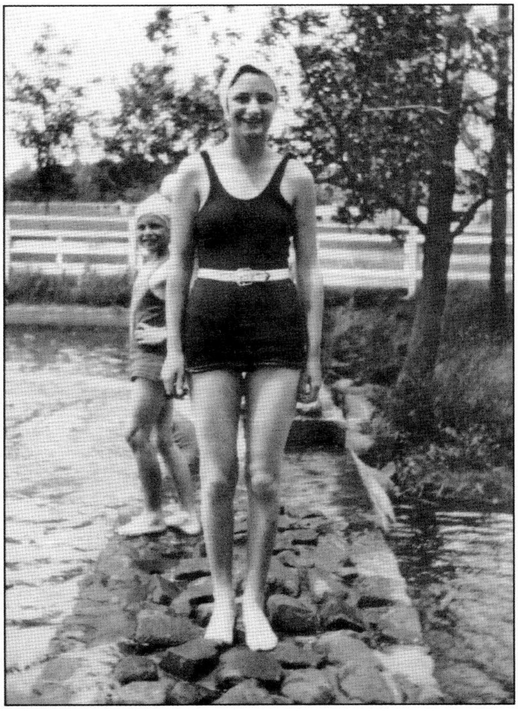

Swimmers hiked from Martinsville in the 1920s and 1930s to spend hours at Schultz's pond. Rumors survive that moonshine operations were conducted on the farm during Prohibition and that numerous discarded jugs were later discovered on the property. In 1933, Virginia "Jinks" Smalley stands on the dam behind Elizabeth Busse. (DOC.)

As autumn leaves began to turn colors, hunters readied their guns for hunting season. Coddington brothers Bill (left) and Harold flank their cousin Elmer Coddington to display the results of a day in the fields. Today, rabbits continue to abound in the area, but the pheasant population has declined over the years with destruction of habitat; wild turkeys, however, now flourish in the woodlands of the mountains. (JCD.)

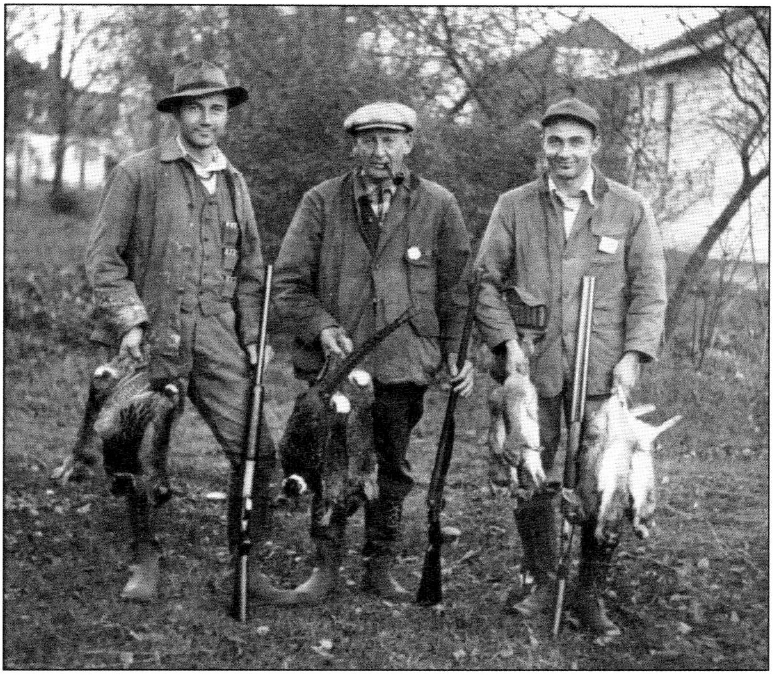

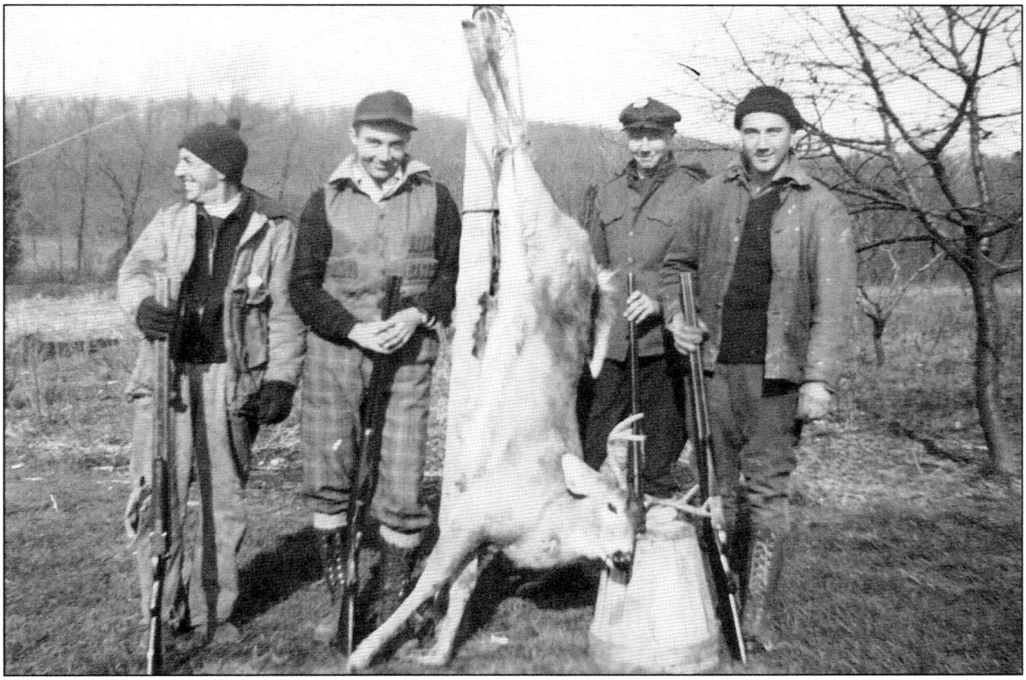

As fall progressed, venison was added to the dinner table. Enjoying a meal of rabbit or squirrel meant chewing carefully and removing shotgun pellets from the meat. Venison was free of such hazards. From left to right, unidentified, Harold, Edwin, and Bill Coddington smile proudly in 1939. Youths also set traplines, checking them before and after school. Catching a skunk before school posed problems. (JCD.)

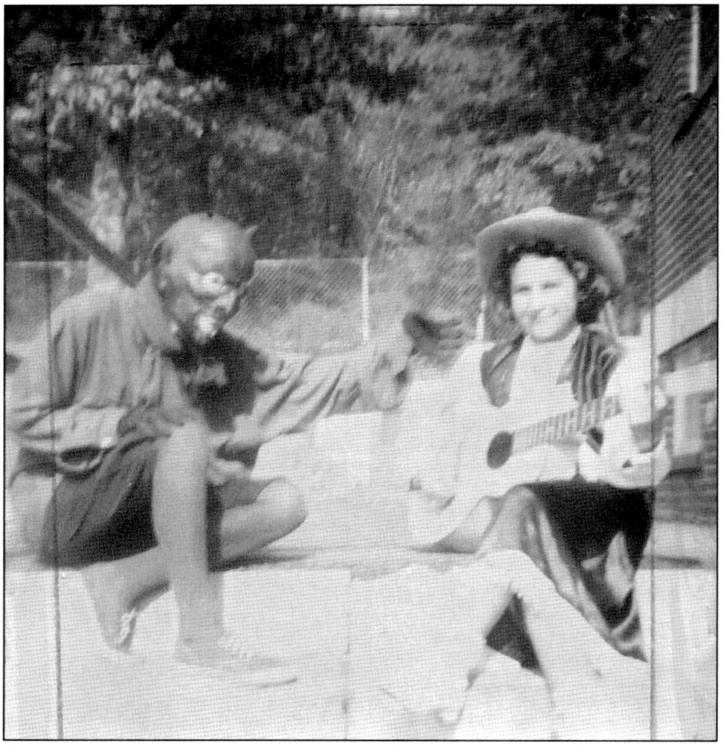

Halloween costumes often consisted of store-bought masks and materials from home. In Martinsville's stable population where residents knew each other, the custom was for costumed visitors to enter the home and remain silent while the hosts tried to guess their identities. With identifications established, the children were given treats and sent on to the next house. In 1948, Pat Valentine is a devil, and Margaret Tullo is a singing cowgirl. (PVW.)

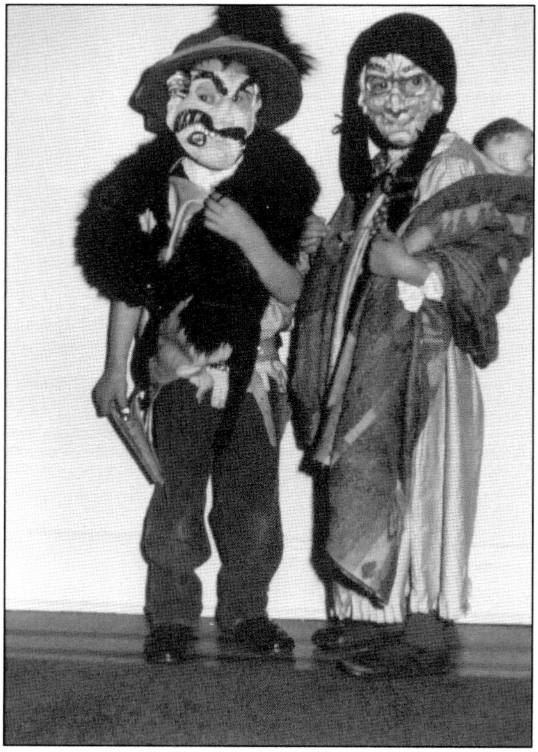

It was rumored that visitors to the bar in the Hoffman House might receive a $5 bill from the patrons, but those who visited only received a quarter. Halloween pranks were sometimes quite complicated, as when an entire farm wagon was dismantled and reassembled on someone's porch roof. Younger children continued to innocently visit homes. Valentine grandchildren David and Debra Whitacre are dressed as a trapper and his squaw. (PVW.)

Girls enjoyed playing dress-up throughout the year, composing outfits from discarded finery, old curtains, and assorted accessories. Diane Dennis (left) and Judy Coddington are glamour girls in the 1950s. A favorite indoor pastime for girls was cutting outfits for paper dolls from booklets. A predecessor of Barbie dolls, which have real fabric clothes, a paper doll has outfits cut with tabs to be bent over the cardboard doll's shoulders. (JCD.)

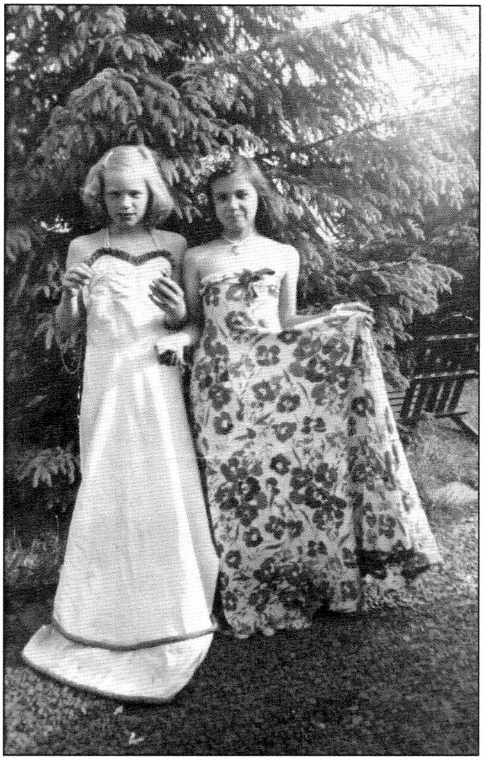

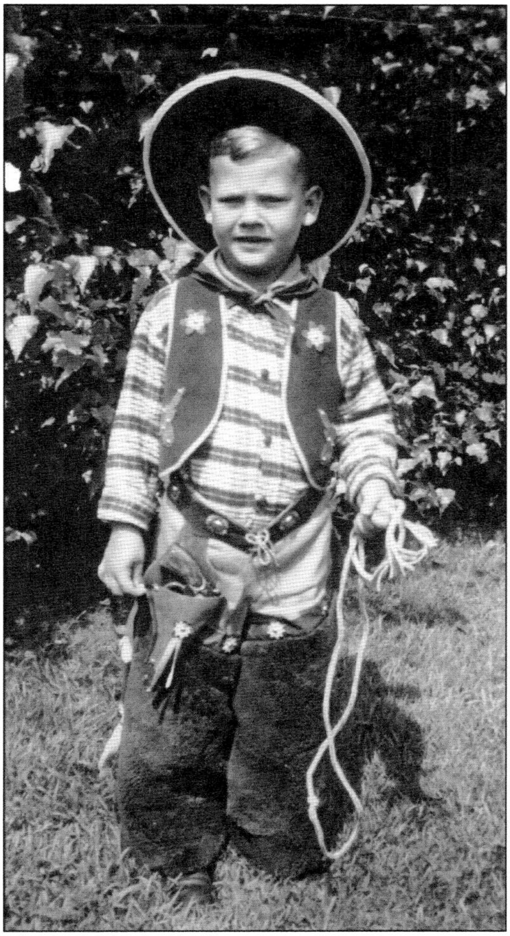

Boys' outfits seldom varied. They were usually cowboys from the time they could walk and sometimes well into adulthood. Their mock warfare, waged with cap pistols or water guns, pitted the "good guys" against the fierce outlaws. Rick Thum, at age three, wears chaps and carries a lasso. (THM.)

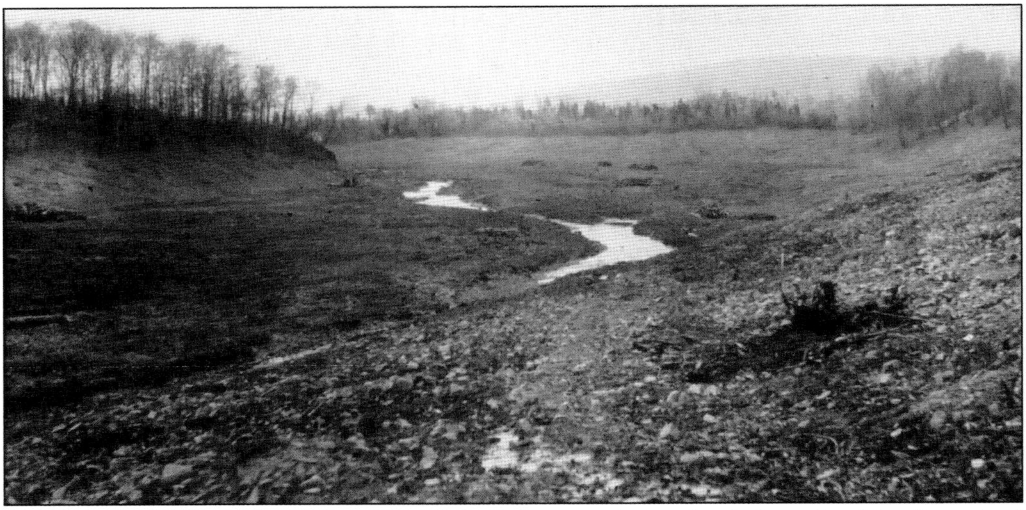

The Bound Brook Water Company began to acquire and clear land along the West Branch of Middle Brook early in the 20th century. A dam was completed in 1907 near Chimney Rock Road, and the water level gradually rose, submerging several early homes along the brook. The water company also planted evergreens in the watershed, and these eventually provided neighbors with Christmas trees. This view from about 1915 looks west. (JWG.)

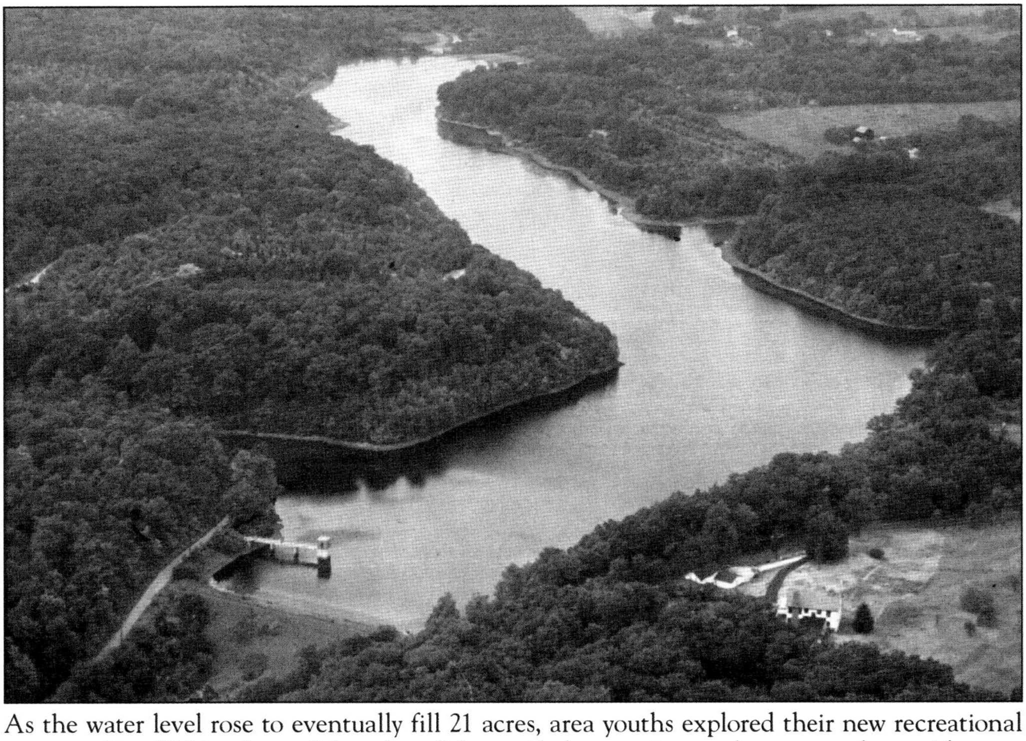

As the water level rose to eventually fill 21 acres, area youths explored their new recreational opportunities. Fishing for catfish and sunfish provided entertainment but not much nourishment. In one venture, a garage door became a raft, which towed a trailer made from a chicken coop door. In this aerial view from above Chimney Rock Road, the dam is in the foreground, while the Newmans Lane Bridge is in the distance. (JWG.)

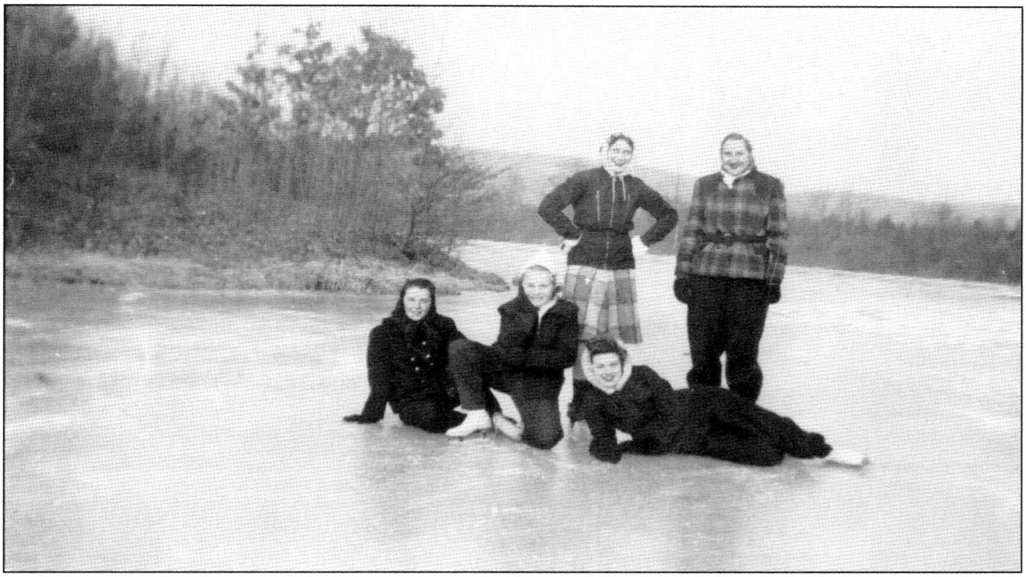

Ice-skating continued for 30 years from about 1930 until the water company, concerned about the safety of the dam, drained the reservoir. The grove of trees behind and to the left of the skaters also appears in the previous view of the empty reservoir. In 1940, from left to right, are (first row) Beverly Brown, Fluff Bartle, and Jeanette Van Nest; (second row) Clara Hulse and Freda Yehle. (YLE.)

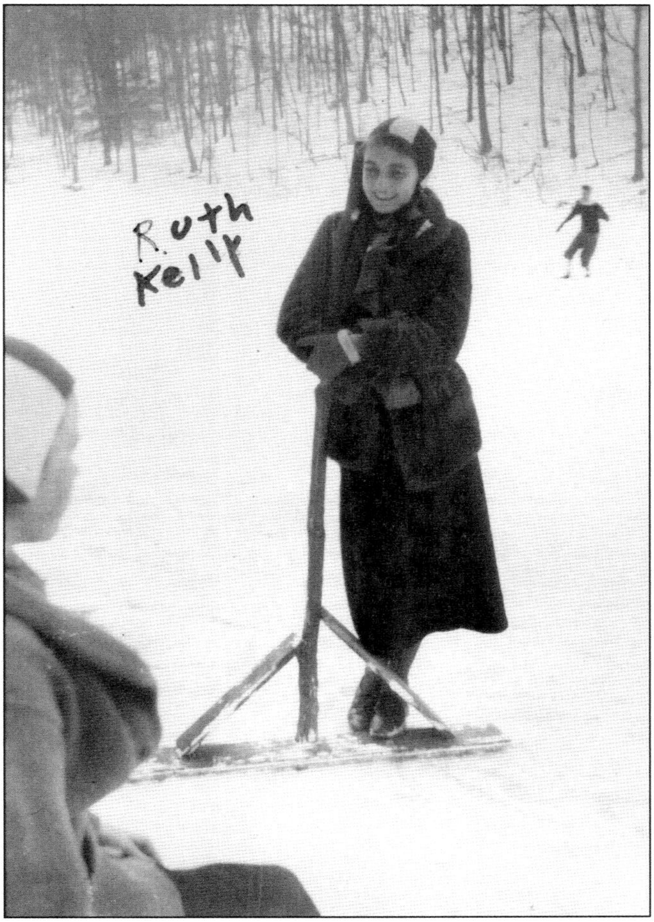

When the reservoir froze smooth as glass, skaters who began at the Chimney Rock Road access could brave their way against the westerly winds for a mile to the Newman's Lane Bridge, turn around with wind to their backs, and glide all the way back to the warming fire where they had begun. When snow covered the ice, paths had to be cleared. Ruth Kelly helps with the clearing in 1933. (DOC.)

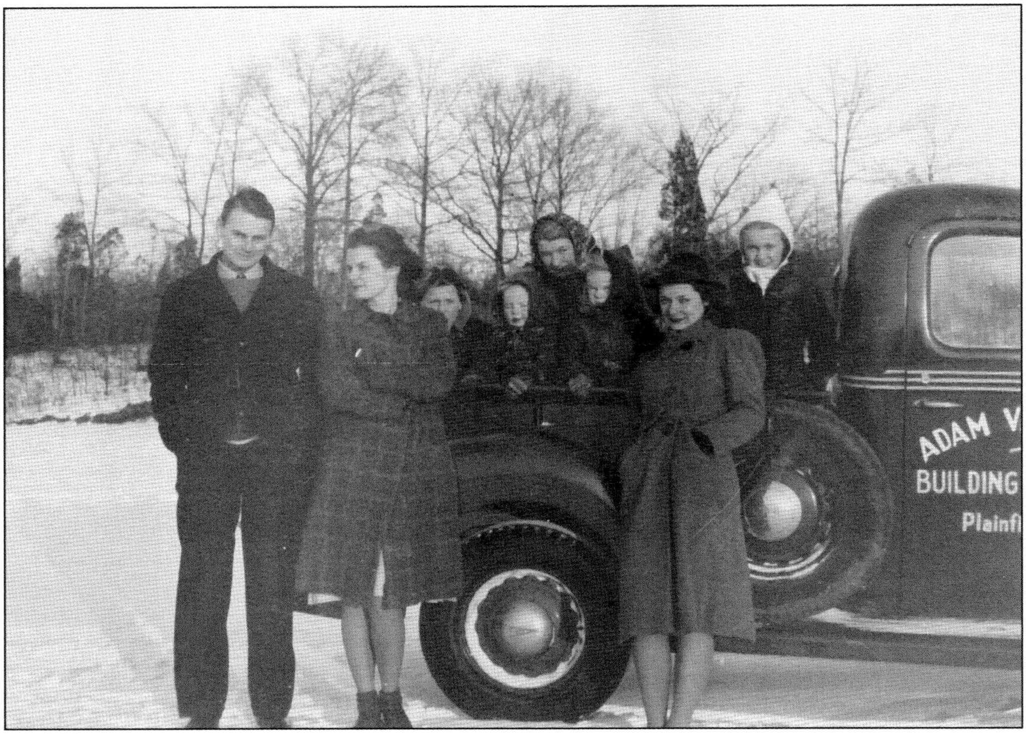

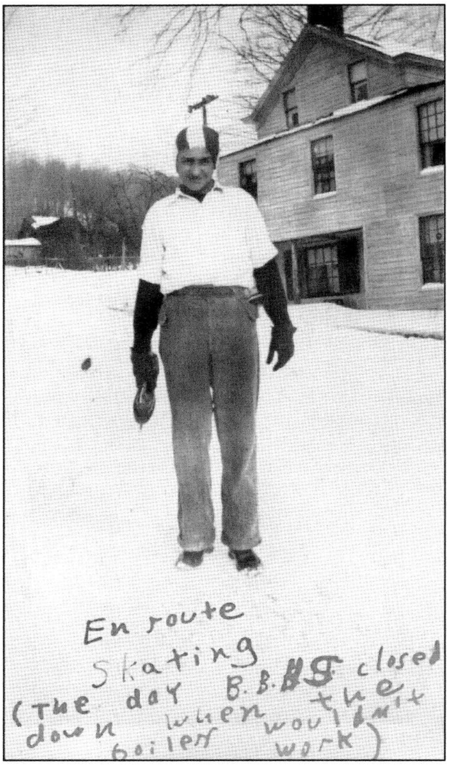

When the ice was a foot thick, Sonny Van Allen drove his car out on it, stepped on the gas, and hit the brakes to spin around. Someone else drove a Jeep on the ice to plow paths in the snow. Doug Valentine took his truck out and honked his horn behind startled skaters in 1941. From left to right are Doug and Eleanor Valentine, unidentified, Don Valentine, Hazel Byrne, Pat Valentine, Ruth Byrne, and Jean Valentine. (PVW.)

Written on this photograph of Ted Mastapeter in 1933 is, "En route skating (the day B.B.H.S. closed down when the boiler wouldn't work)." Youngsters brought their skates to school so they could go directly to the reservoir after dismissal. Tiny tots learned to skate on double runners before they graduated to single-bladed skates. The reservoir is now full again and part of a county park, but skating is no longer permitted. (DOC.)

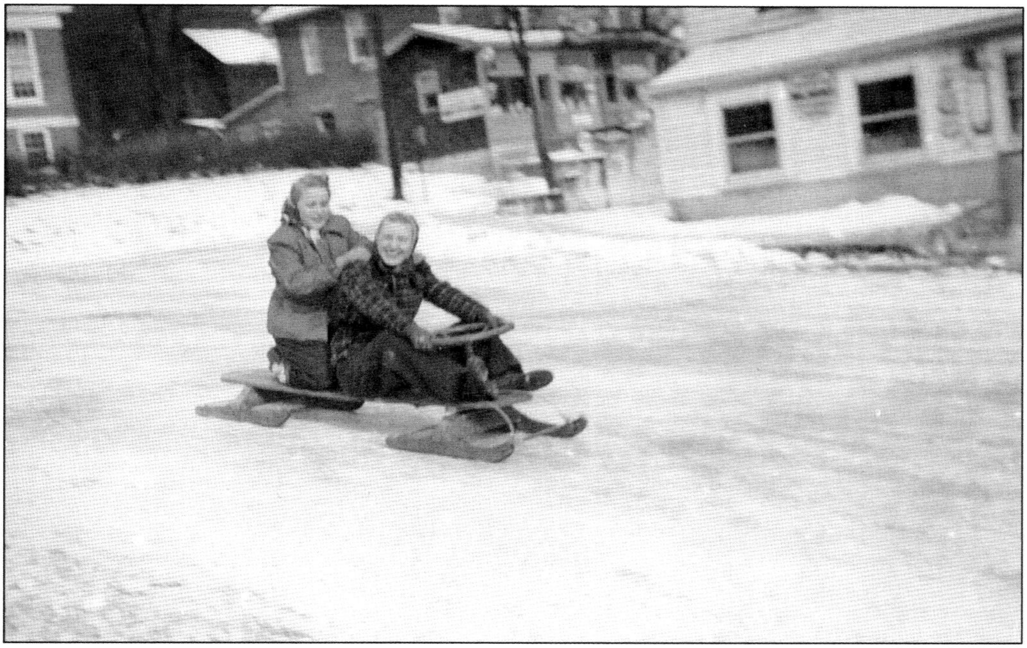

A bobsled run began on the mountain behind the school, crossed Washington Valley Road where lookouts stood to warn occasional traffic, continued past Waldron's store, and went down Chimney Rock Road. It was an exhilarating ride but meant a tedious walk back up for another run. Jeanette Van Nest (left) and her sister Irene enjoy sledding in 1938. (JWG.)

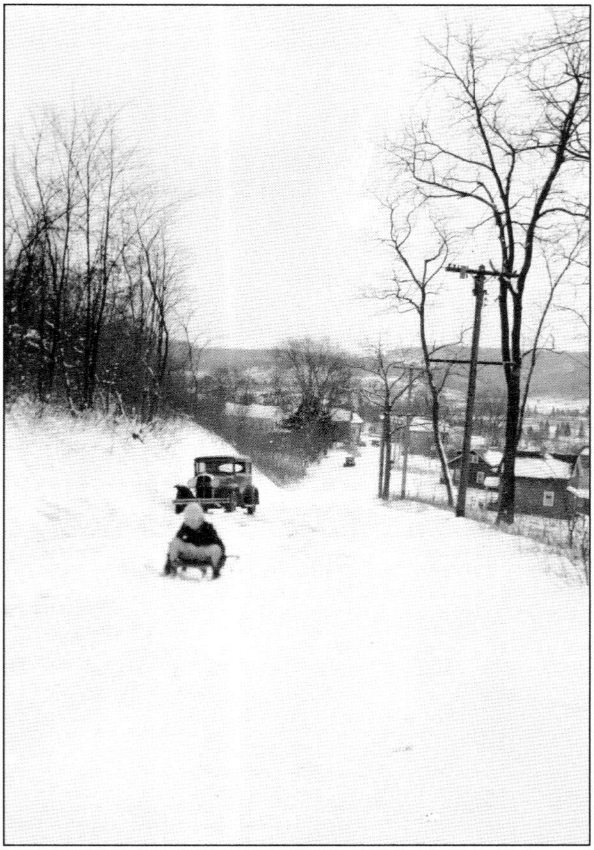

Mount Horeb Road was another favorite sledding hill. When the snowplows had been too efficient for good sledding, riders simply shoveled enough snow back on one side of the road for a single sled run. The road leveled off enough to halt the sleds before they reached the dangerous intersection with Washington Valley Road. In this 1934 view, the snow-covered reservoir is in the distance. (JVC.)

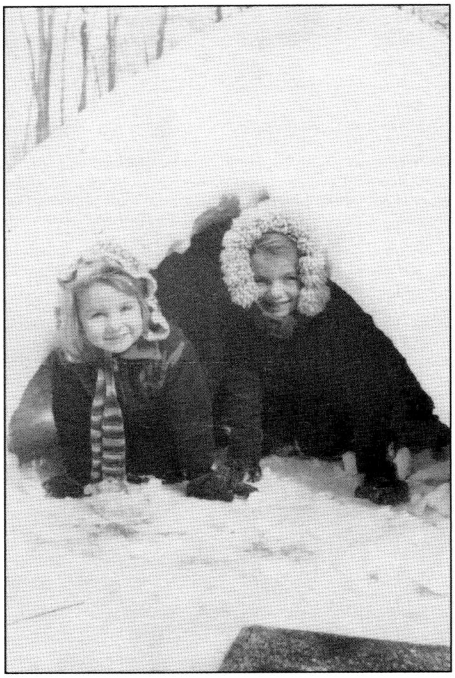

Snow ice cream was made with a bowl of fresh snow, with a bit of milk, sugar, and vanilla added. Children also made snow angels by lying flat in the snow and moving arms and legs to form the shape. When snow was plentiful, they might spend days piling it high and then digging out an igloo. Suzy (left) and Pat Valentine peer from their igloo in 1944. (PVW.)

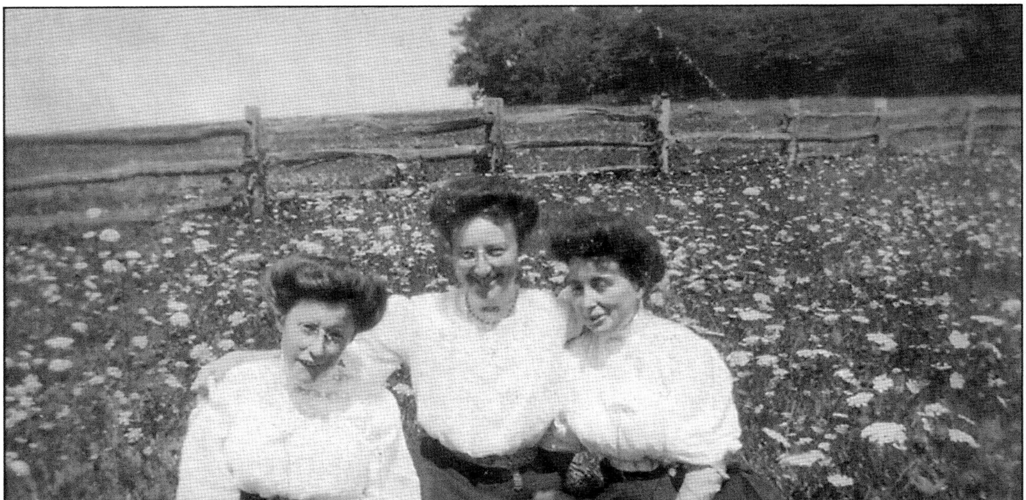

As spring returned, a succession of wildflowers sprang up, including rare plants no longer found here. Yellow violets grew in the woods, Indian paintbrush were in the Van Nest pasture, and both bottle and fringed gentians and orange milkweed appeared in abandoned fields. Indigo buntings, cedar waxwings, scarlet tanagers, and rose-breasted grosbeaks delighted bird-watchers. In this 1908 photograph, Ann Buchanan Alker (right) and two unidentified friends enjoy a field of Queen Anne's lace. (ALK.)

The Girl Scout troop led by Margaret Smith, who was also the teacher of grades five through eight, hiked to Schley's Tower near Pluckemin in 1929. From left to right are (first row) Shirley Bartle (see next photograph) and Elizabeth Busse; (second row) Helen Tullo, Edwina Smalley, Anna Van Allen, Anne Skillman, Miss Smith, and Elizabeth "Bib" Doty; (third row) Doris Horn, Eleanor Byrne, Florence Wilde, and Irene Gesh. (PVW.)

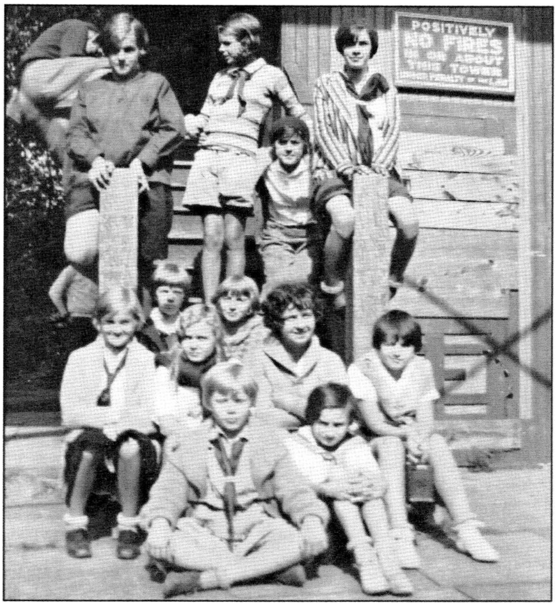

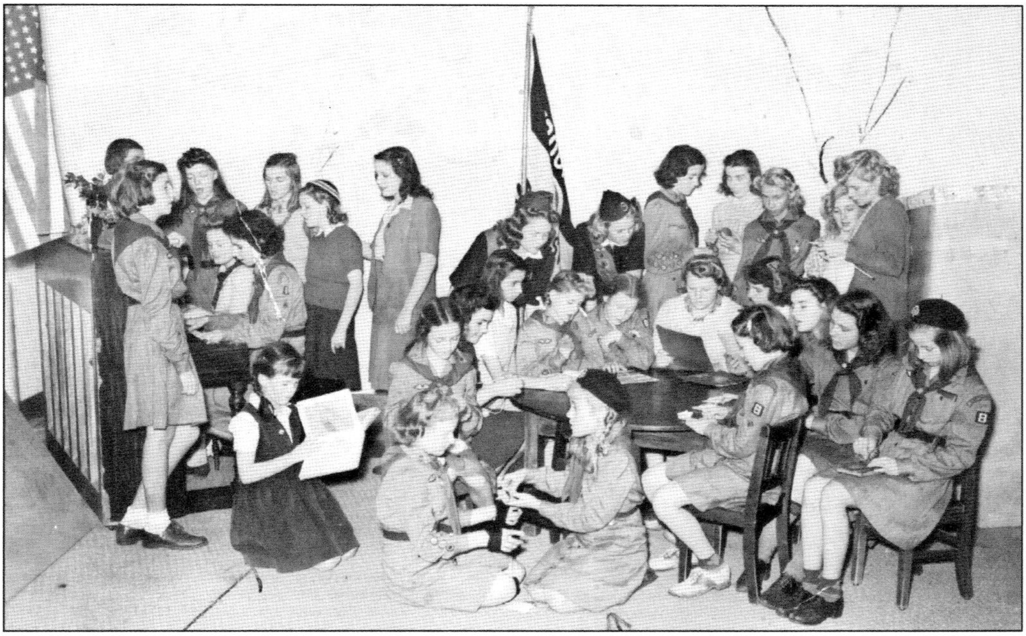

Girl Scouts knitted squares for Blankets for Britain in 1943. Around a piano, from left to right, are (standing) Betty Parry (in front), unidentified (partially hidden), Lois Poffley, Dora Van Heusen, Joyce Duxbury, and Kathleen Aagard; (seated) Sonya Young and Fran Buono. The girl kneeling with a book is unidentified. Standing near the flag, from left to right, are Charlotte Stumpp, Fluff Bartle, Ruth Parry, Betty Hulse, Carol Howarth, Arlene Olson, and leader Shirley Bartle Dennis. Around the table, clockwise from Nancy Hulse, who appears at bottom in the hat, are Betty Stumpp, Nancy Mitchell, Elaine Papen, Meryl Brown, Janet Tingley, Shirley Anderson, Dolores Geschwindner, Shirley Cunningham, Lorraine Totten, Mary Keohne, Katherine Van Heusen, and unidentified. (HLS.)

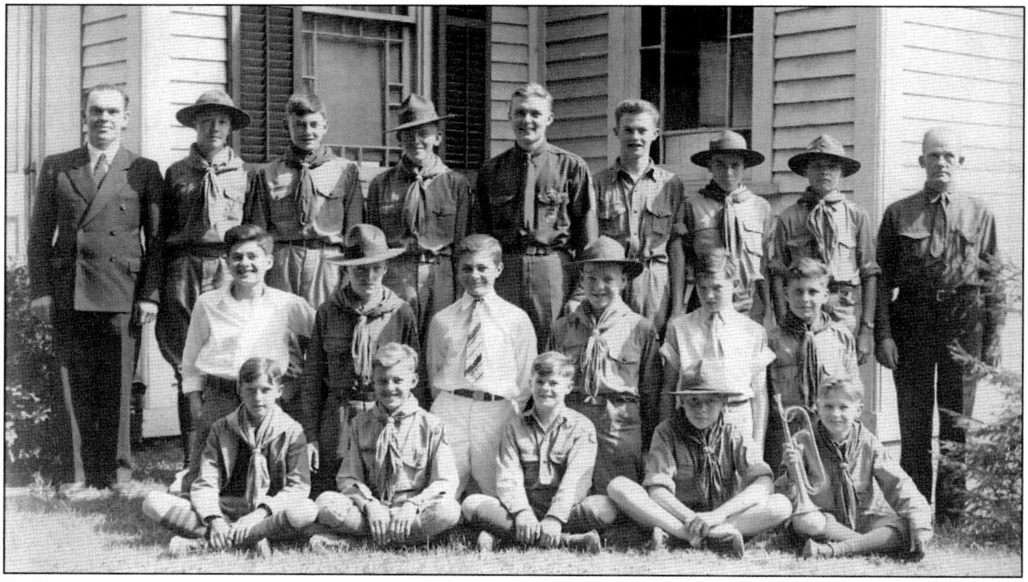

Before Boy Scout Troop 46 left for Camp Watchung in 1935, they gathered at the church. In this photograph, from left to right, are (first row) Otto Klein, Fred Geschwindner, Raymond Frazer, Warren Moore, and William Frazer; (second row) Alden Grant, Harry Poffley, Richard Grant, John Waldron, William Cunningham, and George Mastapeter; (third row) Rev. Roy Mills, Edwin Coddington, Robert Hall, Howard Moody, scoutmaster Elliot Moore, Wilfred Frazer, Russell Brarens, Robert Moore, and assistant scoutmaster James Moody. (JWG.)

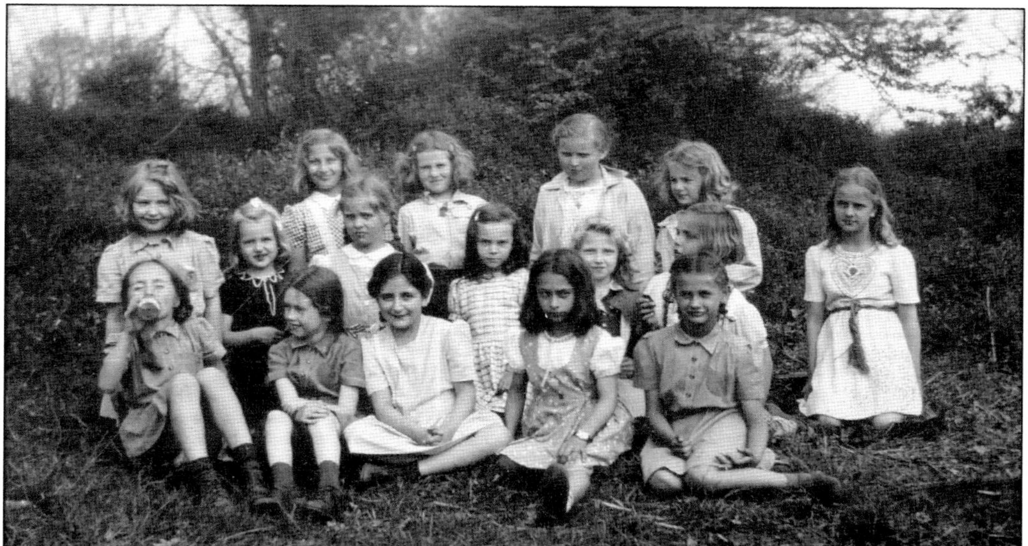

Eleanor Valentine's Brownie troop in 1943 includes, from left to right, (first row) Mary Lynn Mitchell, Nancy Hass, Adele Wishnow, Gail Brown, and Margaret Tingley; (second row) Ethel Schweitzer, Suzy Valentine, Hetty Mitchell, Marcia Hesler, June Gibbs, and Beverly Davis; (third row) Rose Tullo, Jean McGrath, Edna Conyk, Pat Valentine, and Kay Detweiler. As they hiked, they would sing "Little Red Caboose," "Found a Peanut," and the "Brownie Smile Song," also known as "I've Something in My Pocket." (PVW.)

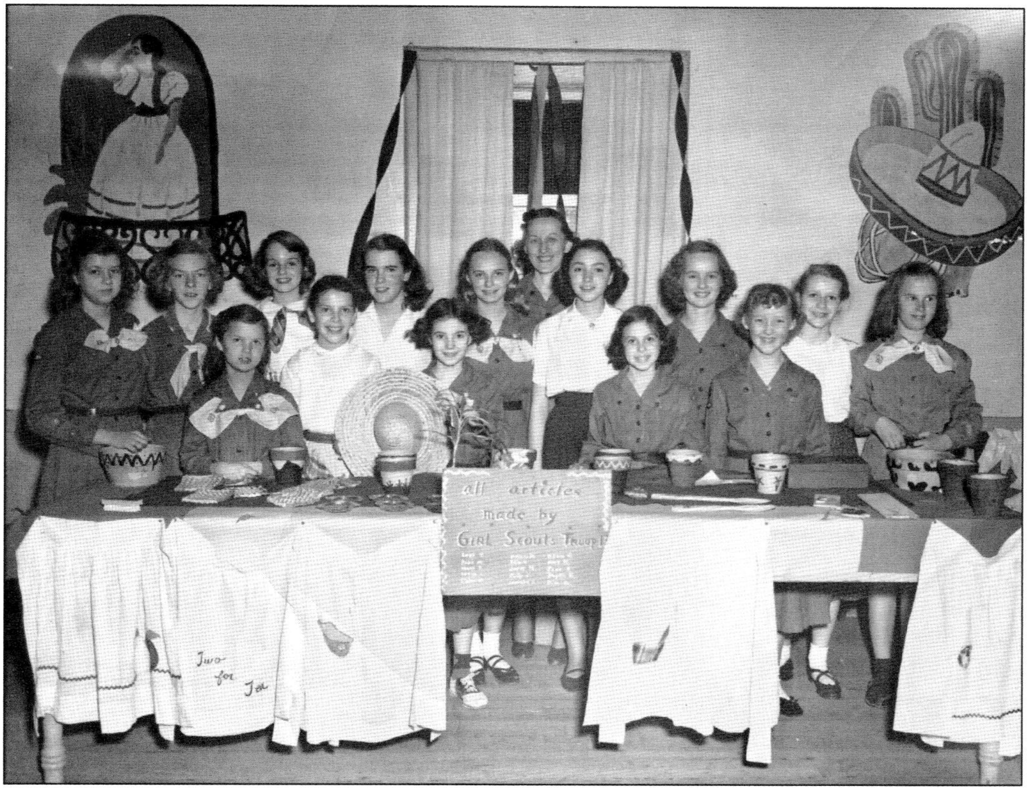

Mildred Musialowski's Girl Scouts benefited from her artistic talents in many interesting projects. In 1950, they studied Mexican traditions and created Mexican pottery. From left to right are (first row) Dawn Munro, Dale Torta, Alice McIlhenny, Judy Coddington, June Stein, and Dona Kae Carpenter; (second row) Joyce Messler, Patti Musialowski, Suzy Valentine, Susan Steinback, Mary Papen, Mildred Musialowski, Elaine Wagner, Lorraine Stein, and Phyllis King. (MUS.)

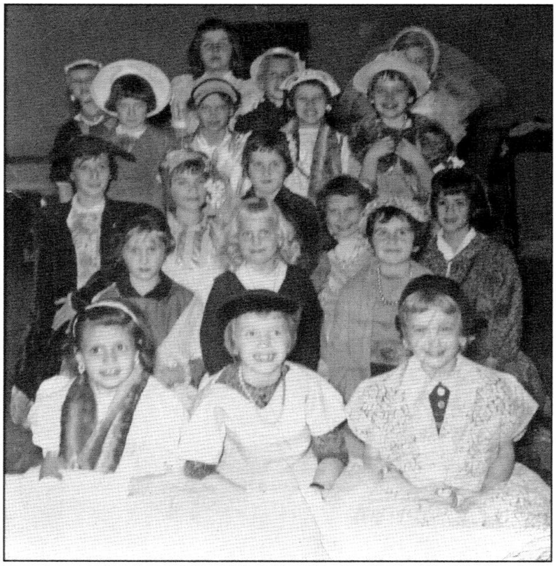

Sis Cramer Longo's Brownies are dressed in glamour garb with Avon cosmetics samples in 1959. They are, from left to right, (first row) Fran Longo, Irene McMullen, and Jeannie Berry; (second row) Patty Urich, Sharon Blake, and Karen Coddington; (third row) Carol Furino, Susan Roberts, Cathy Russell, Marcia Kopf, and Chris Adams; (fourth row) Alice Hallenbeck, Beverly Klein, Eileen Hliva, and Janet Berry; (fifth row) Sandy Lyng, Mary Ann Torta, Kris Olsen, and Candy Clark. (SIS.)

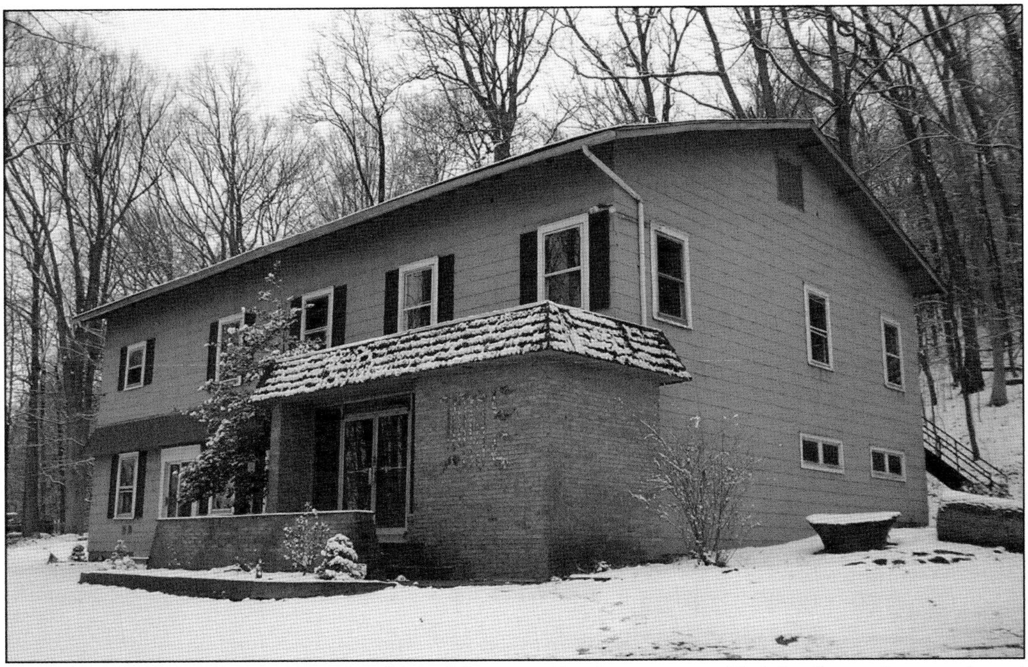

Anna O'Higgins's 1919 suggestion that a Martinsville Community Club be formed as a cultural and social center met with enthusiasm. Fundraising began with a kermess, a traditional Dutch fall festival with games, food, music, and dancing. William Ellis Bartle donated the land, and a series of events raised enough funds to begin building. Bylaws specified that the property serve forever as a public park for the community. Pictured is the MCC in 2010. (BER.)

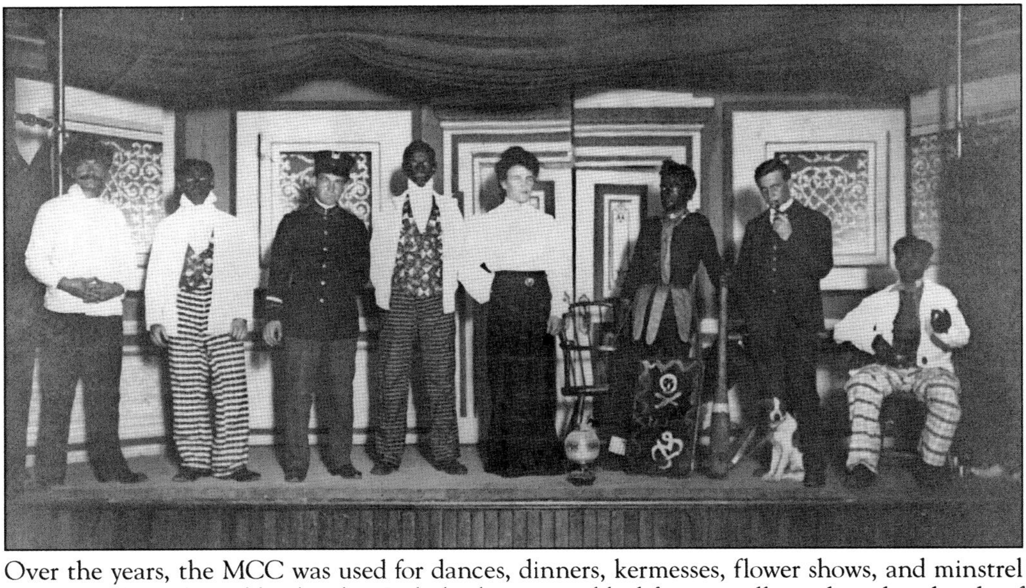

Over the years, the MCC was used for dances, dinners, kermesses, flower shows, and minstrel shows. Fred Bartle and his brother Jack, both wearing blackface, usually anchored each side of the stage while a variety of musical performances and humorous dialogues take center stage. Fred played the banjo and whistled stirring renditions of "Listen to the Mocking Bird." However, none of the participants in this performance around 1925 has been identified. (IKE.)

In 1946, Zuma and Conrad Alexander moved to the village. Zuma, a veteran of many little-theater productions in California and northern New Jersey, quickly organized residents into the Martinsville Community Club Players. For the next two decades, they entertained the area with a series of very popular productions, with each performance surpassing previous ticket sales. This poster was one of the many created by resident Lee Franz over the years. (SIS.)

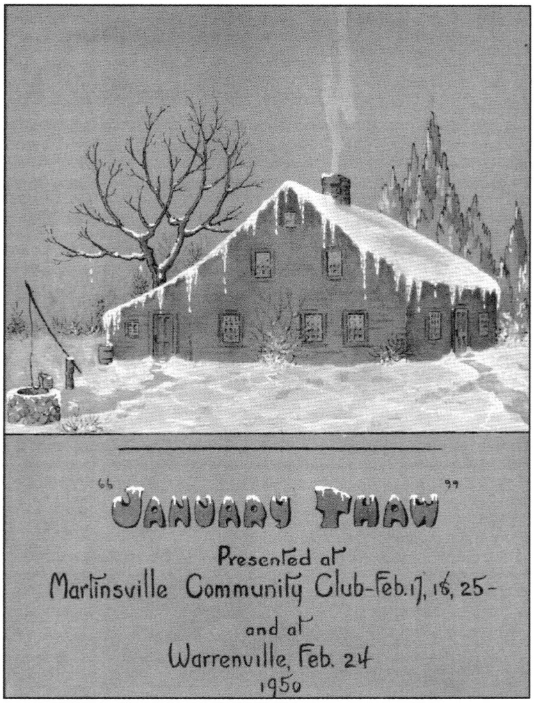

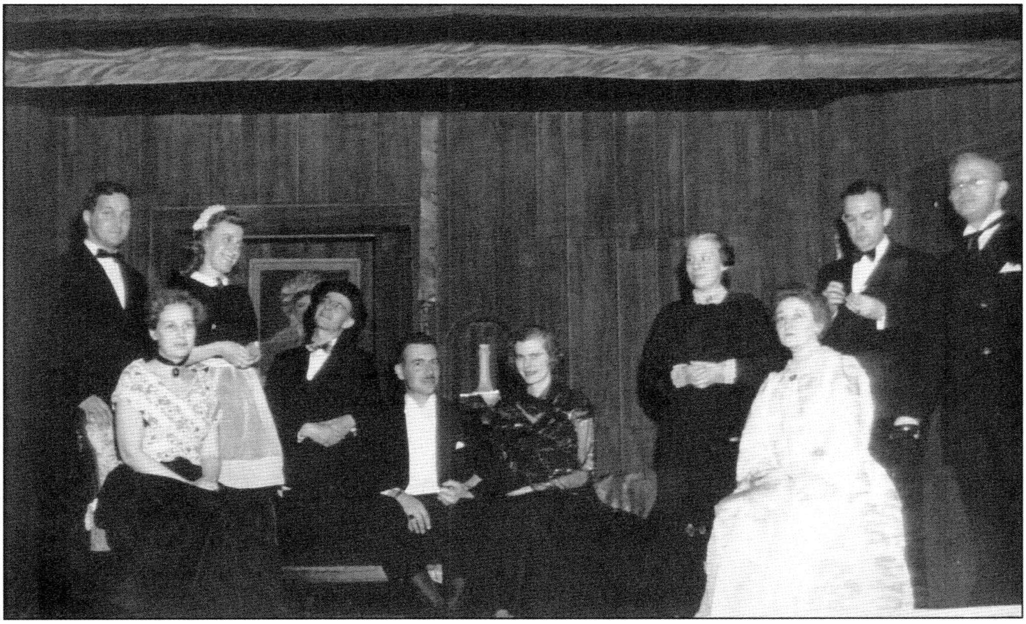

Zuma Alexander starred in the April 1948 presentation of *Double Door*. From left to right, Walter Kritzberger, Arlene Stark, Cherry Coddington, Wendell Munro, William Daughaday, Marjorie Daughaday, Betty Tyree, Zuma and Conrad Alexander, and Ross Tyree appear in costume for the period drama. Zuma later recalled, "Martinsville, with a population of about 500, is the kind of place you dream about. At first, people were a little timid at my suggestion of a theater group, but gradually they agreed to try." (SIS.)

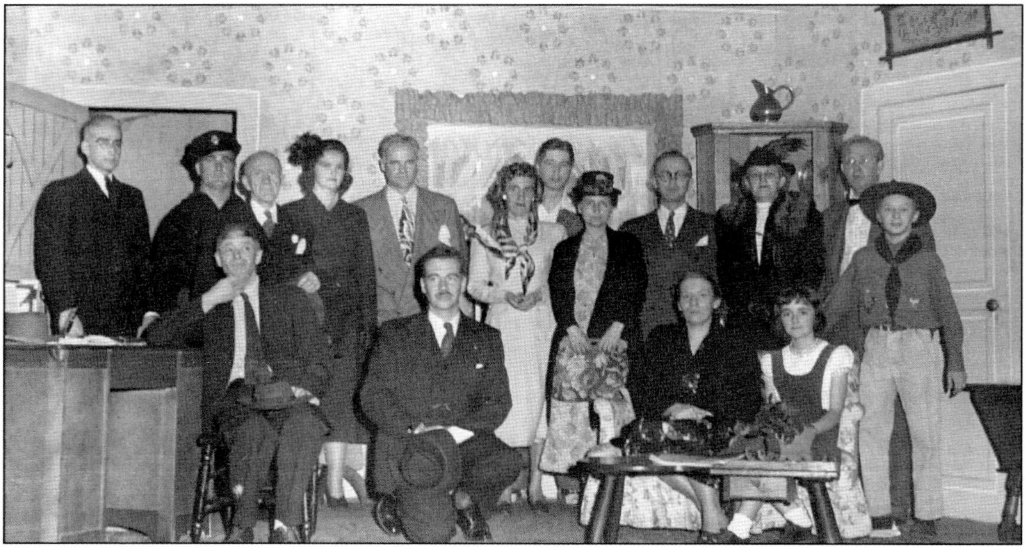

In October 1948, the cast of *Village Green* includes, from left to right, (first row) Wendell Munro, William Daughaday, Betty Tyree, and Mary Lynn Mitchell; (second row) Warren Hine, John Trupo, Waldemar Neiman, Hazel Lydecker, unidentified, Cherry Coddington, Herbert Hall, Pam Coddington, unidentified, Elizabeth "Bib" Doty, Ross Tyree, and Warren Munro. Zuma also directed area children in annual Christmas festivals and organized a Junior Dramatics Club, which presented several plays, including *Alice in Wonderland* in 1950 (SIS.)

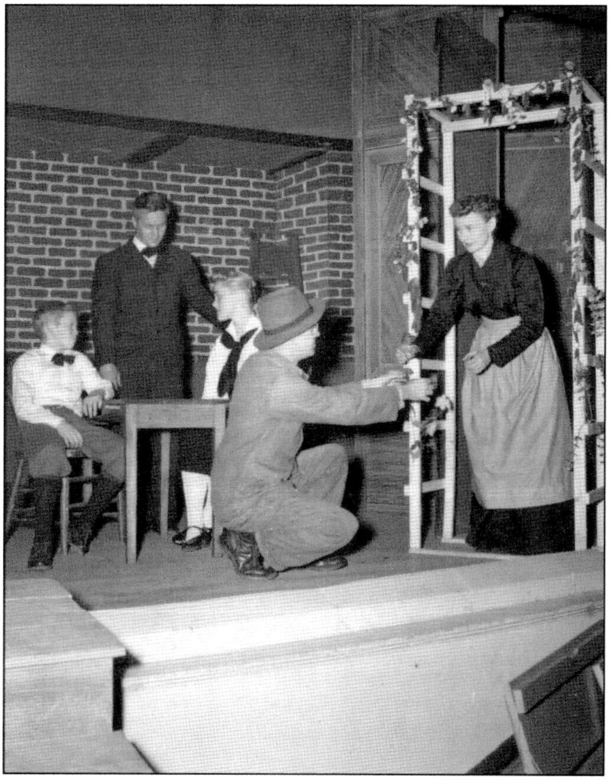

The cast and crew for the November 1950 production of Thornton Wilder's classic *Our Town* included 60 members of the community from many walks of life: three school teachers, the school custodian, the postmistress, the blacksmith, local tradesmen, New York businessmen, scientists and engineers from local industries, and everyday housewives. In this image are Walter Kritzberger, standing; David Dennis and Phyllis Bartle, seated; Ross Tyree, kneeling; and Ruth Lessing, standing. (SIS.)

The 1964 production of *Oh, Mama! No, Papa!* was one of the many plays that included resident comedienne Sis Longo (seated). Larry Egan (left), Judy Coddington (center), and Clint Seeber completed the cast. Perhaps Sis's most memorable role was in the John Patrick play *Everybody Loves Opal* in which she portrayed an eccentric character who lives in the town dump. (SIS.)

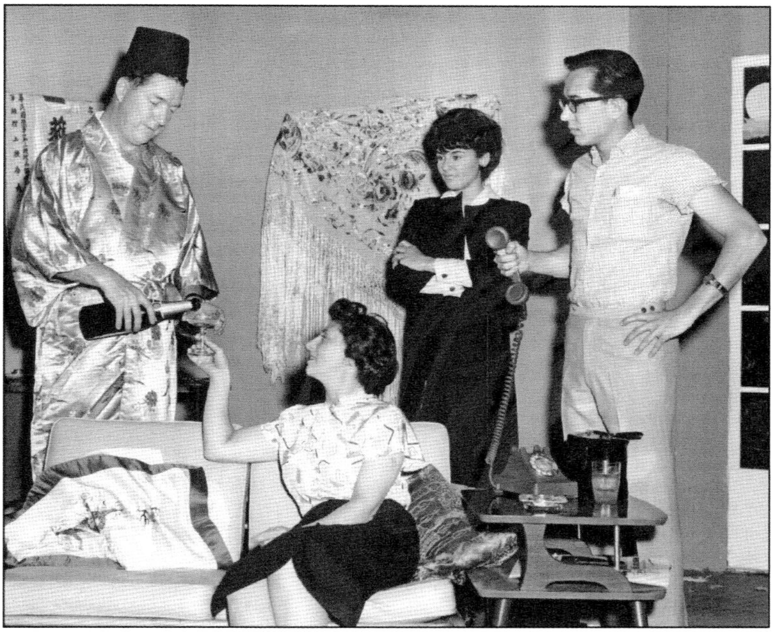

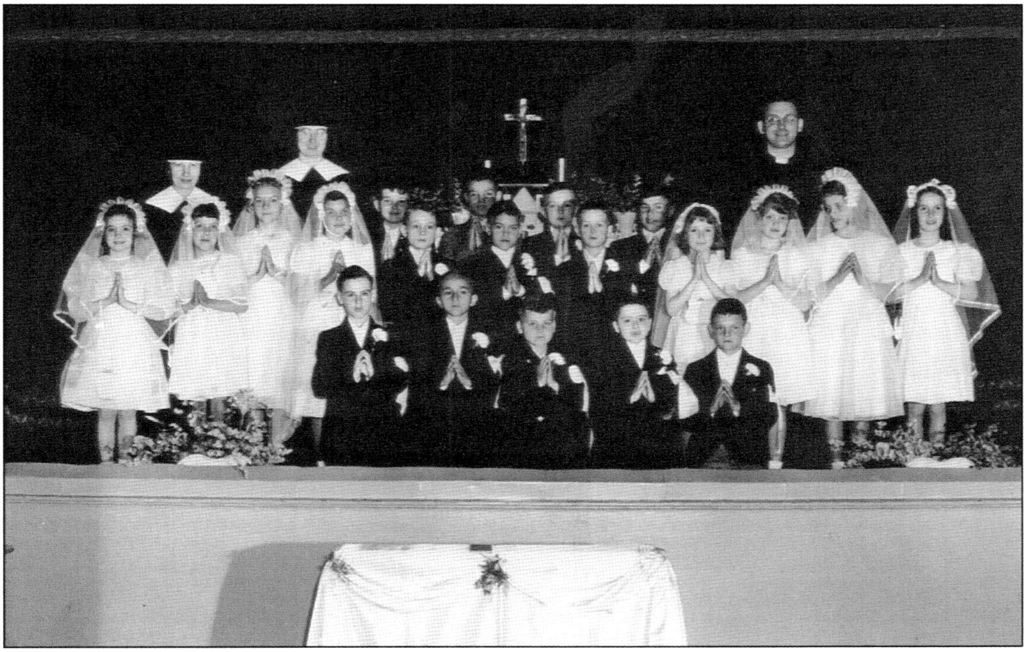

The Blessed Sacrament Church held a First Communion Service at the MCC in 1948. From left to right, the girls are Alice McIlhenny, Dale Torta, Patti Musialowski, Eleanor Pepper, Betsy Kozic, Didi Lamb, Marion Consalvo, and Barbara Kozic; boys include (first row) John Harcharik, Anthony Trinchera, ? Tullo, unidentified, and Bill Pepper; (second row) unidentified, Leonard Assante, and Buddy Biddle; (third row) Robert Gluck, Henry Pepper, Edmund ?, and Michael Assante; (fourth row) Sister Florentine, unidentified, and Father Drous. (PEP.)

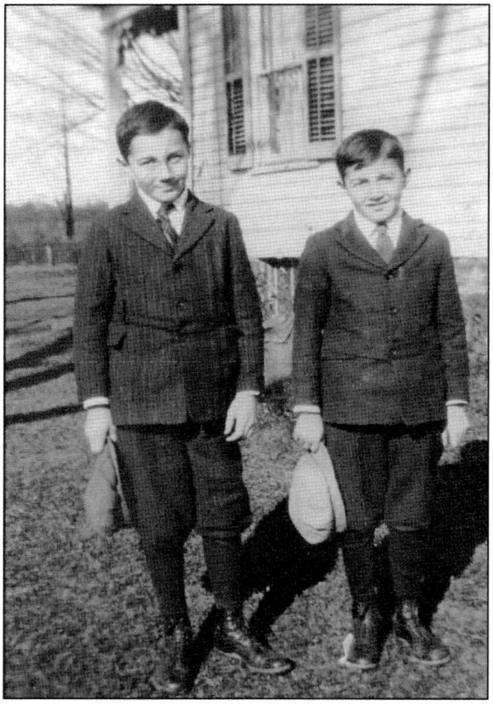

Fashions for both men and women evolved during the first half of the 20th century. As well-dressed young men in the 1920s, Bill (left) and Harold Coddington wear black stockings and knickers and carry their caps. When corduroy pants for men were an option in this period, schoolteacher Lester Codington (note spelling variation) wore them, which earned him the nickname "Whistle Britches." (JCD.)

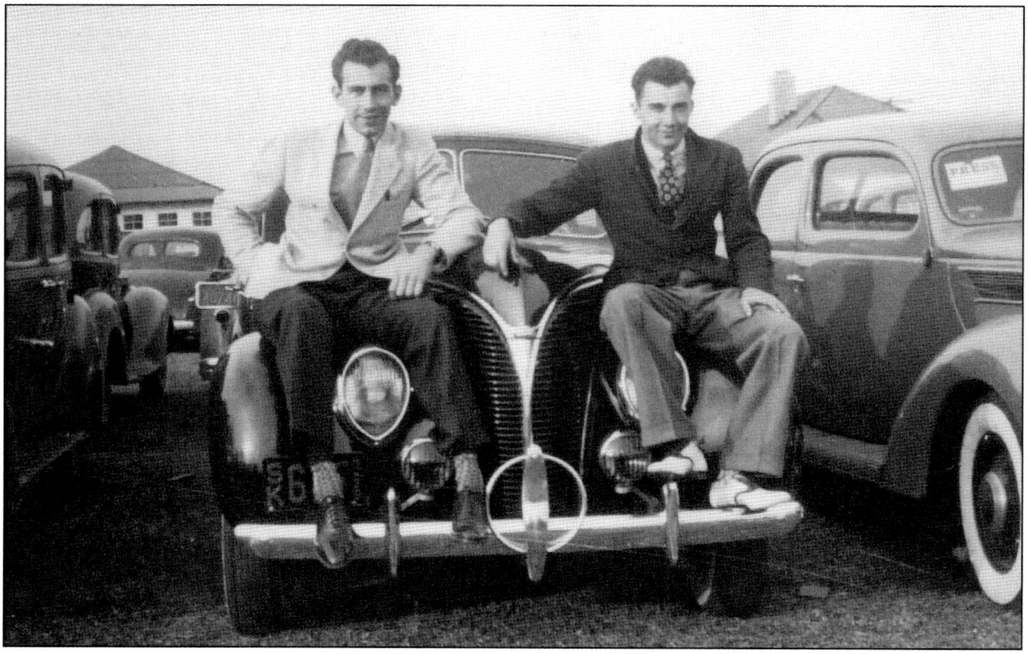

By the late 1930s, men's fashions had progressed, as illustrated by Clinton Boxwell and Harold Coddington. As they sit on a 1938 Ford DeLuxe convertible and admire the equally modernized fashions of the passing young ladies, their shoes are a far cry from the universal black, high-topped footwear of a decade earlier. Fashion changes might also be noted by comparing the photographs of schoolchildren over the years. (KCD.)

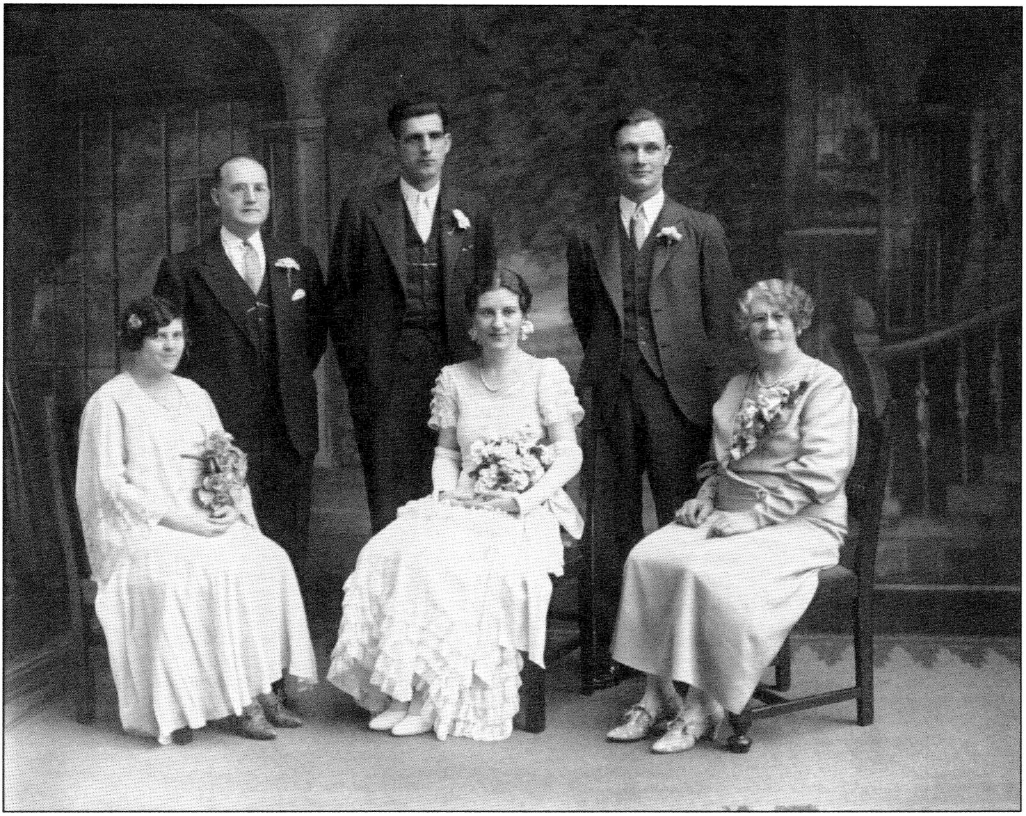

Wedding gowns have alternately reflected earlier fashions and modern innovations, as flappers preferred short skirts, while later brides chose romantic Victorian-era styles. For her 1937 marriage to Francis "Jake" Thum, Gladys Corbin chose this lovely ruffled style, which any modern bride might also choose. The attending couples are unidentified. (THM.)

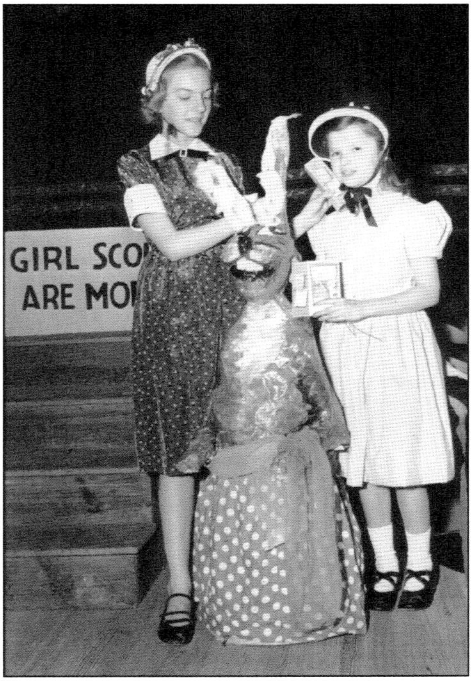

Mildred Musialowski's Girl Scout troop presented a spring fashion show in 1951. The girls learned good posture and built their confidence by appearing before an audience. The troop also created the decorations, including this large Easter rabbit. Patti Musialowski (left) and Dawn Munro pose in their Easter outfits, complete with ribbon-and-flower-trimmed bonnets. (MUS.)

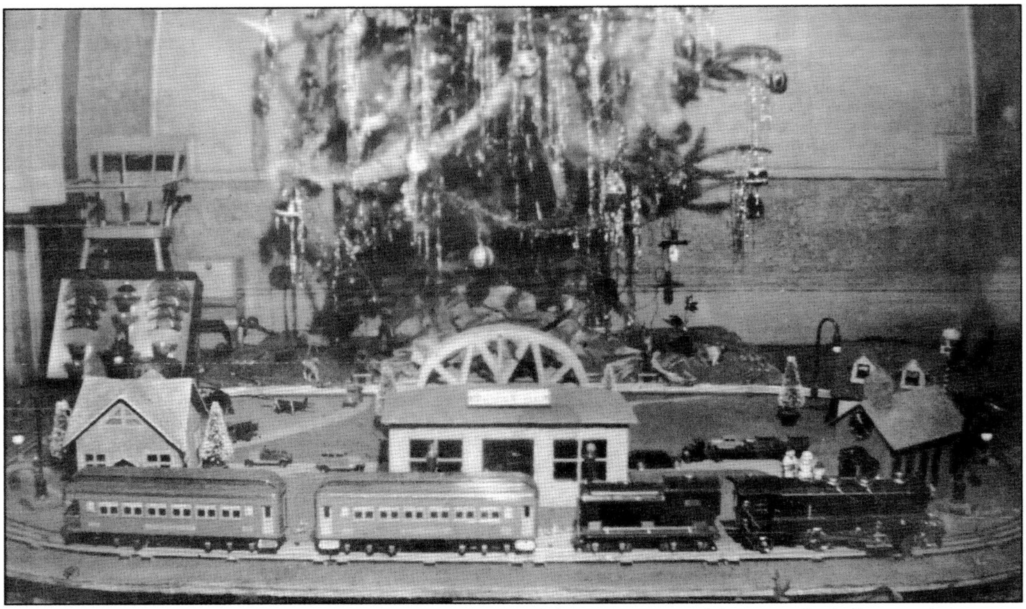

An early project of the Martinsville Community Club was to raise $5,000 to help bring electricity to Martinsville in the early 1920s. Toy electric trains then became popular. From a Lionel train beneath the Christmas tree, pictured in 1934, boys sometimes progressed to building elaborate scale-model railroad layouts as a year-round hobby. They also experimented with chemistry sets, which sometimes exploded in basements. (EGS.)

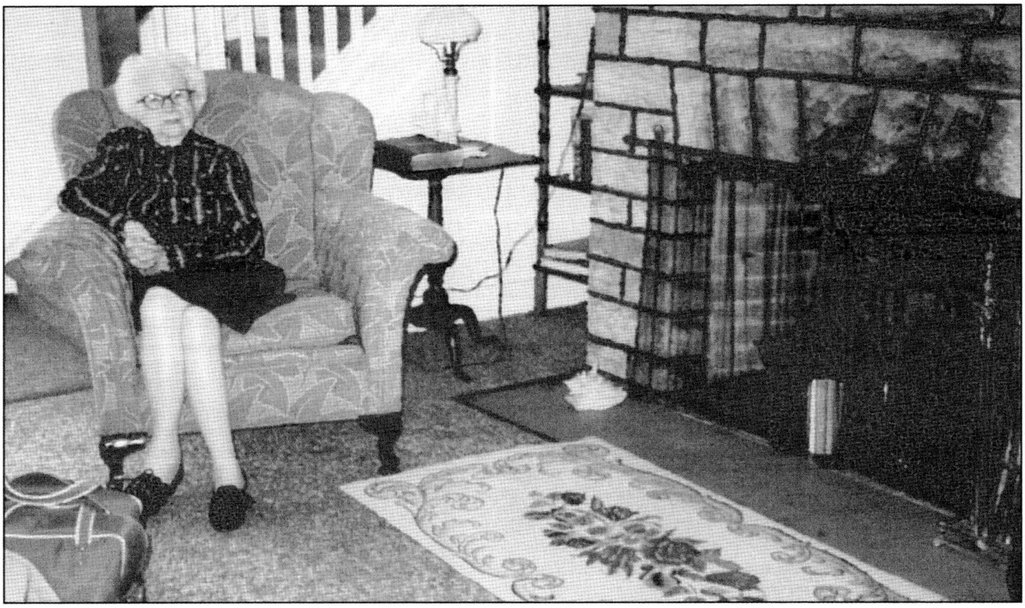

Ladies found various ways of crafting beautiful and useful objects in their free time. Stitching patchwork quilts, knitting, crocheting, and hooking rugs were favorite pastimes. Jessie Smalley, who hooked many beautiful rugs over the years, sits beside one of her creations in 1985. Jessie, who weighed four pounds at birth and was not expected to live, survived past her 106th birthday, remaining fiercely independent and keeping up with current events to the end. (IMB.)

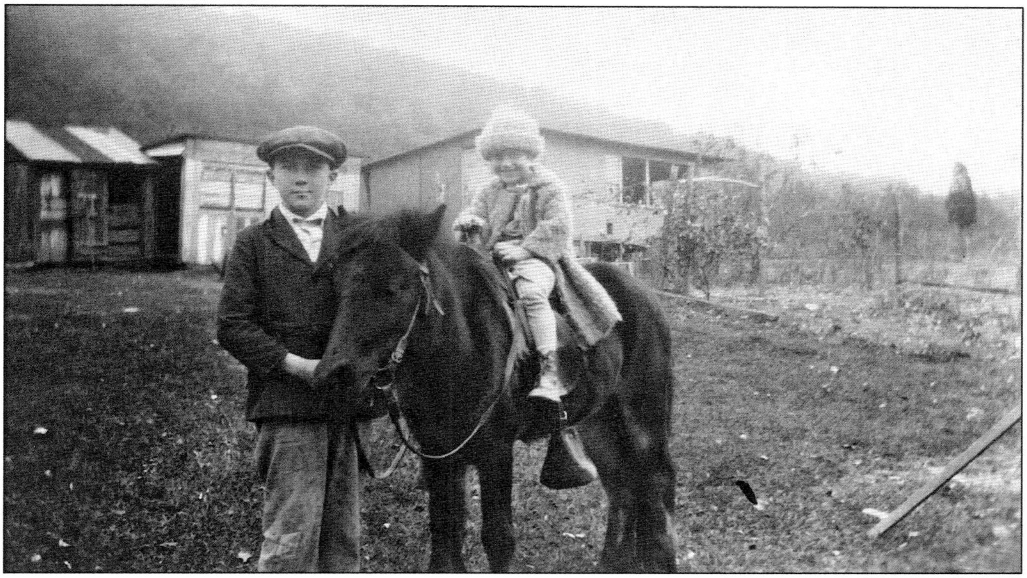

Riding on a pony is a thrill for many children. Those who lived on a farm could be treated to a ride frequently, and as they grew older, they learned to care for the pony. When Bill Coddington gave his cousin Irene Van Nest a pony ride in 1926, her legs were so short that her feet could not reach the stirrups. (KCD.)

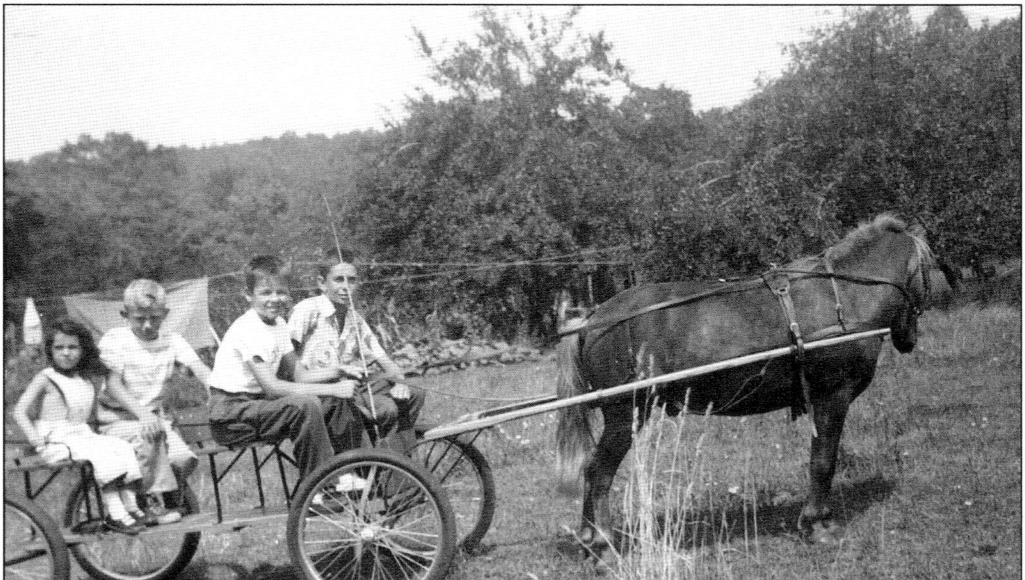

By the 1950s, a number of Martinsville youngsters owned horses, which inspired the formation of the Chaps & Spurs 4-H Club. The club held an annual horse show on Mother's Day in Loft's field on Chimney Rock Road. Ponies remained popular as well, especially for pulling a cart, as shown in this photograph from 1957. From left to right are Karen Coddington, Bob Hall, Jimmy Van Allen, and Gary Coddington. (KCD.)

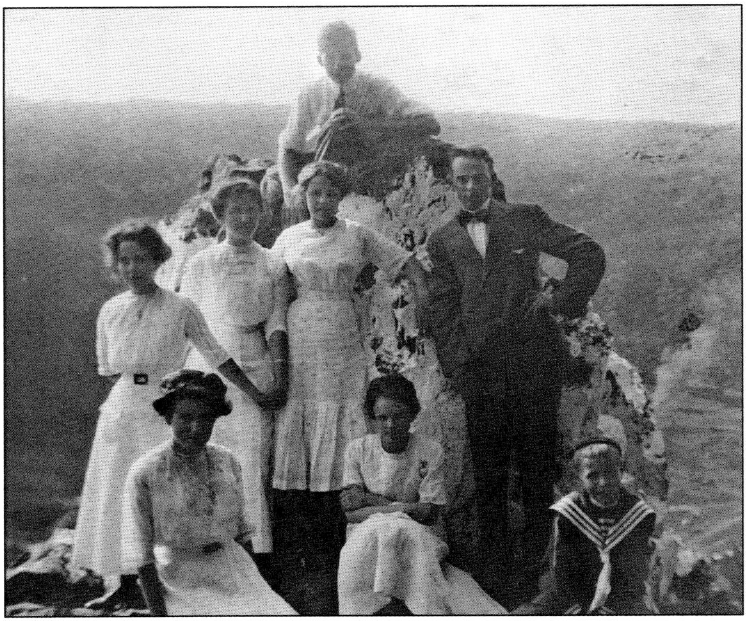

A hike to Chimney Rock has been fun for many generations. Hikers today dress more casually for the climb through the woods and underbrush than Jessie Bartle and friends did for this photograph in 1917. The rock has been whitewashed for many years, making it easily visible from Chimney Rock Road, which skirts the stone crusher operation far below. Jessie stands third from the left, but her companions are unidentified. (JCD.)

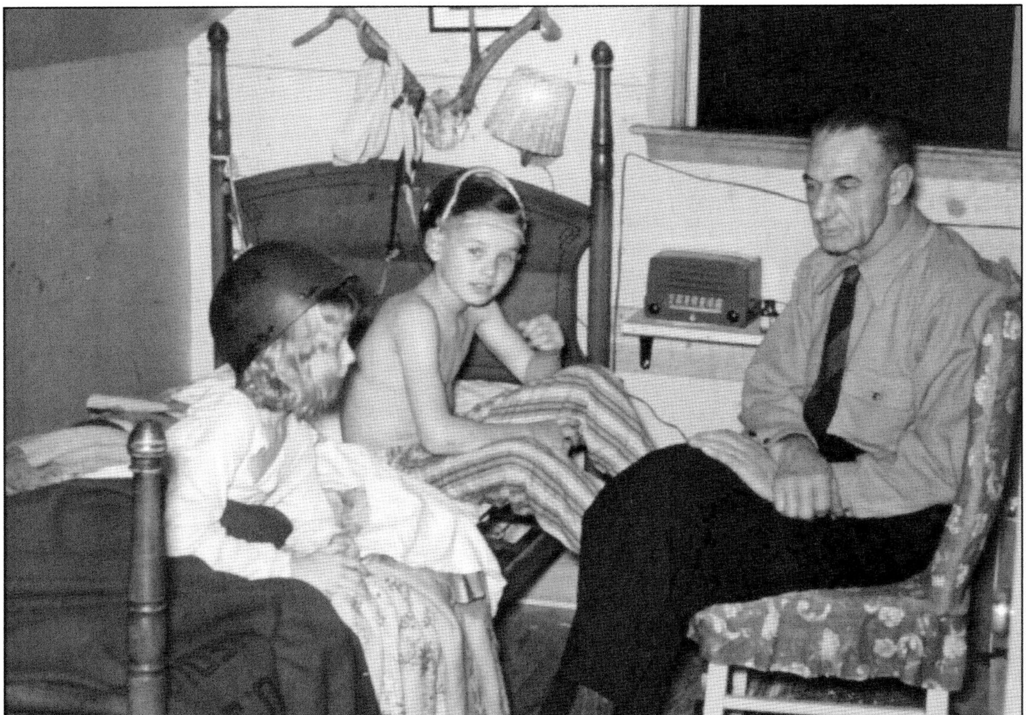

When several generations of a family live in the same community, the relationship of grandchildren and grandparents strengthens. A Sunday evening ritual was the visit of Ed Byrne to tell bedtime stories of family history, his own childhood adventures, and fables. "The Boy Who Cried Wolf" was a favorite with grandchildren Suzy Valentine, wearing a soldier's combat helmet, and brother Don, captured in this 1944 photograph. (PVW.)

Seven

Survivors in the Path of Progress

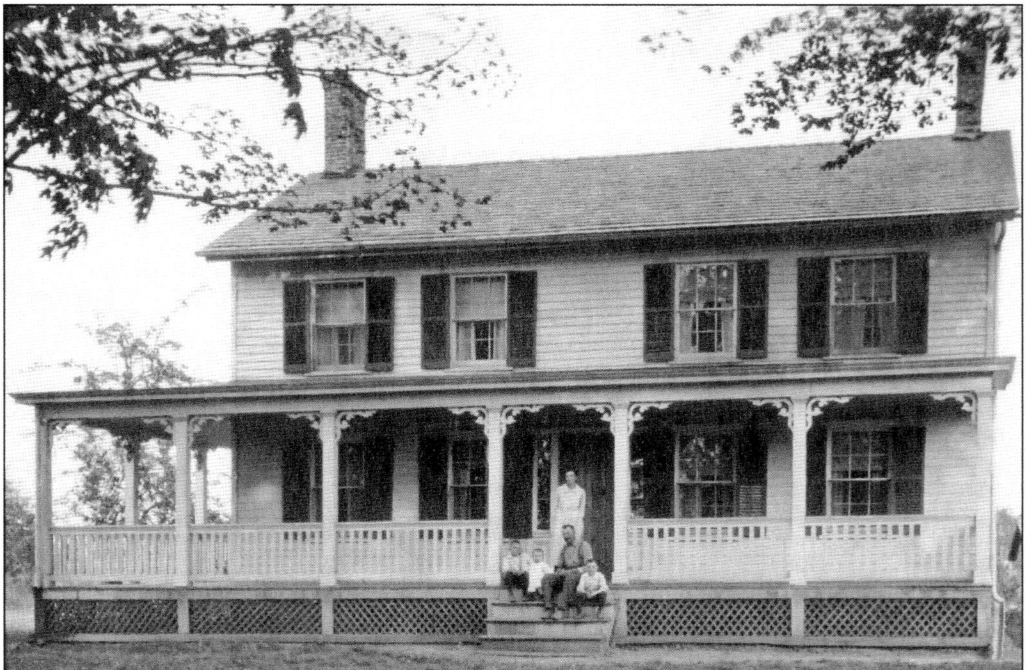

When Reuben Coddington presented a basket of peaches to his neighbors the Edward Byrne family, he brushed off their thanks with the jest: "Well, if I fed them to my pigs, they'd choke on the pits." Today, his beautifully preserved farmhouse appears as it does in this 1920 photograph. It is down the road from the equally well-preserved Mount Horeb Methodist Church, which was built on land donated by the Coddington family. (KCD.)

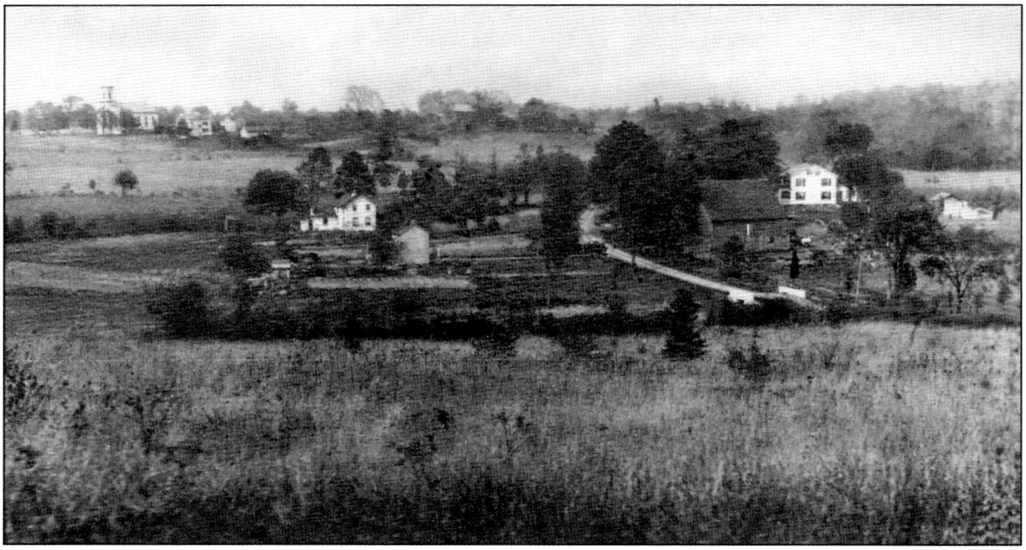

In this 1920 north-facing overview of the Mount Horeb area, the church stands atop the hill in the distance, Reuben Coddington's white farmhouse is on the right, and Amelia Mason's home, which also survives, is opposite. Today, a few more houses have joined the Mason residence, and homes fill the field above the Coddington farm, but the fields across from the church, now the grounds of the Pingry School, remain open. (KCD.)

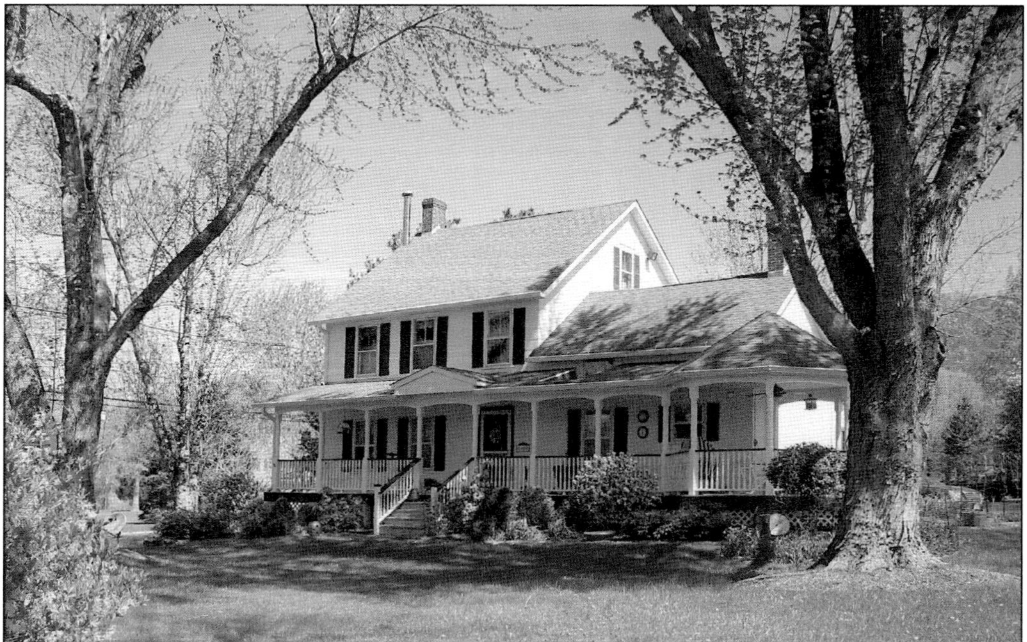

In the western area of the valley, the Papen farm fields now contain houses, but the Papen farmhouse, seen here, is preserved in pristine condition. The Cornelius Van Nest farmhouse once stood near the present Arrowbrook Drive, on the farm which later became Joe's Fruit Farm. Although that house is gone, the Musialowski family chose to permanently preserve five acres of open farmland as township parkland. (PVW.)

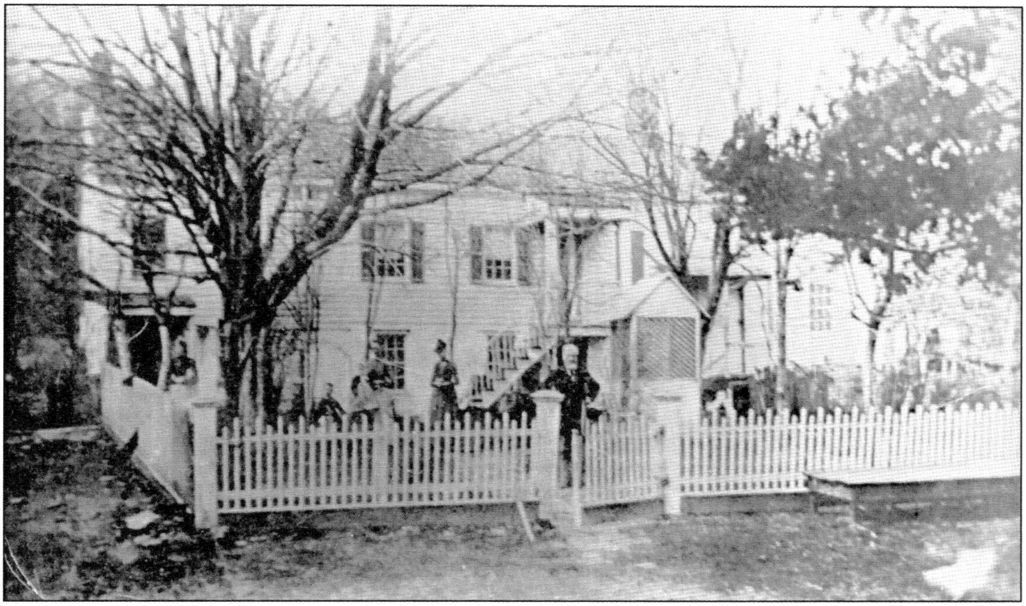

One of the oldest surviving homes in the eastern area of the valley was the Jennings property, built as early as 1766. Jacob Jennings sold it to a Zimmerman in 1863. In this early photograph, Zimmerman alterations obscure the lines of the original bank dwelling. Buildings nestled against a slope feature ground-level access in the front, while doors from the second story on the back also exit at ground level further up the bank. (MRN.)

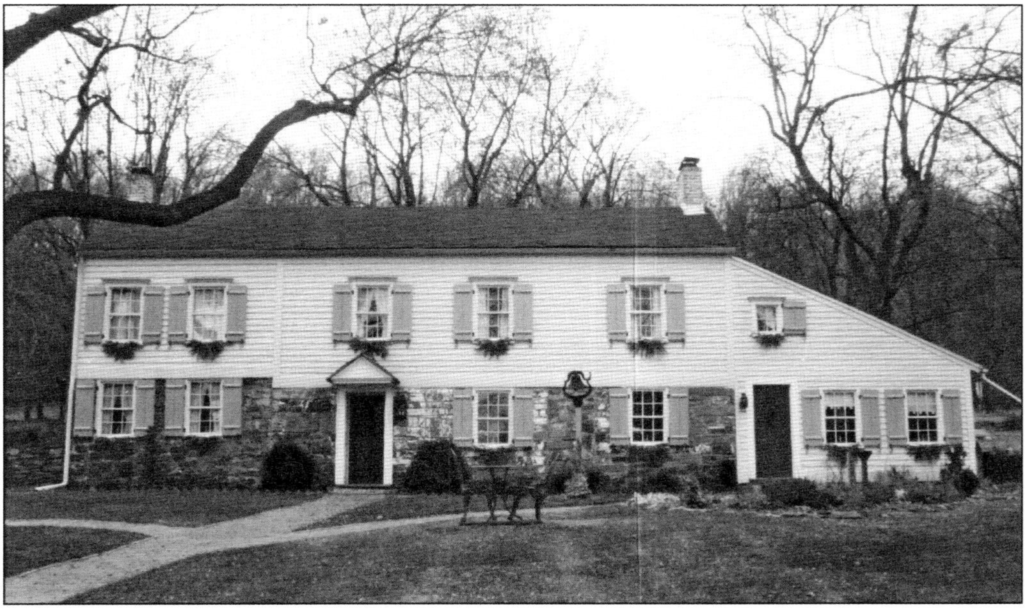

Conrad and Zuma Alexander, who bought the farm in 1946, may be credited with restoring the home to more closely resemble its original appearance, as in this 1998 photograph. The stone walls of the ground floor, nestled against the bank, keep the rooms pleasantly cool on the warmest summer days, while the winter sun, low in the sky, helps to warm the house in colder weather. (MRN.)

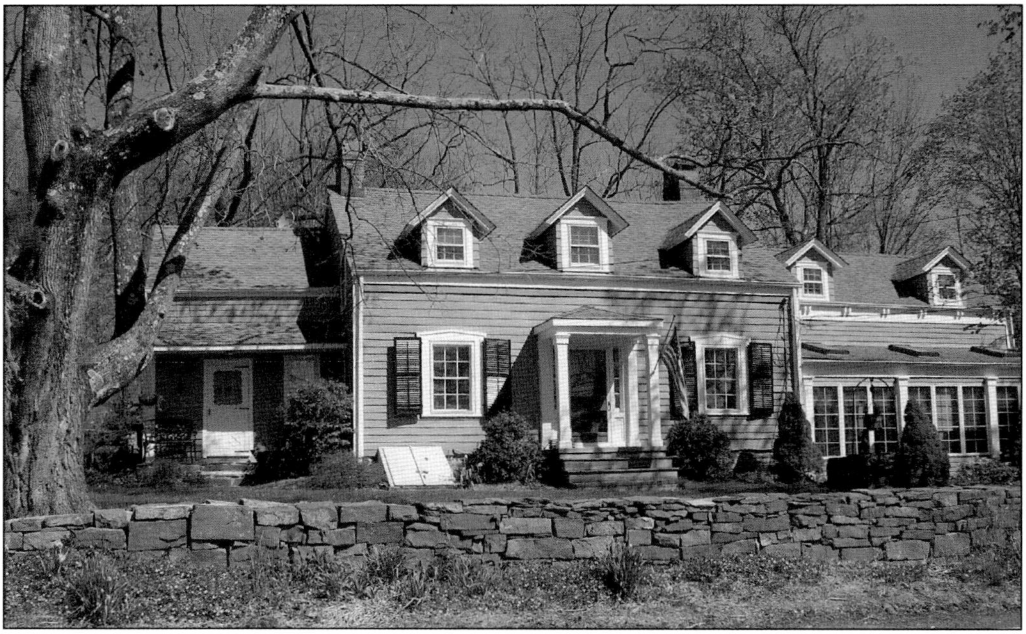

Also surviving, Double Duck Farm, the next house east, was the home in 1908 of Harvey and Anna O'Higgins, who inspired the formation of the MCC. In 1821, the will of owner Oliver Goltry left the farm to his two sons, "Unless Abraham concerns himself with the wife he once owned, who now lives with John Long, he shall be forever barred from having the right to the bequest." (PVW.)

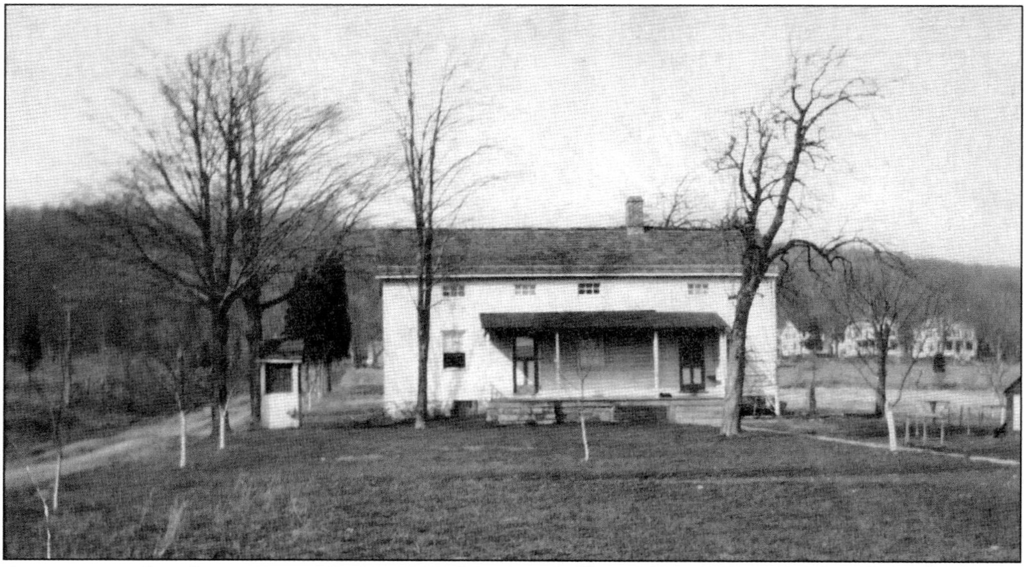

A surviving farmhouse near the center of Martinsville is the Yehle home on Chimney Rock Road, which was purchased from Elam Perrine in 1921, the approximate year of this photograph. The houses in the background on Washington Valley Road also survive, but their view from the Yehle home is now blocked by a shopping center. The small windows on the second story are referred to as eyebrow windows. (YLE.)

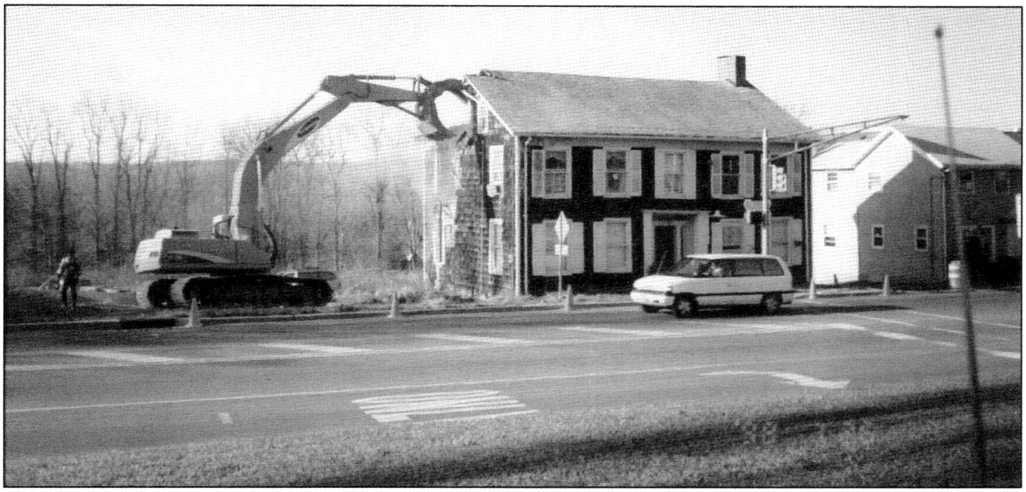

Although a number of early homes have survived and are being preserved by their present owners, many others have perished over time. In 1998, Fred Bartle's house met the same fate as his blacksmith shop when it fell to wrecking machinery. The site is now occupied by Blacksmith Commons, a shopping complex. (AND.)

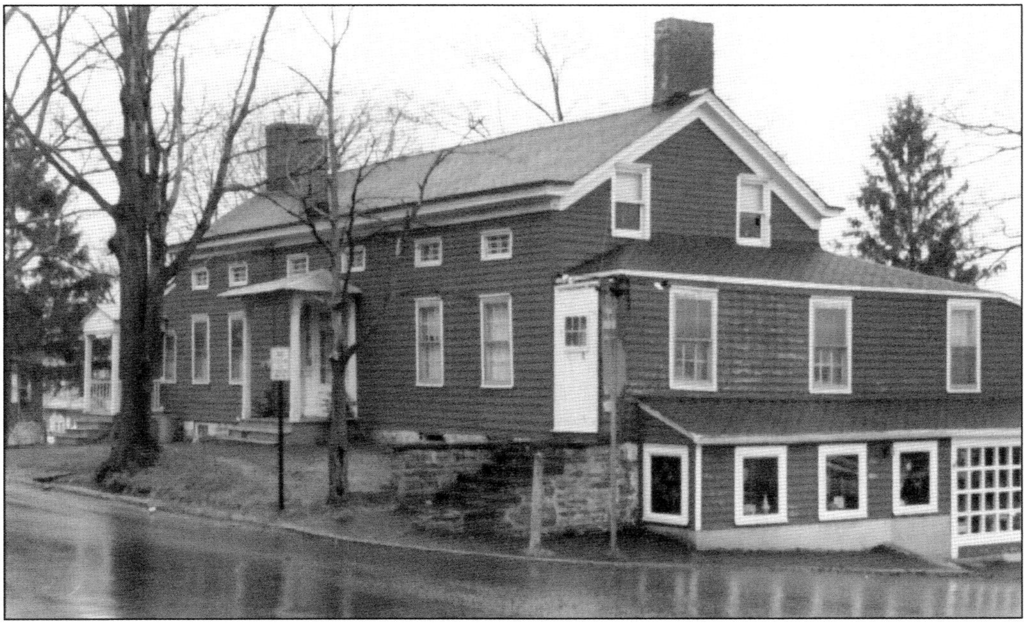

The Waldron house, which stood on the corner of Chimney Rock and Washington Valley Roads for two centuries, was the post office and stationery store for many years. It continued as a gift shop, as in this 1975 photograph, for several years after the Waldrons retired. It was demolished in 1987, and Squire's Corner shopping complex now occupies the site. (ECD.)

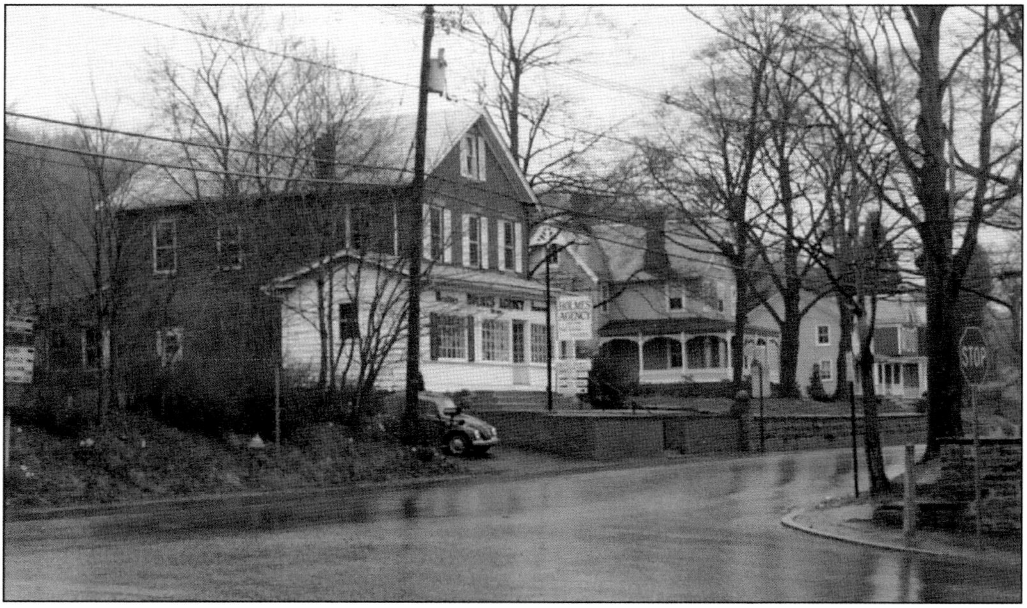

Across the road from the Waldron house, the general store owned by Edwin Smalley and then the Lyng family has survived with few modifications over the years. When Martinsville's first fire engine was stored in the Lyng barn, fire emergency calls came to the store, and word was sent to the schoolhouse next door. Schoolboys then ran up to the belfry to dangle from the rope and ring the bell in alarm. (ECD.)

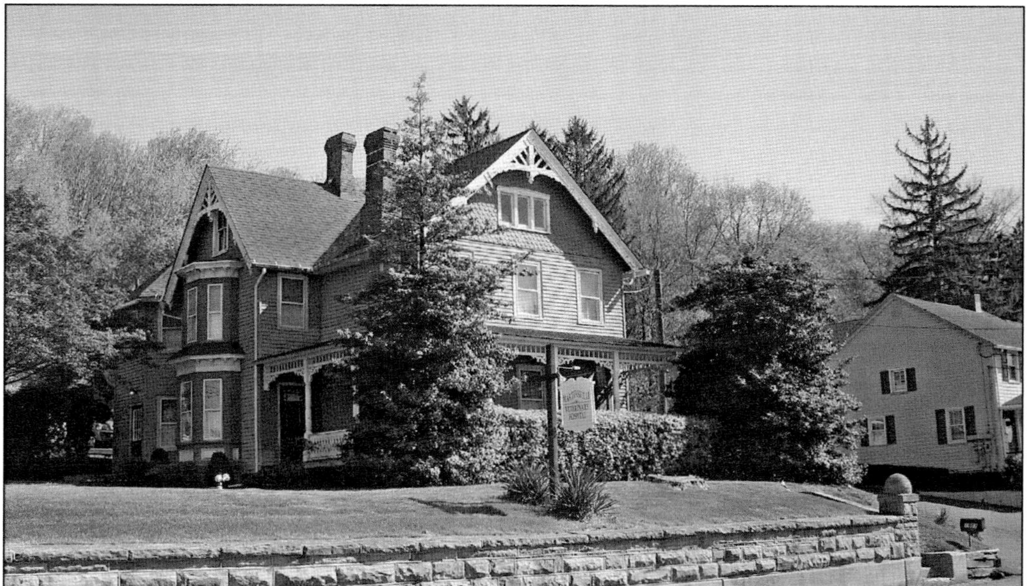

Beside the Lyng store is the handsome Victorian home built in 1888 by William Ellis Bartle as a wedding gift for his bride, Elizabeth Zimmerman. She was the daughter of Sebastian and Catherine Zimmerman, who were born in Heppenheim in Hesse, Germany. Jessie Bartle, daughter of William Ellis, was courted by her next door neighbor, Edwin Smalley. The home is now a veterinary clinic. (PVW.)

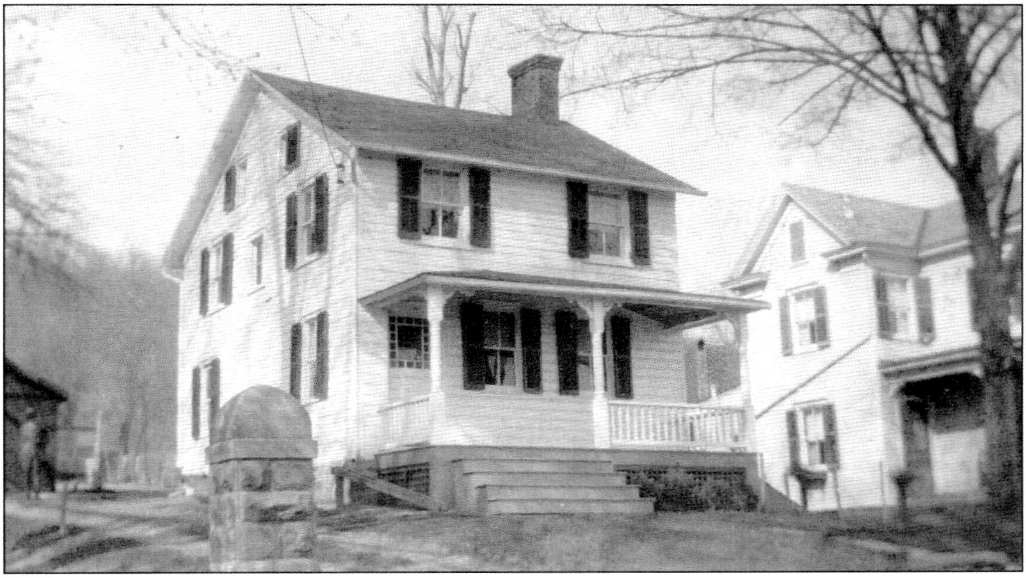

Next to the former Bartle home is the former residence of Nancy and David Coddington; he was the older brother of Reuben Coddington. Their two sons, Chester and Elmer, served in World War I, never married, and lived here all their lives. Their home is now occupied by Talk of the Town, a barbershop whose owner, Sal Longo, found the original hardware surviving on some of the doors of the structure. (KCD.)

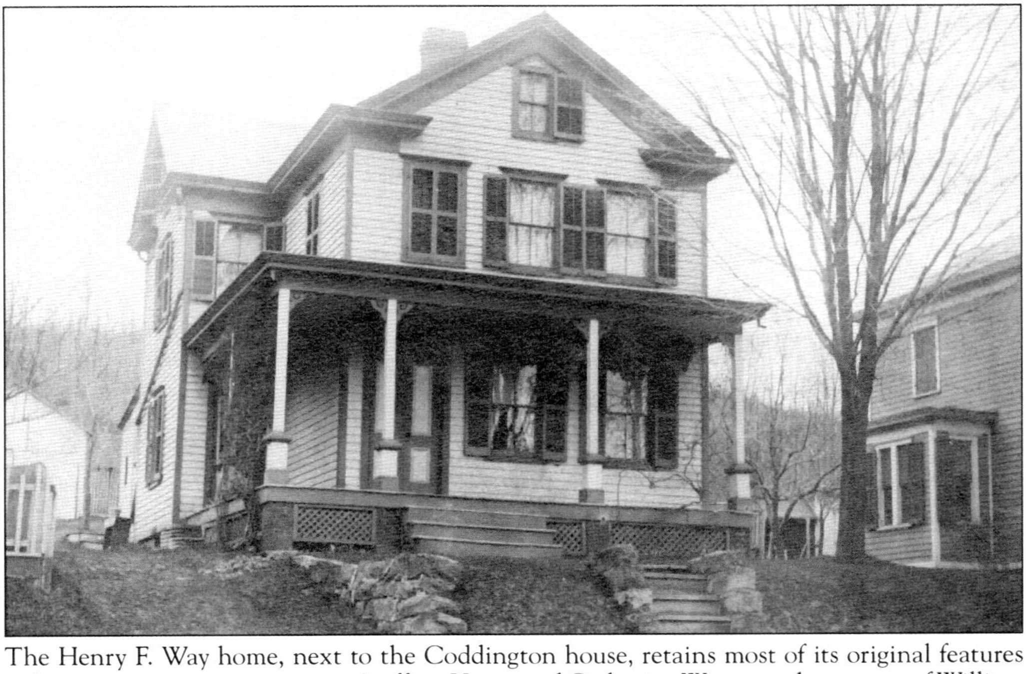

The Henry F. Way home, next to the Coddington house, retains most of its original features today as it serves as an accountant's office. Henry and Catherine Way were the parents of William F. Way, whose daughter Evelyn was a schoolteacher before marrying Harold Howarth. Henry's daughter Maria married Charles Van Winkle. Their daughter Doris became the bride of Fred Bartle, the blacksmith. (KCD.)

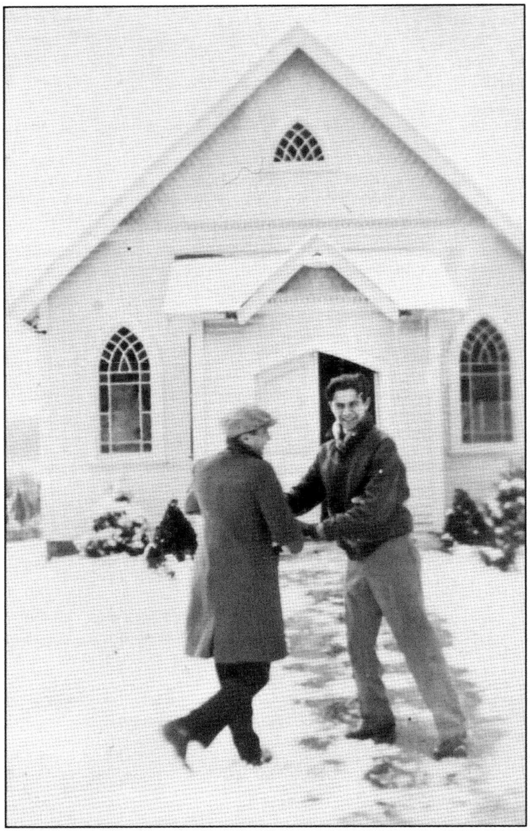

The original Martinsville Methodist Church, built in 1894, survives, but it requires a sharp eye to find it. Across the road from the current Methodist church, the building is surrounded by commercial additions, but the small Gothic-style window near the peak of the gable is still visible. In this photograph from about 1940, Harold Coddington (left) clowns with Albert Roberts, another grandson of John Peter Roberts and cousin of Chub Haines. (BCD.)

Martinsville celebrated its 150th birthday in 1978, having established the founding date as the year that the village was granted a post office. A parade included this float on which Cub Scouts portrayed a scene from "The Great Martinsville Fire 1923." To add realism, they obtained a smoke bomb used for fire department training. It later proved to be more realistic than expected as the entire float became engulfed in a cloud of smoke. (JWG.)

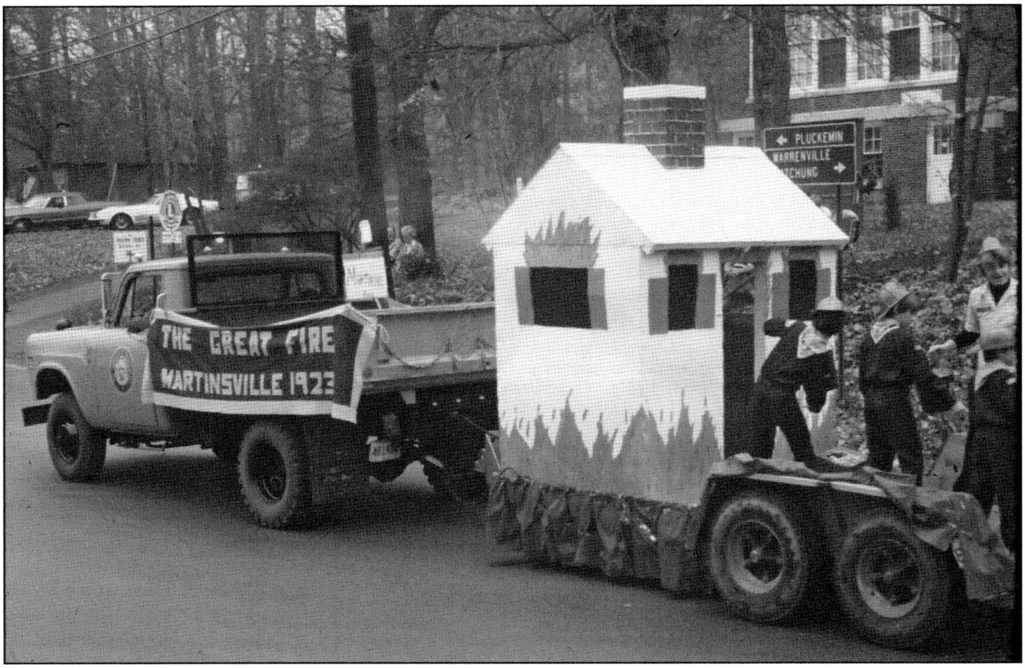

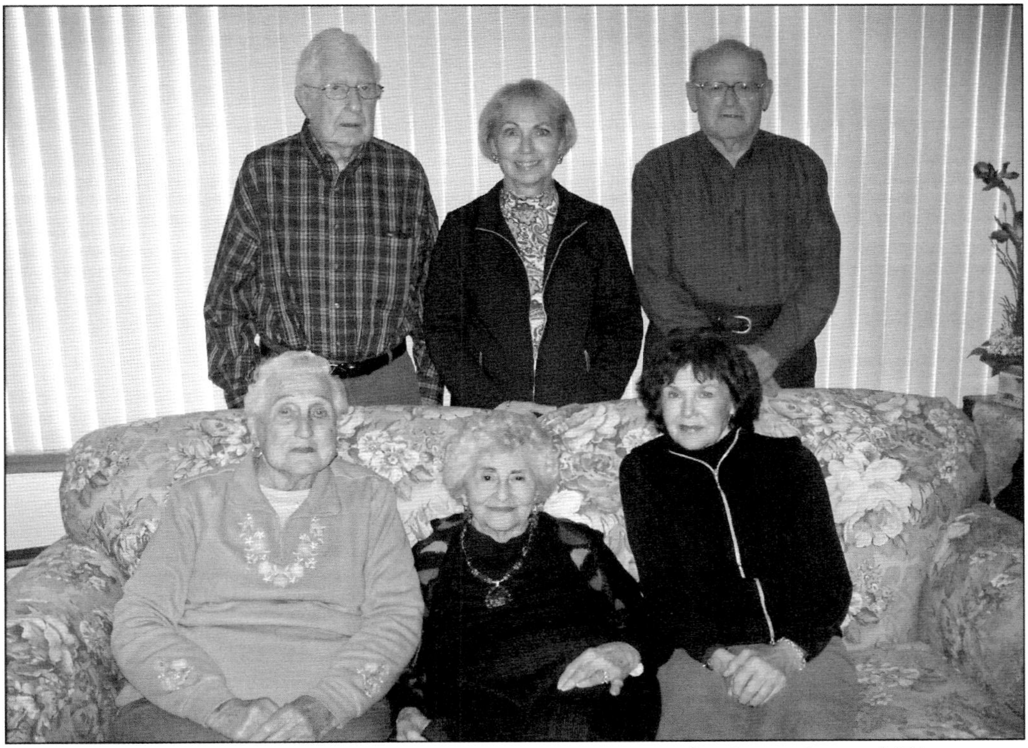

In addition to the buildings that still stand, other survivors are the descendants of 17th-century settlers ("old-timers") and of early-20th-century "newcomers" who continue to dwell here. In this image are, from left to right, (seated) newcomers Freda Yehle and Sis Cramer Longo and old-timer Barbara (Bartle Smalley Van Nest Coddington) Marton; (standing) old-timers Bob Tunison and Jane (Byrne Waldron) Gandolfe and newcomer David London. (PVW.)

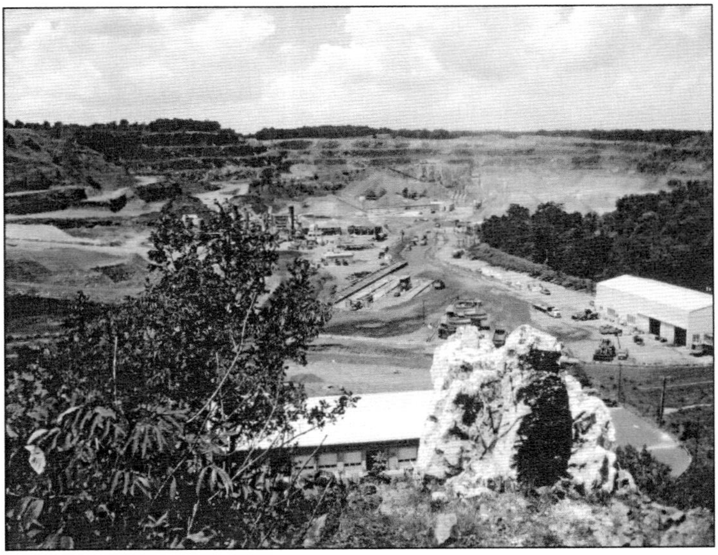

One enduring survivor is Chimney Rock, which stands as a sentinel over the gorge in the First Watchung Mountain. It has survived centuries of erosion by the elements and now overlooks the rapid destruction by man of the opposite mountain. Looking north into the Washington Valley at the right of this photograph when leaves conceal the houses nestled among the trees, the view is as it must have appeared to the first settlers entering the valley. (JMN.)